Perfectly Legal
Competitor
Intelligence

Perfectly Legal Competitor Intelligence

How to get it, use it and profit from it

DOUGLAS BERNHARDT

PITMAN PUBLISHING
128 Long Acre, London WC2E 9AN

A Division of Longman Group UK Limited

© Longman Group UK Limited, 1993

First published in Great Britain 1993

British Library Cataloguing in Publication Data
A CIP catalogue record for this book can be obtained from the British Library.

ISBN 0 273 60753 9

Typeset by PanTek Arts
Printed and bound in Great Britain by
Biddles Ltd, Guildford and Kings Lynn

CONTENTS

PREFACE

In his introduction to *The Competitive Advantage of Nations*, Professor Michael Porter asks 'Why do some social groups, economic institutions, and nations advance and prosper?[1] As a consultant in the field of competitive intelligence I confront the corollary to this question every day; that is, why do some firms in an industry succeed where others, many with superior resources, do not? Is the answer to be found in the way in which different companies translate strategy into action? Or is innovation the nucleus around which competitive advantage is built? Is market share the key? Are better companies simply those firms which are run better by better managers?

In 1982 Peters and Waterman, in their classic study *In Search of Excellence*, described IBM as one of America's 14 best-run companies. Consider a representative list of IBM strengths: the company's extensive global marketing and services network, a huge software business (bigger than Microsoft's), leading edge research and technology (three Nobel Prize winning scientists), a dominant position in semiconductor manufacturing, and a powerful, universally recognised 'brand' name. Yet within 10 years of the publication of *In Search of Excellence* IBM's share of worldwide computer industry revenues plummeted from 30 per cent to less than 20 per cent, profits crashed from $6 billion in 1984 to a $5 billion loss in 1992, 100,000 jobs were eliminated, and its market valuation shrank nearly 50 per cent to $29 billion. In contrast, Dell Computer, a pioneer in the 'factory direct' selling of personal computers, grew its total revenues from $258 million in 1989 to approximately $2 billion at the end of 1992. People still buy computers.

There are numerous examples of other industry leaders, ranging from Michelin, the French tyre maker, to the Netherlands-based Philips Electronics, struggling to restore competitiveness. Even the once impregnable Mercedes-Benz, the flagship car- and truck-making division of Daimler Benz, Germany's largest industrial concern, has seen production and profits fall. In the now fiercely contested luxury car market, for example, it must fight BMW, Nissan (Infiniti), Toyota (Lexus), and others for market share. In March of 1991 I asked a Mercedes-Benz sales manager who he thought were his major competitors; 'we don't have any,' he replied.

Throughout Europe many private sector and state-owned enterprises are threatened with closure as companies and industries come under assault from global competition, no longer protected by 'safe' home markets. Unemployment in Europe rises steadily, political instability in the Balkans and former Soviet republics shatters any hope of early or lasting peace, and since Margaret Thatcher's departure from office as Britain's prime minister no European political leader offers anything in the way of vision or direction.
According to Oxford Economic Forecasting (OEF):

> . . . there is now a real possibility that . . . we will see a number of years of Eurosclerosis. . .
>
> The first structural problem Europe faces is the regional composition of its exports. . . . nearly 40 per cent of European exports go to the relatively slow-growing areas of Africa, OPEC and Eastern Europe, whilst only a small proportion go to the fast-growing areas of the Far East.
>
> Secondly, Europe's wage costs are on average far higher than the USA and Japan. . . . hourly wage costs including social security are likely to be $16 in Japan and the USA. In a number of European countries they are over $20. This makes life particularly difficult for medium-to-low productivity sectors.
>
> Besides these Europe-wide problems, there are the particular difficulties in Germany. Problems financing unification are exacerbated by the competitive disadvantage of very high labour costs and a strong deutschmark. Add to this the probability that investment in plant, equipment, and eventually construction is expected to fall and the outlook for the short term looks distinctly bleak . . . Incorporating all these factors the OEF model predicts a suitably gloomy growth rate [for western Germany] of −1% for 1993.[2]

Nevertheless I remain optimistic, because in spite of intensifying competition, deep-seated economic problems, and the uncertainty always associated with fundamental change, firms as diverse as Benetton, Britain's GEC, the French luxury goods company LVMH,

Nestlé, Hoffmann-La Roche and Unilever flourish. These companies consistently deliver solid profits and above average returns on assets and sales. Each of these outstanding organisations demonstrates an exceptional ability to add value to the goods and services it provides its customers, and to the investments in labour and money of its employees and shareholders. So what's the difference?

Quinn suggests that 'most of the value-added [the difference between the value of output and the cost of input] in manufacturing or product companies . . . is created by knowledge-based service activities such as research and development, marketing research, product design, customer information functions, advertising, or distribution.'[3] Winning firms, it seems, are organisations which most successfully master the business issues critical to their performance, and develop the clearest, most precise understanding of value definition and value creation. Put another way, gaining competitive advantage has a lot to do with leveraging the knowledge assets of the firm, while at the same time determining how competitors are likely to leverage theirs.

This work explores one more knowledge-based service activity Quinn may well have added to his list; that of competitive intelligence.

The purpose of this book therefore is four-fold:

i. to encourage the reader to adopt a strategic approach to the use of competitive intelligence; to see the intelligence function as an integral part of the strategy process
ii. to show how competitive intelligence is used by firms to achieve competitive advantage
iii. to examine the process, some of the tools, and the output of competitive intelligence
iv. to dispel some of the myths and misunderstandings associated with the intelligence function in business.

Competitive intelligence in European industry is growing in importance. In a detailed survey I conducted of a sampling of *Financial Times* 500 companies in France, Germany, Great Britain, Italy, the Netherlands and Switzerland, 60 per cent of the respondents said the CEO was a main user of competitive intelligence; and 70 per cent reported that executive directors or vice presidents were main users of competitive intelligence. When asked how much use the company makes of competitor information when formulating strategy, 55 per cent of the survey respondents said 'a lot'. Each firm that participated in the survey is a leader (in terms of performance) in its industry.

Finally I have one overriding reason for producing this book. I believe that the enormous economic, political and social challenges we as individuals, as companies, and as nations face cannot, must not, be left for government to resolve. The source of economic prosperity in Europe and elsewhere springs from the efforts, the innovation, and the resourcefulness of companies, big and small, however imperfect; not from government. Government does not create wealth, it taxes it, and with varying degrees of success it spends it. When state enterprises are privatised, they almost always perform better and give customers better value. When air transport and telecommunications services are deregulated, customers get better service and lower prices. Where exchange rates are permitted to float freely, to find their natural levels, the economic adjustments which follow, however painful, reflect reality, not politically correct pipe dreams. Companies and industries prosper through continuous improvements in competitiveness, not in any other way. I believe that competitive intelligence is at the very heart of the firm's pursuit of improved competitiveness, of competitive advantage, and I hope that in some small way this book will contribute to the quest.

Notes

[1] Michael E. Porter, *The Competitive Advantage of Nations* (New York, NY: The Free Press, 1990), p. xi.

[2] Oxford Economic Forecasting, *World Economic Prospects: Winter 1992/93* (Oxford: Oxford Economic Forecasting, 1992), pp. 20–21.

[3] James Brian Quinn, *Intelligent Enterprise* (New York, NY: The Free Press, 1992), p. 33.

ACKNOWLEDGEMENTS

I have had the benefit of much encouragement and help in the production of this book. Margaret, my wife, ensured that the time (and space) I needed to work was always available, and, together with our children, was my greatest source of inspiration.

Compaq Computer AG, Basserdorf, Switzerland were especially generous; they provided me with a new Contura 3/25 notebook computer on which all my writing was done. The superb little machine was my constant and indispensable companion for many months. It never let me down.

The European Association of Information Services (EUSIDIC) also made an important contribution to the project; providing me with a copy of their research report, *Competitive Information Programmes*.

Of course it is to my silent partners, my clients, that I owe the biggest debt. For it is only through the opportunity I have of working together with managers in industry that I continue to learn about the real challenges of intelligence and strategy firms face.

I must also acknowledge my American associate, Kirk Tyson, whose company is regarded today as one the world's leading business intelligence firms. Kirk's innovative and invaluable contributions to the theory and practice of competitive intelligence are at the core of much of my own thinking.

The International Institute for Management Development (IMD), Lausanne, Switzerland, too, deserve special mention. Early in my research I was permitted access to their excellent business library.

I did not write this book alone. Each co-author willingly gave up many hours of his time to prepare an original manuscript. Although I take full responsibility for the notions and opinions which are clearly mine alone, this book is as much a product of their efforts as it is mine.

Last, I wish to thank the two women at Pitman Professional Publishing who made this book possible: Helen Pilgrim, Publishing Director, and Laura McGeary, editor. Helen originally proposed the idea to me in July of 1992, and ensured that the project was not only completed, but completed on time. She somehow managed to combine considerable moral support with firmness. She is a manager who makes things happen. Laura, I am afraid, had the unenviable task of ploughing through, then editing, a somewhat cumbersome manuscript. How she completed the job so cheerfully, yet so quickly, remains a mystery to me.

1 WHY COMPETITIVE INTELLIGENCE

INTRODUCTION

Competitive intelligence is the lifeblood of competitive strategy. Used effectively it becomes a prime source of power in the firm's bid to create competitive advantage. Neglected, and it is not long before urgent and now all too familiar pleas are heard for government, creditors, customers, and shareholders alike to rally to the defence of the firm against new, unexpected, or 'unfair' competition. Indeed the frequent spectacle of captains of major American and European industries calling 'foul' when they discover international competitors 'guilty' not only of breaking the rules of the game, but of repeatedly moving the goal posts, begs a number of questions:

- Why is it that these richly-paid custodians of our economic welfare are so surprised? Why have we witnessed recently so many abrupt departures of chief executives from companies such as American Express, British Petroleum, Digital Equipment, General Motors, IBM and Westinghouse?
- Why do evidently great firms with world class products, skilled managers, dominant market positions, leading edge technologies, and other strengths we typically associate with successful businesses, go out of business?
- And why does the term *globalisation of industries* so often serve as a euphemism for the wholesale disintegration of key industry sectors and competencies in Europe and in North America?

Of course there are no simple answers to any of these questions, just as there are no ready-made solutions to the dilemmas and problems which these questions mirror. As one *Financial Times* journalist put it when writing about the crisis of large corporations today:

A corporate culture with its roots in the 19th century is thus, in many companies, combined with a management structure that dates back to the 1920s. Not surprisingly, many such businesses cannot cope with a wave of pressing problems:

- Global competition is now a reality in many sectors, spelling an end to protected domestic markets and safe, reliable profits.
- The lean production system, pioneered by Japanese car makers, requires a complete transformation of manufacturing and distribution techniques – and may in time pose a similar challenge to service-sector companies as well.
- The microprocessor wipes out the competitive advantages of companies relying on (or selling) older generations of computing equipment. More generally, today's vast, cheap information flows make the traditional management hierarchies of large companies obsolete.
- Economies of scale, the solid foundation on which big companies have based their dominance for decades, may no longer be an overwhelming advantage. Changes in information technology, in the financial system, in flexible production techniques, in the growth of companies offering all-comers the distribution and support systems which previously only the largest companies could afford – all of these are nibbling away at the advantages of economies of scale. The *diseconomies* of scale – communications overheads, inflexibility, the not-invented-here syndrome – are becoming increasingly clear.[1]

Unfortunately for many firms, post-mortems such as this are, like all post-mortems, too late. The increasingly complex and ever-changing characteristics of global competition, of production processes, of distribution systems, of organisations and their structures, and of scores of other factors must be anticipated, must be monitored, must be understood, and, last, must be acted upon if firms are to survive and prosper. In business, there are no happy surprises.

WANG

In late summer 1992, Wang Laboratories, the company credited with having pioneered the word processor, filed for bankruptcy protection in the United States. Wang at the time had piled up three-year losses of $1.5 billion, and were forced to acknowledge in their bankruptcy announcement that the company's resources and cash flow were not sufficient to complete the restructuring started in 1990. Under Chapter 11 protection, the company went on to suffer declining revenues, and a further loss of $9.8 million in their first fiscal quarter for 1992. By the time *Fortune* magazine published their 11th annual ranking of corporate reputations in February 1993, Wang had become America's 'least admired' company.

Once worldwide leaders in the microcomputer industry, and highly regarded for their technical capabilities, Wang failed to anticipate the rapid changes that were to occur in their industry and their markets. Why did Wang's top management not respond in time to new and proliferating competition? Why did they not re-orientate their technologies and the strategic direction of their business towards changing customer needs, and new industry standards? The easy explanation is that the failure of Wang was a failure of strategy. But equally it was a failure of intelligence. Wang's top decision makers either chose to ignore the competitor and market intelligence warnings, or their intelligence, and perhaps their assessment of that intelligence, were flawed.

One month after filing for bankruptcy protection, Wang's Chief Financial Officer, Michael Mee, announced that the company was re-examining its strategies, and would in the future concentrate on services and software, rather than manufacturing. Subject to decisions taken by the US bankruptcy court on Wang's plan of reorganisation, the company may not have the opportunity to test their new strategies. Rather like the passengers and crew of the *Titanic* – who would clearly have benefited from early warnings about the location, shape and size of the iceberg which claimed their ship and most of their lives – Wang's management are likely to find that fresh insight, new strategies, and what Richard Miller, the CEO, describes as 'continued commitment to the company from our customers' will have as much impact on saving the company as would have re-arranging the deck chairs on the 'unsinkable' vessel.

GM

It is in the motor industry, however, where we see one of the most glaring examples of what can happen to a firm that falls victim to what I call strategic failure.

By October 1992, General Motors, the world's biggest industrial corporation, was haemorrhaging cash, and losing money at a rate of $3.5 million a day. The year before, on a turnover of $123 billion, GM lost nearly $4.5 billion (IBM lost $5 billion in 1992), at the time the largest annual deficit ever posted by an American company. But this was only a prelude; after a giant write-off for future health care costs GM was forced to report a net loss for 1992 of $23 billion.

Evidently GM failed to appreciate the full extent of the global competitive war their adversaries waged, and continue to wage, against them. Even the comparatively bright performance of GM Europe (Opel, Saab and Vauxhall), which generated cumulative net profits of $9.7 billion from 1987 to 1992, was of little help. In 1991 and 1992 alone GM's North American motor business lost $10 billion, and the corporation has yet to overcome big gaps in its product range, and the problem of inefficient factories.

Why did GM's management not respond more decisively to their company's weaknesses in areas such as productivity (it takes GM 40 man-hours of labour to produce a Cadillac Seville, two and a half times longer than Toyota require to build a Lexus at their manufacturing facility at Tahara in central Japan), or labour costs (GM spend nearly $800 more to make a car than arch rival Ford)?

Why was GM's share of the US car market permitted to slip from 44 per cent in 1982 to 33 per cent in 1992, when during the same period their four main Japanese competitors – Honda, Mazda, Nissan and Toyota – increased their combined share from just over 19 per cent to 27 per cent?

Last, where was the intelligence that 10 years earlier could have alerted GM's bosses to what these powerful and resourceful companies had in store for them? Where, in other words, was the intelligence that would have enabled GM's top management to understand that each one of these competitors was not only creating 'an obsession with winning at all levels of [their] organisation',[2] but was vigorously pursuing a strategy predicated on sustaining 'that obsession over the 10- to 20-year quest for global leadership',[3] or what Hamel calls strategic intent.

THE VALUE OF COMPETITIVE INTELLIGENCE

Today our bookshelves groan under the weight of management literature aimed at sharpening our thinking on questions such as:

- On what foundations, with what models, and with what tools are sound competitive strategies built? 'What might give us continued competitive advantage?'[4]
- How do we most usefully define the mission of the firm, its strategic intent, its goals, its objectives and its strategic options?
- What do we need to know to develop and to select strategies which are not only successful, but sustainable?
- 'What new products should we make or markets should we enter and how?'[5]
- How do we successfully manage the implementation of competitive strategy?

Whatever strategic approach or framework the firm chooses to embrace for the management of its business (or businesses), no single element or influence remains more fundamental to competitive strategy than that of competitive intelligence. This is not to say that other management functions and skill sets are of lesser importance, but none are more important. Yet much of what managers do, and certainly much of what is written about what managers should do, is concerned with 'doing the thing right'. Competitive intelligence is about 'doing the right thing'.

According to Porter, 'The objective of a competitor analysis is to develop a profile of the nature and success of the likely strategy changes each competitor might make, each competitor's probable response to the range of feasible strategic moves other firms could initiate, and each competitor's probable reaction to the array of industry changes and broader environmental shifts that might occur.'[6] Or as one strategy consultant in Canada put it, 'Competitive intelligence should have a single-minded objective – to develop the strategies and tactics necessary to transfer market share profitably and consistently from specific competitors to the company.'[7]

A firm which does not rigorously monitor and analyse key competitors is ill-equipped to formulate or implement sound competitive strategy. Too great an emphasis on financial objectives when formulating or reviewing strategy, or failure to predict, or respond to, on-going changes in the competitive environment leads to missed opportunities, and can leave the firm and its markets vulnerable to attack.

Competitive intelligence serves to underpin decisions made by managers about the 'positioning [of] a business to maximise the value of the capabilities that distinguish it from its competitors.'[8] Positioning of course is about the perceptions a firm creates both of itself and of its products in the minds of its customers relative to the competition. In today's real world of global competitive warfare, where corporate household names suddenly become yesterday's news, and new competitive entrants just as suddenly, and perhaps more unexpectedly, rise to market dominance, the failure to systematically collect, analyse and act upon competitive information can lead to the downfall of the firm itself.

What, then, is competitive intelligence? How do we define it? In what ways does it differ from market intelligence? How is it used to make companies (and indeed nations) more competitive? Who needs competitive intelligence? How is it managed? How is it produced? How should competitive intelligence be used? By whom? What are its costs? Where does competitive intelligence fit within the strategic management system of the firm? And lastly, what are the measurable 'bottom line' benefits for managers and their organisations? This book seeks to answer these important questions.

INTELLIGENCE AND THE STATE

This is a book about competitive intelligence; that is, about the adaptation and application of modern intelligence principles and practices to strategies concerned with 'how to create competitive advantage in each of the businesses in which a company competes.'9 But the origins of formal intelligence concepts and methods are firmly rooted in politics and in warfare – environments not entirely dissimilar from those in which today's global competitive battles are being waged. Therefore a brief examination of intelligence and the state provides valuable insight into how intelligence serves organisations.

In China 2,400 years ago the military strategist, Sun Tzu, stated the case for intelligence plainly. He wrote, 'Now the reason the enlightened prince and the wise general conquer the enemy whenever they move, and their achievements surpass those of ordinary men, is foreknowledge.'10 In war, as we know, foreknowledge, or lack of it, determines whether men live or die, whether the battle is won or lost, whether a nation emerges as victor, or is instead vanquished.

The Duke of Wellington put it this way: 'All the business of war, and indeed all the business of life, is to endeavour to find out what you don't know from what you do', or, as he added, 'guessing at what is on the other side of the hill'.

In the competitive wars being fought today by the world's leading firms the value of 'foreknowledge' is no less important. In the words of the United States Central Intelligence Agency (CIA), 'Intelligence is knowledge and foreknowledge of the world around us – the prelude to Presidential decision and action.'11 The benefits of successfully anticipating a competitor's future plans and strategies are self-evident. And the consequences of making decisions based on information that is incomplete, inaccurate, or late, are no less severe. They are just different. When companies fail in their struggle for profits, and are forced to downsize (or 'restructure'), or sometimes close their doors altogether, we refer to the human casualties as unemployed, and we calculate losses in economic, social and sometimes political terms, rather than in numbers of aircraft, guns and tanks lost.

BUSH AND CLINTON – THE STRUGGLE FOR THE PRESIDENCY

George Bush lost the presidential election to Bill Clinton in 1992 because, unlike Clinton, he and his campaign managers did not interpret correctly the intelligence we presume was at their disposal. Bush underestimated what he needed to do (or say) in order to win the hearts and minds of American voters disenchanted with recession and economic uncertainty. Moreover, Bush's response to Clinton's meticulously planned and executed campaign strategy (which focused almost exclusively on prescriptions for the nation's economic ills) was both inadequate and inappropriate.

Clinton's relentless attacks against the management and performance of the economy under the Bush administration were not convincingly defended. To make matters worse (for Bush), the Republican offensive mistakenly targeted Clinton personally (lack of experience in national politics and foreign affairs; a history of anti-Vietnam War activities during his student days at Oxford; his wife Hillary's apparent ambitions for 'co-presidency'; and what the editor of *The New Republic* is said to have described as 'Bill's history of compulsive philandering').

It was not Bill Clinton who voters perceived as their enemy, but rather government policies and practices which had failed to deliver solutions to economic and social problems. And Bush was unable, or was unwilling, to forge the one political alliance that might have made a difference to the outcome of the election, one with Ross Perot.

Bill Clinton, the governor from Arkansas, not only had better intelligence – including a better assessment of the electorate (his customer base?) and of Bush himself (the competitor) – he used this to create and implement, a better, and ultimately successful, campaign strategy. George Bush was not defeated by a stronger team, he was beaten by a more intelligent one.

INTELLIGENCE AND THE MILITARY

The great Prussian soldier, General Carl von Clausewitz, offered his interpretation of information in war. According to von Clausewitz, 'By the word "information" we denote all the knowledge which we have of the enemy and his country; therefore, in fact, the foundation of all our ideas and actions.'[12]

Not surprisingly the military regard intelligence as an indispensable element of combat support, fulfilling both strategic and tactical needs. A general with even perfect knowledge of the battlefield (the market?) and his own army's capabilities, strengths, and weaknesses (his 'company'?) would not intentionally engage the enemy (his competitors?) in combat without first gathering and evaluating enemy intelligence reports. Unfortunately managers at all levels in industry – many with ostensibly 'perfect' knowledge of their industry, their markets, their products and their strategic objectives – with great commitment and enthusiasm march forward onto the competitive battlefield with no understanding whatsoever of what their competitors can and will do.

In his account of the war in Vietnam, General Bruce Palmer, jr, who between 1966 and 1968 served first as Commander of the 18th Airborne Corps, and then as US Army deputy to General William Westmoreland, reminds us that 'even sustained, outstanding operational performance can go for naught if the intelligence that guides operations and generates the thrust of operational efforts is lacking in quality.'[13]

General Palmer also refers to 'longer-term strategic aspects'[14] of the conflict in Vietnam upon which there was a strong intelligence focus. These 'included such matters as the assessment of opposing US/allied and North Vietnamese strategies; North Vietnamese perceptions of the US war effort; the effectiveness of the US air war against North Vietnam; North Vietnamese capacity to wage a prolonged war and their dependence on the Soviet Union and China; and the prospects for survival over the longer term of a free and independent South Vietnam.'[15]

The key terms used by General Palmer could well be adapted as main headings of a Competitor Intelligence Report. For example:

- assessment of strategies
- competitor perceptions
- effectiveness of current operations
- competitor capacity (or capabilities)
- long-term market prospects.

Although the means by which intelligence is collected in warfare may differ quite radically from those more common to the commercial environment, the goal is the same: to enable decision-makers to make winning decisions.

TYPES OF INTELLIGENCE

For our purposes we can classify intelligence into three main types. These are:

i.   strategic intelligence
ii. tactical intelligence
iii. counter-intelligence.

In business, strategic intelligence is concerned mainly with competitor analysis, or, more precisely, with gaining an understanding of a competitor's 'future goals, current strategy, assumptions [held about itself and the industry] and capabilities.'[16] Porter refers to these as 'diagnostic components'.

Intelligence about a firm's major customers, suppliers and partners (for example, partners in a marketing or research and development alliance) is often also of strategic value. For example, it is of strategic importance for companies in the flavours and fragrances industry to know the longer-term product strategies of their biggest customers so that they can predict, and at the right time be ready to match, their needs.

The focus of tactical intelligence is generally upon operational, usually smaller-scale issues. Examples of tactical issues include competitors' actual (as opposed to official) terms of sale, their price policies and the plans they have for changing the way in which they differentiate one or more of their products from yours. Middle-level marketing and sales managers who have a tendency to think weeks (not years!) ahead represent some of the main users (and collectors!) of tactical intelligence. They want to know how to avoid surprises on the competitive minefields they must cross each day. They seldom have real practical concern or sense of responsibility for the prosecution of the overall war.

The subject of counter-intelligence, or how to defend your company's secrets, is examined in Chapter 10.

It is at the business unit level, where competition occurs, where the firm formulates and finally tests its strategy. Thus competitive intelligence is concerned with what Aaker reminds us are the principal factors, or determinants, of sustainable competitive advantage:[17]

- Basis of competition (on what set of assets, capabilities, and skills is the competitor's strategy based?)
- Where the firm competes (what target product markets has the competitor selected?)
- Who, other than ourselves, does the competitor compete against (competitor selection)?
- In what way does the firm compete (product strategy, positioning strategy, manufacturing strategy, distribution strategy, etc.)?

Competitive intelligence involves the pursuit of the answers to these questions.

The war in the Gulf is instructive in helping us understand the different, albeit complementary, types of intelligence. American satellites provided target data to allied aircraft and tanks: tactical intelligence. 'Field operatives' reports on morale among Saddam Hussein's Republican Guard meanwhile influenced presidential decisions in Washington on suspending hostilities':[18] strategic intelligence.

It has been argued that Iraq's invasion of Kuwait in August 1990 succeeded largely because of serious failures in Western intelligence. Whether the intelligence itself was deficient, or whether policymakers simply chose not to act upon it, we are not certain. What is clear is that the so-called intelligence gap – the gap between what the intelligence community knew, or should have known, and what leaders in Europe and the US understood to be the case – was too wide. Fortunately the military conflict was quickly resolved, due in part to good military intelligence, and ultimately to the effective and timely application of that intelligence.

According to General Norman Schwarzkopf, commander of Allied Forces in the Gulf War, 'ever since the tanker war, the United States had kept the region under stepped-up surveillance, both human and high-tech, so each day [before Iraq's invasion of Kuwait] brought a huge haul of fresh information.'[19]

But could the war in the Gulf have been avoided in the first place by better political intelligence? At least three British ministers – Alan Clark (Trade), Lord Trefgarne (Defence Procurement) and William Waldegrave (Foreign Office) – may have been somewhat more eager to facilitate the feeding of Iraq's hungry, cash-rich defence industry (with British-made machine tools) than see tens of millions of pounds worth of export orders dry up.

THE VALUE OF INTELLIGENCE

The issue of intelligence is one with which governments constantly grapple. In democratic societies the debate over the role and practice of intelligence is particularly intense. My purpose is not to enter this debate, over the rights and wrongs, or the fairness or unfairness, of secret intelligence services, but rather to consider what managers can learn from the ways in which intelligence serves the interests of the state.

One recent work about the apparent 'tension' between intelligence and democratic values (in America) makes it clear that some 'see intelligence as preserving democracy and American values through vigorous use of the full battery of intelligence techniques within the international system to protect and further US interests.'[20] The notion of (or, perhaps more accurately, the rationale for) a pro-active intelligence function is important for two reasons:

- it highlights for us the strategic nature of intelligence, and its key role as an instrument of foreign policy
- it suggests that an essential task of intelligence is to facilitate the quest for strategic, or competitive, advantage.

The end of the Cold War has focused renewed attention on the subject (and costs) of intelligence. To what extent do the nations of Europe and North America still need, and indeed to what extent can they still afford, the 'spooks', their spy satellites, their listening posts (GCHQ at Cheltenham), and the rest of the vast infrastructures of men, women, equipment and facilities that make up the intelligence establishment? It would be unrealistic to assume that the intelligence apparatus in even the most democratic of states will simply wither away, or, indeed, that this would even be desirable (it is not). What is reasonable to expect is that the energies and resources of the intelligence establishment will, in large part, be redirected.

How then do we as managers and as citizens reconcile this essentially secret craft – the 'second oldest profession' – with the new spirit of co-operation and openness meant to prevail among nations today? The answer is that the reality of international co-operation and openness stops rather short of the spirit. International competition for markets and for resources has never been more intense, and there are no indicators, economic or otherwise, which suggest that this will soon change.

Even the Japanese feel the uncomfortable pressures of world recession, and are preparing for new and tougher competitive clashes in the years ahead. Business leaders in Japan realise that despite heavy investment in new plant and equipment during the recent 'bubble years' the country's industry must become more productive. Productivity, of course, is the most fundamental measure of economic performance, therefore a more productive Japan means a more competitive Japan.

In addition, many Japanese firms are adopting more global strategies. For example, by 1998 Japanese motor manufacturers could be making more than 1.5 million cars in Europe. When added to imports from Japan, this would increase their share of the European car market from 12 to 18 per cent.

Toyota, already the world's most efficient manufacturer of motorcars and trucks, 'is rethinking almost everything it does'.[21] In 1992, with Japan in an economic slump, the company accelerated the process of 'reorganising its operations, putting still more high technology into its factories, and reworking its legendary "lean production" system'.[22] Toyota intend to stay on the attack. According to their president, Tatsuro Toyoda, Toyota intend to increase their unit sales of cars and trucks from under five million now to six million by the year 2000.

In 1990, William H. Webster, at the time Director of the Central Intelligence Agency (CIA), said in a speech at American University that 'in the years ahead international friction is likely to be increasingly expressed in economic terms'. He added: 'The right information will be critical. Providing that information is, of course, the business of intelligence'. Within weeks of Bill Clinton's election victory, Congressional Democrats who advise the President, including the Chairman of the House Permanent Committee on Intelligence, were saying that he would 'need a more complete and timely analysis of . . . messy problems',[23] including the problem of economic competitiveness.

Robert Gates, Director of Central Intelligence under Bush, endorsed this view. Although Gates denied suggestions that the US intelligence community had any intention of engaging in industrial espionage, he did confirm in April 1992 that about 40 per cent of the intelligence requirements of government policy-making agencies and departments 'are economic in nature'.[24] He told one group of businessmen that 'the most senior policy-makers of the government clearly see that many of the most important challenges through and beyond the end of this decade are in the international economic arena – and they have fleshed out that insight with a detailed set of requirements for the intelligence community'.[25] With an intelligence budget of some $30 billion – from which the CIA, the National Security Agency, the Defence Intelligence Agency, the National Reconnaissance Office, and other sectors of the National Foreign Intelligence Program are funded – it is clear the United States attaches considerable value to intelligence and allocates sizeable resources to meet its intelligence needs.

European-based firms need to consider their response to an important new challenge. In the post-Cold War era American businesses are unlikely to remain satisfied with seeing billions of tax dollars spent for intelligence from which they do not benefit directly. The government of the United States will find it increasingly difficult to resist pressures to share more (and, indeed, more focused) economic intelligence with industry. Admiral Stansfield Turner, who served as Director of Central Intelligence from 1977 to 1981 under President Jimmy Carter, cautions Americans of a 'growing need to discern threatening intentions, subterfuge, and ill will among our competitor nations',[26] and advocates that the United States expand its 'efforts to collect international economic data, by espionage where necessary'.[27] More recently, in response to an article in *The Economist*[28] suggesting it is wrong that America's 'vast intelligence bureaucracy' be used for purposes of 'economic intelligence', R. James Woolsey, Clinton's new Director of Central Intelligence, wrote to the magazine saying:

> . . . it is interesting that you urge us to reallocate responsibilities within the government in such a way as to rule out of bounds for intelligence to be used to help protect [American] companies operating abroad from foreign intelligence services used against them. This would be a brand-new shackle on our ability to protect American interests, and we will give your proposal the consideration it deserves.
>
> Piffle, *Economist,* piffle.[29]

Knowledge, especially foreknowledge, is power. In a world characterised by increasing competitive intensity it is not unreasonable to assume that both firms and governments alike will dedicate greater and more sophisticated resources to intelligence activities.

At present some countries in western Europe probably do more to provide intelligence support to their private sectors than do the Americans. There is evidence to suggest that the French are particularly active in seeking financial and technological secrets. Their intelligence and counterintelligence services, respectively the *Direction Générale de la Sécurité Extérieur* (DGSE) and the *Direction de Surveillance de Territoire* (DST), are reported to have 'tried to plant "moles" inside overseas offices of IBM and Texas Instruments Inc'[30] and to have posed 'as flight attendants or passengers on Air France jets to glean information useful to French companies'.[31] Boeing and Corning Glass have also been targets of the DGSE.

In September 1991 Pierre Marion, former director of the French secret services, said there was 'no need to suffer from a guilt complex' about bugging businessmen. And in 1992, at a time when the budgets of many western intelligence agencies were being pruned, President

François Mitterrand authorised a 10 per cent increase in the budget of DGSE. The year before DGSE had recruited about 1,200 extra staff.

There are other known examples of French intelligence intervening on behalf of French industry: in the River Oaks suburb of Houston in 1991 two men were seen sifting through rubbish outside the home of an executive of the American computer and electronics firm Texas Instruments. An off-duty policeman took a note of the registration number of their van, which was later traced to the French consulate. The French consul-general, Bernard Guillet, claimed the men were collecting grass cuttings to fill a hole in the consulate garden.

The same year the French embassy in Washington, DC, organised a tour for a team of French engineers who, it was claimed, were nuclear experts. Instead, they 'tried to gather details of America's top-secret stealth technology before the FBI intervened'.[32]

In the spring of 1993 the Pentagon and a number of American defence companies, including Hughes Aircraft, cancelled plans to participate in the Paris Air Show, one of the most important events in the calendar of the international aerospace and defence industries. This followed reports from the CIA that American firms were targets for French economic espionage. Earlier the CIA had come into possession of copies of top-secret American documents which US administration officials claimed originated from the DGSE.

A US Presidential order signed in December 1981 sets clear goals for the American intelligence community. It defines the mission of the national intelligence system as one which is to 'provide the President . . . with the necessary information on which to base decisions concerning the conduct and development of foreign, defence and economic policy, and the protection of United States national interests from foreign security threats.'[33]

How many CEOs of firms in Europe and North America have issued directives to the same effect? The leaders of global organisations such as Airbus Industrie, ABB, Daimler-Benz, Glaxo, Philips and Royal Dutch Shell may not be heads of state; but each of them are powerful men, directly responsible to many tens of thousands of stakeholders for the survival and success of the enterprises they run and the communities of which their companies are a part. They, too, have a growing need for 'the necessary information on which to base decisions concerning the conduct and development' of each of their firm's strategies and policies, and the protection of their organisations against threats from their competitors, and from fast changing sociological, technological, economic and political (STEP) factors.

It is not possible for any major enterprise, or for any one of the portfolio of businesses which make up that enterprise, to achieve full commercial potential if an effective competitive intelligence programme responsible directly to the CEO and other top decision-makers is not in place.

COMPETITIVE INTELLIGENCE AND JAPAN

Although Japan has no official intelligence service, the Ministry of International Trade & Industry (MITI), and MITI's Japan External Trade Organisation (JETRO) more than make up for any handicaps this might cause. JETRO was established in 1958 to promote Japanese exports, and now has 78 offices worldwide, including a total of 21 in western European countries, of which four are located in Germany. There are also JETRO offices in Bulgaria, Poland and Romania.

Over time, JETRO has become the Japanese government's main arm for the gathering of foreign competitor intelligence, much of it shared with private industry in Japan. This is what JETRO has to say about itself in its own promotional literature:

> By marshalling the resources of its . . . offices in 57 countries around the world, JETRO is able to collect, process and study data on overseas economies, trade, industry, products, technology and the climate for investment in a great many areas.
>
> Functioning very much like a global research institute, our organisation digests, analyses and evaluates this mountain of information for its significance. We then publish our findings . . . for study by domestic researchers and other interested parties.[34]

According to Minoru Masuda, Chairman of JETRO, the work of his organisation 'will continue to increase in significance'.[35]

MITI itself has a major responsibility for assessing the information it collects, and for transforming it into usable intelligence products and recommendations for Japanese industry. The big Japanese trading houses – the *sogo shosha* – and the research departments of the large Japanese corporations also do good jobs of systematically gathering and processing competitive intelligence.

THE PURPOSE AND ROLE OF INTELLIGENCE IN BUSINESS

Intelligence is at once both a process (the intelligence cycle) and a product. Competitive intelligence can therefore be defined as:

- an analytical process that transforms disaggregated competitor and market data into actionable strategic knowledge about competitors' capabilities, intentions, performance and position
- the end-product of that process.

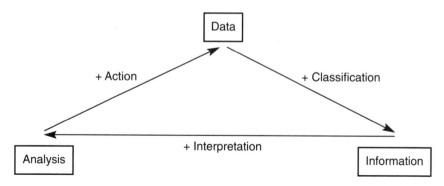

Figure 1.1 Business intelligence

Source Presentation to the SCIP 8th Annual International Conference, Los Angeles, by Gil Press, Global Strategy R & D, Corporate Marketing, Digital Equipment Corporation (Maynard, Massachusetts).

Competitive intelligence is not market research, nor is it always synonymous with market intelligence, although the activities are interrelated. Competitive intelligence managers often draw upon the resources of their firms' market research departments, but the perspectives and goals of competitive intelligence and market research units are quite different from those of competitive intelligence managers and co-ordinators.

The focus of market research tends to be on problems associated with the profitable marketing of a firm's products and services. The scope of competitive intelligence is broader. Competitive intelligence is a 'value added' concept that layers over the top of business development, market research and strategic planning.

The research objectives of a competitive intelligence project will typically involve issues such as:

- the manufacturing capabilities of the competitor
- analysis of alliances and/or joint ventures entered into by competitors
- the competitor's future plans and strategies for specific markets, or range of product offerings
- reasons behind a shift in the corporate or business unit strategy of the competitor, customer, distributor or supplier.

Competitive intelligence is at the heart of those strategic management activities which are anticipatory in nature, in particular those concerned with 'assessing business strengths/weaknesses and environmental opportunities/threats in relation to competitors and formulating, evaluating and selecting strategic alternatives.'[36]

Competitive intelligence is driven by, and carried out for, policymakers. Although it is the task of the intelligence professional to deliver a useful – an actionable – intelligence product, it is the responsibility of the consumer of intelligence, the policymaker, to define and explicitly articulate the organisation's front-end intelligence requirements. At the same time it is the policymaker's responsibility to ensure that these requirements are indeed satisfied.

In the modern diversified company competitive intelligence, like strategy, is conducted at two levels:

i. Corporate
ii. Business unit

According to Porter, 'Corporate strategy concerns two different questions: what businesses the corporation should be in and how the corporate office should manage the array of business units.'[37] But, also according to Porter, 'Competitive strategy concerns how to

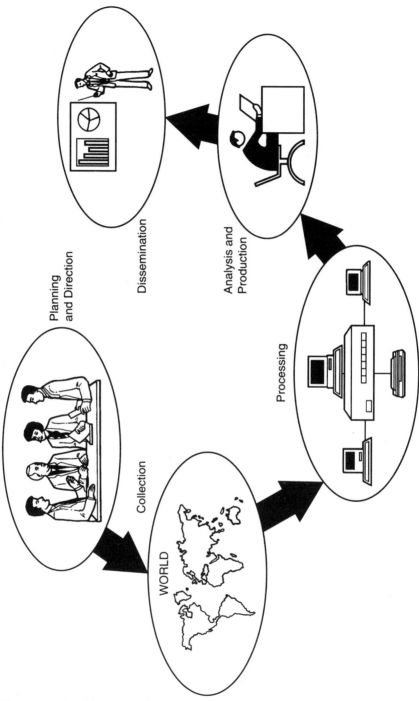

Figure 1.2 Intelligence cycle

create competitive advantage in each of the businesses in which a company competes.'[38]

We are concerned in this work primarily with how competitive intelligence serves the firm at the business unit level. In other words, we are concerned here with how managers use competitive intelligence to create and sustain superior competitive performance.

THE INTELLIGENCE CYCLE

The CIA describes the intelligence cycle as 'the process by which raw information is acquired, gathered, transmitted, evaluated, analysed and made available as finished intelligence for policymakers to use in decision-making and action.'[39] The five steps which constitute this cycle are:

i.   planning and direction
ii. collection
iii. processing
iv. analysis and production
v.   dissemination.

Each of these steps represents an essential element within an intelligence system, and each will be examined in detail in later chapters.

Managers should address seven questions as they prepare to invest time, money, and manpower in the collection and processing of intelligence:

i.   What do we need to know?
ii. What do we already know, or what are our assumptions?
iii. Why do we need to know it (what is the strategic impact likely to be)?
iv. When do we need to know it?
v.   What will we do with the intelligence once we have it – is it actionable?
vi. What will it cost to get it?
vii. What could it cost not to have it?

Only when these questions have been answered both by managers and by those responsible for producing the intelligence can an effective intelligence project be said to be under way. The case examples in Chapter 6 serve to illustrate this.

THE INTELLIGENCE PRODUCT

The product of the intelligence cycle, or process, is evaluated information. It is finished intelligence, packaged in a format appropriate not only to the intelligence itself, but to the customer for the intelligence, the policymaker.

The question of what approach managers should take in assembling the intelligence product is covered in Chapter 5, The Packaging and Dissemination of Intelligence. But a few comments are in order here.

In practice, the intelligence product is unlikely to be created from perfect information. For example, we can only know with absolute certainty when and where the competitor's new product is to be launched once the launch has taken place. By then, of course, it is too late. The firm finds itself in a position where it can only react (or choose not to react) to the competitor's move; it has lost the initiative it might have had if the right intelligence had been available earlier. So, although we cannot know with absolute certainty the details of the competitor's new product launch until it actually happens, we can nevertheless learn from 'less-than-perfect' information exactly when and where the competitor intends to launch, and formulate competitive strategy accordingly.

In other words, it is possible to acquire, gather, evaluate and analyse sufficient intelligence, in ample time, to reveal within satisfactory limits of accuracy what the firm needs to know, when it needs to know it. It is the competitive intelligence function which provides managers with the organisational mechanism to learn what the competitor will do, not what the competitor has already done.

A word about ethics. In a world where ethical behaviour is perceived as 'a boon to a company's reputation and competitiveness'[40] it would be counterproductive for a firm to undertake its intelligence activities without regard to ethical or legal constraints. Business is not a Sunday School picnic, but it is not a free-for-all either; even warfare has its conventions. Everything a firm needs to know about the competition can be obtained by legal means. The incremental costs of stepping over the line – into the black – are far too high, and entirely unnecessary.

Finally, what are some of the proven 'bottom line' benefits of competitive intelligence to the firm? They include:

- improved market knowledge
- improved cross-functional relationships in the organisation
- greater confidence in strategic plans
- improvements in product quality relative to the competition.

In short, better business performance through doing things better.

NOTES

[1]Peter Martin 'Life Gets Tougher at the Top', *Financial Times*, 30/31 January 1993, p. 6.

[2]Gary Hamel and C.K. Prahalad. 'Strategic Intent', *The McKinsey Quarterly*, Spring 1990, p. 39.

[3]Ibid.

[4]Paul J.H. Schoemaker. 'How to Link Strategic Vision to Core Capabilities', *Sloan Management Review*, Fall 1992, p. 67.

[5]Ibid.

[6]Michael E. Porter, *Competitive Strategy: Techniques for Analysing Industries and Competitors* (New York, NY: The Free Press, 1980), p. 47.

[7]Ian Gordon, *Beat the Competition*: *How to Use Competitive Intelligence to Develop Winning Business Strategies* (London: Basil Blackwell, 1989), p. 26.

[8]Ibid.

[9]Michael E. Porter, 'From Competitive Advantage to Corporate Strategy', in *Michael E. Porter on Competition and Strategy* (Boston, MA: Harvard Business School Publishing Division, 1987), p. 15.

[10]Samuel B. Griffith, ed., *Sun Tzu: The Art of War* (New York: Oxford University Press, 1982), p. 144.

[11]_____. *Factbook on Intelligence* (Washington, DC: Central Intelligence Agency, 1991), p. 13.

[12]Anatol Rapoport, ed., *Clausewitz: On War* (London: Penguin Classics, 1984), p. 162.

[13]Bruce Palmer, Jr, *The 25-Year War: America's Military Role in Vietnam* (New York, NY: Simon & Schuster, Inc., 1984), p. 161.

[14]Ibid., p. 162.

[15]Ibid., pp. 162–163.

[16]Michael E. Porter, *Competitive Strategy: Techniques for Analysing Industries and Competitors* (New York, NY: The Free Press, 1980), p. 49.

[17]David A. Aaker, *Developing Business Strategies*, 3rd ed. (New York, NY: John Wiley & Sons, 1992), pp. 182-187.

[18]Ernest R. May, 'Intelligence: Backing Into the Future,' *Foreign Affairs*, Vol. 71, No. 3 (1992), p. 64.

[19]H. Norman Schwarzkopf with Peter Petre, *It Doesn't Take a Hero* (New York, NY: Bantam Books, 1992), p. 293.

[20]Kenneth G. Robertson, 'The Study of Intelligence in the United States', *Comparing Foreign Intelligence* (London: Pergamon-Brassey's, 1988), p. 8.

[21]Alex Taylor III. 'How Toyota Copes With Hard Times', *Fortune International*, 25 January 1993, p. 46.

[22]Ibid.

[23]'Clinton Urged to Redefine Intelligence Needs', *International Herald Tribune*, 30 November 1992, p. 3, col. 1.

[24]George Lardner Jr. 'US Demands for Economic Intelligence Up Sharply, Gates Says', *The Washington Post*, 14 April 1992, Section A, p. 5.

[25]Ibid.

[26]Stansfield Turner, *Secrecy & Democracy: The CIA in Transition* (London: Sidgwick & Jackson, 1986), p. 273.

[27]Ibid.

[28]_____. 'Indiana Jim and the temple of spooks'. *The Economist*, 20 March 1993, p. 60.

[29]R. James Woolsey, letter to *The Economist*, 24 April 1993, p. 6.

[30]Amy Borrus, et al. 'Should the CIA Start Spying for Corporate America?', *International Business Week*, 14 October 1990, p. 52.

[31]Ibid.

[32]James Adams. 'Paris Steps Up Spying on Both Friends and Foes', *The Sunday Times*, 5 April 1992.

[33]Executive Order No 12333, 4 December 1981.

[34]_____. *JETRO: Leading the Way to More Imports* (Tokyo: Japan External Trade Organisation, undated), p. 14.

[35]Ibid., p. 1.

[36]Rajaram Veliyath, 'Balancing Short-run Performance and Longer Term Prospects', *Long Range Planning*, June 1992.

[37]Michael E. Porter, 'From Competitive Advantage to Corporate Strategy', in *Michael E. Porter on Competition and Strategy* (Boston, MA: Harvard Business School Publishing Division, 1987), p. 15.

[38]Ibid.

[39]_____. *Factbook on Intelligence*, loc. cit.

[40]Christopher Lorenz. 'Flying in the Face of Corporate Ethics', *Financial Times*, 22 January 1993, p. 7.

2 INTELLIGENCE AND COMPETITIVE STRATEGY

INTRODUCTION

A great deal of the management literature produced since the mid-1960s has been concerned with explaining the theoretical and practical complexities of strategic management and of strategic thinking. Various interpretations of the concept of competitive strategy in particular have captured the interests of scholars and managers alike over the period. Today no professional manager will dispute that firms must be able to integrate their vision, their objectives, and their key goals into a formal strategic process that accommodates the formulation and implementation of corporate, business and functional strategies.

Whatever model, or models, of organisation companies choose to follow – global, international, multinational or transnational – the overriding strategic considerations remain broadly the same. Managers must continuously re-assess their strategic situation (where are we relative to our competitors?). Managers must make strategic choices (how should we compete? how do we gain competitive advantage?). And of course managers must act; at the end of the day they must implement strategy. George Yip, professor of business strategy and international marketing at University of California Los Angeles, argues that 'being able to develop and implement an effective global strategy is the acid test of a well managed company.'[1]

It was apparent as we entered the 1990s that no company, no industry, and no market would escape the shock waves of economic, political, social and technological change sweeping over the globe. The competitive environment had changed fundamentally, it had changed radically, and it had changed everywhere.

The Paris-based consulting firm, Strat*X, offers one list of radical changes occurring in the business environment:

- deregulation in various industries (e.g. airlines, financial services, and telecommunications)
- globalisation of major industries
- information 'explosion'
- major shifts in distribution patterns
- quality as the norm, not the exception (e.g. Total Quality Management programmes)
- slower global economic growth
- transition from product to systems offerings (firms like DEC now emphasise information solutions, not hardware)
- unexpected competition (the greatest challenge to the toy makers Lego of Denmark comes from Nintendo, Sega and other electronic games).

These changes and others have led to rising competitive intensity.

Since 1989 we have witnessed the seemingly continuous re-drawing of the map of Europe, and still wait as the final act of the tragedy that was Yugoslavia is played. And despite the fact that the 12 nations which make up the European Community were officially united on 1 January 1993, economic and political harmony in Europe remain distant goals.

Unemployment in the European Community reached 10 per cent in 1992 and climbed towards 11 per cent in early 1993 as economic growth continued to slow. Corporate dinosaurs such as GM and IBM (which lost $5 billion in 1992) seemed headed for extinction, and President Clinton's wife, Hillary, in her Rasputin-like role as head of a taskforce responsible for reforming America's healthcare system, wasted little time before firing her opening volleys in the new administration's war against the pharmaceutical companies.

In sharp contrast to these events organisations such as Merck, Microsoft, Intel, Philip Morris and Toys 'R' Us continue to inspire managers by setting new and improving standards of business excellence, particularly in the ways in which they develop and implement strategy. Moreover the tireless and intensely competitive 'dragons' of east Asia – Hong Kong, South Korea, Singapore and Taiwan – look forward to real economic growth. Why, one must ask, are some firms and some nations able to grow and prosper consistently while others appear content simply to survive?

The managing of strategic change has emerged as the major challenge to managers for the 1990s and probably beyond. We observe that successful firms are those able (and willing!) to set in motion a process of strategic transformation whereby the organisation 'seeks to regain a sustainable competitive advantage by redefining the business objectives, creating new competences and harnessing these capabilities to meet the new market opportunities.'[2] We see too that the speed with which such a process is initiated by a company, and the relative effectiveness with which that enterprise is able to implement strategic transformation, and sustain it as a continuous process, is likely to signal its long-term prospects as a viable commercial entity.

Even functional excellence does not guarantee success. Practices built around popular notions such as high-performance teams, just-in-time (JIT) delivery, learning organisations, time-based competition and Total Quality Management (TQM) may represent important organisational priorities, and may indeed be essential for operational efficiency, but they do not automatically translate into competitive success, or even increased profits.

For example, producing a camera of such robust design and materials that dropping it from a 10-storey window would cause it no serious damage may well qualify its makers for technical and design awards, but if the camera does not in all other respects meet the perceived needs of customers at the price they are prepared to pay for it (which in each instance is measured in terms of its relative position to competitor cameras), it will not be a commercial success. The efficiency with which the camera manufacturer manages its human resources, its logistics, its marketing activities and its production operations will be meaningless.

It is not enough to rely upon internal factors alone as drivers of businesses, or of planning activities. While it is right to extol the virtues of customer or quality focus, we should remember that the most focused beast on earth must be the ostrich with its head in the sand. Competition has emerged as the key driver of strategic decision-making.

And as the drivers, the role and the structure of strategic planning have evolved, so too have the information needs of managers. Competitive intelligence has therefore become a central component of the strategic management process. It has become the means by which firms can gauge the competitor objectives and strategies which lie beneath the surface.

Porter, in the seminal work *Competitive Strategy* (1980), offers a penetrating look at competitor analysis and its role in the formulation of competitive strategy. Porter points out that 'sophisticated competitor analysis is needed to answer such questions as "Who should we pick a fight with in the industry, and with what sequence of moves?" "What is the meaning of that competitor's strategic move and how seriously should we take it?" and "What arenas should we avoid because the competitor's response will be emotional or desperate?"'[3] Put another way, how are our competitors trying to beat us and therefore how are we going to beat them?

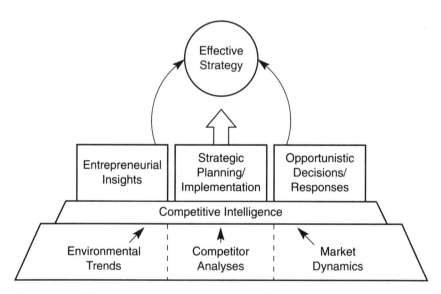

Figure 2.1 Effective strategy/competitive intelligence

Reprinted by permission of John Wiley & Sons, Inc. from *Business Competitor Intelligence: Methods for Collecting, Organising and Using Information* by William L. Sammon, Mark A. Kurland and Robert Spitalnic. Copyright © 1984 by John Wiley & Sons, Inc.

This is how the link between intelligence and strategic planning is presented by a former vice chairman of the CIA's National Intelligence Council (the office responsible for producing national intelligence estimates and for providing intelligence goals to the Directorate for Operations):

> . . . intelligence is nothing less than the crucial second half of strategic planning. It is the mechanism which enables a company that has a good strategic plan to chart and pursue a course that will bring the company to its objectives in the shortest possible time, no matter how rapidly or radically external conditions may change. And when external conditions change so radically that the plan itself needs to be altered, it is intelligence that sounds the first alert for the strategic planners themselves.[4]

Without competitive intelligence the formulation of strategy is impossible. Without competitive intelligence a firm cannot be managed strategically.

Of course it is not sufficient only to gain competitive intelligence. Intelligence must be used. Managers must know what actions they can, should and will take when they acquire the intelligence they need. The 'shelf life' of intelligence is short, and its costs in absolute terms are high. The task of managers is to use intelligence in a timely manner to create or sustain competitive advantage – to make decisions, to take action. Schwarzkopf put it this way to his senior commanders before launching the Gulf War ground offensive:

> I cannot afford to have commanders who do not understand that it is attack, attack, attack, attack, and destroy every step of the way. If you have somebody who doesn't understand it, I would strongly recommend that you consider removing him from command and putting in somebody that can do the job.[5]

The value of intelligence is realised in the using of it.

PLANNING AND DIRECTION

In Chapter 1 the five steps which comprise the intelligence cycle were introduced. The first step is that of Planning and Direction. In the words of the CIA:

This involves the management of the entire effort, from the identification of the need for data to the final delivery of an intelligence product to a consumer. It can be seen as the beginning of the cycle – the beginning because it involves drawing up specific collection requirements and the end because finished intelligence, which supports policy decisions, engenders new requirements.[6]

This is how Sherman Kent, who retired in 1968 as Director of the CIA's Office of National Estimates, presents his analysis of organisational difficulties which arise between the consumers of intelligence and the intelligence producers:

There is no phase of the intelligence business which is more important than the proper relationship between intelligence itself and the people who use its product. Oddly enough, this relationship, which one would expect to establish itself automatically, does not do this. It is established as a result of a great deal of persistent conscious effort, and is likely to disappear when the effort is relaxed.

Proper relationships between intelligence producers and consumers is one of the utmost delicacy. Intelligence must be close enough to policy, plans, and operations to have the greatest amount of guidance, and must not be so close that it loses its objectivity and integrity of judgement . . .

[The job of intelligence staff] is to see that the doers are generally well-informed; its job is to stand behind them with the book opened at the right page, to call their attention to the stubborn fact that they may be neglecting, and – at their request – to analyse alternative courses without indicating choice. Intelligence cannot serve if it does not know the doers' mind; it cannot serve if it has not their confidence; it cannot serve unless it can have the kind of guidance any professional man must have from his client.[7]

Managers often ask their company's competitive intelligence unit, their market research staff or corporate librarians for competitive information without giving adequate consideration to the purpose of the information required, or to its relevance to decision-making. The result is that the time of both consumer and researchers is wasted, and the manager ends up without a useless intelligence product. Intelligence, as all company resources, costs money, often large sums of money, and can consume many man-hours of time for collection, processing and dissemination. It is therefore essential that policymakers be crystal-clear about what it is they need to know, why exactly they need to know it, what it is they already know, or think they know, and what they plan to do with the intelligence once they have it.

If the finished intelligence product is to add value to strategic decision-making, and if the intelligence process is to work smoothly, briefings to researchers, analysts and external consultants should be comprehensive and as narrowly focused as practicable. In the words of one well-known consultant, competitive intelligence 'objectives must be set so that the intelligence effort has the greatest impact on [the firm's] ability to generate a competitive advantage.'[8]

For example, the format of a competitive intelligence project briefing will typically include at least three main sections plus supporting documentation:

Background information

Researchers and analysts are not magicians. They are skilled professionals who, often on short notice, are expected to produce intelligence products on which critical strategic or tactical decisions are based. A firm would not make or market a product before understanding the customer needs it fulfils; likewise intelligence professionals cannot be expected to deliver a relevant intelligence product without the benefit of thorough 'backgrounding'.

Background information will cover issues such as:

- who is the intelligence for?
- why is the intelligence needed? what are the strategic or tactical implications? what specific decisions is the policymaker trying to make?
- what do we already know?
- what are the current assumptions? on what data or information are these assumptions based, and what is the reliability of these sources?
- which are the priority issues (ranking)?

Research objectives

Researchers and analysts need to understand the expectations of the intelligence consumer; knowing what policymakers are really looking for guides intelligence staff. It enables them to set the right focus, and develop a research strategy appropriate to the sources available and to budgetary and time constraints. Moreover, it improves their sensitivity to the more obscure pieces of the intelligence puzzle which might otherwise go unnoticed. The best intelligence comes from primary – usually human – sources, so researchers need to know what to listen for, as well as what to look for.

If one purpose of competitive intelligence is to help make specific decisions, it is the decision makers who must initiate, and in broad terms must define, the intelligence needs.

The author was once asked to provide a client in the health care industry with intelligence about a co-marketing alliance into which two main competitors had entered. One competitor was based in Scandinavia, and the corporate headquarters of the other company was in the United States. Our client wished to know which firm was taking the lead role in the alliance, what were the terms of the partnership, in which product areas were the companies planning to co-operate, and in which countries.

The client explained first why the information was needed, and, second, what the implications were to their own strategies. In other words, there was no ambiguity about what was required, what needed to be done, or why it was being done. The research strategy was quickly designed, and the client received exactly what they wanted by way of a finished intelligence product, in time for them to take appropriate action.

Research questions

Research questions must be precise. Where measures are called for there should be no ambiguity (does the 'size' of a competitor's new manufacturing facility refer to the total area of the facility, its production capacity, the number of employees, or all three?).

Research questions should also reflect exactly what the consumer needs and wishes to know, not what he or she believes is possible to learn, or might simply be nice to know. If the questions cannot be related to the strategic plan of the firm, they are probably the wrong questions. If, on the other hand, it is important to know a competitor's key customers or suppliers, or say, the volumes and terms of business between them, then that is what must be asked for. An intelligence briefing is not the place to pull punches.

COMPETITIVE FORCES – THE PORTER MODEL

It is Porter's contention that the extent or 'state of competition in an industry depends on five basic competitive forces',[9] and that strategy formulation is predicated on an understanding of these forces. We shall review each of the elements of the Porter five-forces model:

i. *Threat of new entrants*. Mainly this concerns 'barriers to entry that are present [in an industry], coupled with the reaction from existing competitors that the entrant can expect'.[10] Costs associated with successfully differentiating a new entrant's product offerings from those of established players is one barrier. Limitations in distribution channels represent another. What is important to know 'is what makes the industry vulnerable to entry'.[11]

ii. *Intensity of rivalry among existing competitors*. The intensity of rivalry – of competition – in an industry is determined by many factors, including 'high strategic stakes'. In telecommunications, for example, BT has fought hard against European PTTs and American and Japanese competitors to be one of the key global providers of voice and data services. Its $4 billion link-up with Electronic Data Systems (EDS) in early 1993 represented a major step towards reaching this goal.

iii. *Threat of substitute products or services*. Porter argues that 'substitute products that deserve the most attention are those that (1) are subject to trends improving their price-performance trade-off with the industry's product, or (2) are produced by industries earning high profits'.[12] A good illustration of the competitive dangers posed by substitute products is found in the pharmaceutical business. A growing number of generic manufacturers – many of them privately held and well funded – are making and supplying generic versions of top selling drugs that come 'off patent'. These products are sold at, say, 20–30 per cent less than the original formulations from firms like Ciba-Geigy, Glaxo and Roche, thereby creating additional obstacles in the relatively short revenue streams enjoyed by the companies that developed the compounds in the first place.

iv. *Bargaining power of buyers.* Buyer power is a well-known phenomenon. The airline, banking, film and motor industries are good examples of where buyer power is strong. Porter claims that a buyer group is powerful where the following circumstances apply:

- 'It is concentrated or purchases large volumes relative to seller sales.'
- 'The products [or services] it purchases from the industry represent a significant fraction of the buyer's costs or purchases.'
- 'The products it purchases from the industry are standard or undifferentiated.'
- 'It faces few switching costs.'
- 'It earns low profits.'
- 'Buyers pose a credible threat of backward integration.'
- 'The industry's product is unimportant to the quality of the buyers' products or services.'
- 'The buyer has full information.'[13]

Firms competing in industries where buyer power is strong are fiercely competitive. There is usually considerable downward pressure on prices, so profitability must be achieved by other means. In industries characterised by strong buyer power it is particularly important for the firm to probe issues such as competitor costs, competitor distribution and promotional strategies, and the competitor's approach to product positioning.

For example, the cost of cement in Europe approximately doubles with every 100 kilometres of inland transportation. One of the key success factors for cement manufacturers is therefore the distribution network. This is one reason why cement manufacturers pay close attention to when and where competitors are 'setting up shop'.

v. *Bargaining power of suppliers.* Porter notes that 'the conditions making suppliers powerful tend to mirror those making buyers powerful.'[14] He lists the following as characteristic of a powerful supplier group:

- 'It is dominated by a few companies and is more concentrated than the industry it sells to.' This of course is the situation in the commercial sector of the aerospace industry. Three firms, Boeing, McDonnell Douglas and Europe's Airbus Industrie dominate the world market for new passenger jets.
- 'It is not obliged to contend with other substitute products for sale to the industry.'
- 'The industry is not an important customer of the supplier.'
- 'The supplier's product is an important input to the buyer's business.'
- 'The supplier group's products are differentiated or it has built up switching costs.'
- 'The supplier group poses a credible threat of forward integration.'

Obviously, the interaction between buyers and suppliers is dynamic, and over time (sometimes a short space of time) can shift. Intel's early, almost total dominance of the market for 386 memory chips (for personal computers) eroded in a few short years. Competitors captured over 50 per cent of the 386 market, forcing the company to focus on the 486 and Pentium chips.

Intel is now the world's largest semiconductor company, and enjoys a near monopoly on the 486 chip. But as Pentium replaces the 486 as the 'standard' high-performance chip, Intel will again face new competition, this time from a competitive offering by DEC, the new Alpha chip.

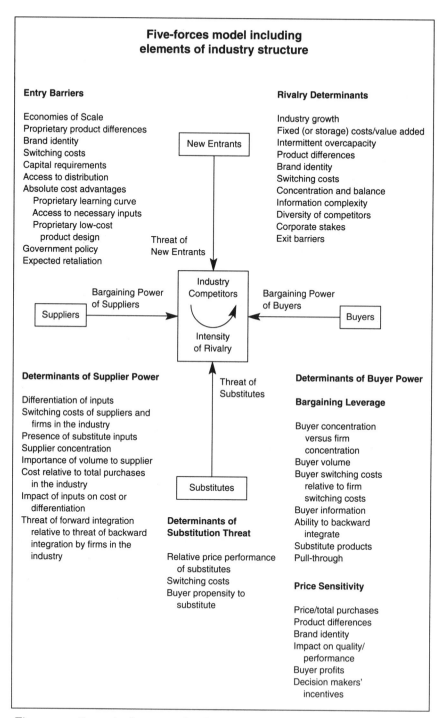

Five-forces model including elements of industry structure

Entry Barriers

Economies of Scale
Proprietary product differences
Brand identity
Switching costs
Capital requirements
Access to distribution
Absolute cost advantages
   Proprietary learning curve
   Access to necessary inputs
   Proprietary low-cost
      product design
Government policy
Expected retaliation

Rivalry Determinants

Industry growth
Fixed (or storage) costs/value added
Intermittent overcapacity
Product differences
Brand identity
Switching costs
Concentration and balance
Information complexity
Diversity of competitors
Corporate stakes
Exit barriers

New Entrants

Threat of
New Entrants

Bargaining Power
of Suppliers

Suppliers

Industry
Competitors

Intensity
of Rivalry

Bargaining Power
of Buyers

Buyers

Determinants of Supplier Power

Differentiation of inputs
Switching costs of suppliers and
   firms in the industry
Presence of substitute inputs
Supplier concentration
Importance of volume to supplier
Cost relative to total purchases
   in the industry
Impact of inputs on cost or
   differentiation
Threat of forward integration
   relative to threat of backward
   integration by firms in the
   industry

Threat of
Substitutes

Substitutes

**Determinants of
Substitution Threat**

Relative price performance
   of substitutes
Switching costs
Buyer propensity to
   substitute

Determinants of Buyer Power

Bargaining Leverage

Buyer concentration
   versus firm
   concentration
Buyer volume
Buyer switching costs
   relative to firm
   switching costs
Buyer information
Ability to backward
   integrate
Substitute products
Pull-through

Price Sensitivity

Price/total purchases
Product differences
Brand identity
Impact on quality/
   performance
Buyer profits
Decision makers'
   incentives

Figure 2.2 Porter's elements of industry structure

Porter also argues that 'the fundamental basis of above-average performance in the long run is sustainable competitive advantage.'[15] He advocates three ways – three 'generic strategies' – through which competitive advantage can be achieved:

  i. cost leadership
 ii. differentiation
iii. focus (cost focus or differentiation focus).

Porter's theories and prescriptions on strategy are well known, and have served as catalysts for much debate since 1980. Nevertheless, it is Porter's thinking on competition and strategy that has provided the principal intellectual framework for competitive intelligence for nearly a decade and a half. More recently the ideas of Hamel and Prahalad have given new impetus to how academics and managers use and think about competitive intelligence. As Hamel points out, 'Honda didn't out-invest GM; it out-learned GM!'[16]

There are three key lessons from the ideas of Porter and Hamel that managers can apply to competitive intelligence:

1. At all times managers must understand how the competitive forces, and how continuous change in these forces, can and will influence the strategies of competitor firms, and of their own companies. The government of the United States, for example, consistently and repeatedly proclaims its enthusiasm for an innovative, profitable and strong micro-computer software industry. This has stimulated the development of an environment where companies such as Borland, Lotus, Microsoft, WordPerfect and Novell flourish. It therefore came as something of a surprise to many industry observers when the Federal Trade Commission (FTC) launched a $2\frac{1}{2}$-year non-public investigation into the business (i.e. competitive) practices of Microsoft (1992 sales $3.75 billion).

    The FTC probe was closed at the end of 1992, and at this writing the FTC commissioners have not decided to act on any of their staff's recommendations. Microsoft Chairman William H. Gates III insists, perhaps rightly, that his firm's success is based on good products (and, I would suggest, excellent management) not on market dominance. Whatever the outcome of the FTC decisions, the implications for Microsoft (and the future competitive strategy) and the industry are significant. Microsoft will be compelled to change the way it does things, as will Microsoft's growing army of competitors. Gaining an understanding of exactly what these changes mean is the domain of competitive intelligence.

2. Managers must be able rapidly to translate changes in competitive forces into new or revised strategies and action. Knowing the whole of a competitor's strategic plan for the next five years would be of no use if well-considered action was not taken upon it.

3. Change is seldom incremental, and strategies which do not recognise this are bound to fail. Business as usual is a thing of the past. To defeat competitors means to leapfrog, and to out-manoeuvre them, not keep up with them. Hamel claims that companies must be more than customer led. 'Give them what they haven't yet dreamed of,' he rightly urges.[17]

Ultimately a firm's intelligence needs will relate directly to decisions that are influenced by one or more competitive forces. For example: is there any danger our customer has decided to integrate backwards into one of our upstream business areas? Or, what emerging competitors can we expect to face in the future? Who are they, what are their strengths, where are they vulnerable (threat of new entrants)? How much is our competitor prepared to spend, and what plans do they have, to seize market share at our expense? How will they position their newest product offerings against ours, where will they launch, and when (intensity of rivalry)? What are the capabilities and intentions of low-price firms offering products which compete with or may provide alternatives to ours (threat of substitutes)? Our buyers are powerful, but how powerful? What are their perceptions of supplier alternatives, and of us? Which of our competitors are they in contact with (bargaining power of buyers)? How important is our business to our suppliers? What are their alternative customer sources? What are the weaknesses of these sources, and how can we leverage our bargaining power to shift the balance in our favour (bargaining power of suppliers)? Competitive strategy and competitive intelligence are interdependent, two elements of the same dynamic system.

STRATEGY AND PLANNING

Strategy, as we have said, exists at three levels of the firm, corporate, business unit and operational. At all three levels strategies are inextricably linked, sub-systems of a wider strategic management system. It is instructive to consider the role of competitive intelligence at each level separately.

Corporate

In 1986 Ghoshal and Westney completed a detailed study of competitor analysis (CA) systems in three big MNCs; Eastman Kodak, GM and British Petroleum. They found at the corporate level that 'the CA unit had two mandates: to follow companies that were "corporate competitors" competing with the firm across multiple lines of business, and to function as a "centre of expertise", keeping abreast of the most effective and efficient tools of competitor analysis and disseminating them to analysts elsewhere in the organisation.'[18]

The strategic perspectives of top corporate managers, of country general managers when they wear their 'corporate hats', and of corporate planners, obviously differ from those of managers, including senior managers, at the business unit level. Often in fact these differences are the source of considerable conflict, or tension within the organisation, even where broad consensus exists on the organisation's mission, and its major goals, objectives and policies. What matters of course is how successfully these differences in perspective – and therefore differences in intelligence needs – are blended together in the strategic management mix.

Corporate managers and planners are chiefly concerned with 'what businesses the corporation should be in and how the corporate office should manage the array of business units.'[19] Put another way, they are concerned with formulating and implementing strategies which make 'the corporate whole add up to more than the sum of its business unit parts.'[20]

Intelligence needs at corporate level are primarily a function of the following five factors:

i. The diversification strategies of existing competitors and of organisations which – possibly through acquisition – are likely to become rivals.

ii. The strategic intent of competitors at corporate level. According to Hamel and Prahalad, where a company possesses strategic intent it is used 'consistently to guide resource allocations'.[21] Intelligence which reveals how and where competitors plan to allocate financial or other strategic resources enables a firm to make smarter resource allocation decisions of its own.

iii. The core competencies of competitors. Hamel and Prahalad argue that 'the most powerful way to prevail in global competition'[22] is 'to be found in management's ability to consolidate corporate-wide technologies and production skills into competencies that empower individual businesses to adapt quickly to changing opportunities.'[23] Therefore it is essential to monitor the degree of success competitors achieve in building their core competencies, and in integrating these competencies throughout their organisations.

A core competence is a competitive strength that meets three tests:

- it is lasting – it 'provides potential access to a wide variety of markets'[24]
- it is relevant – it makes 'a significant contribution to the perceived customer benefits of the end product'[25]
- it is unique – it is difficult to imitate.

iv. Changes in the structure of each industry in which it operates (competitive forces), and in each market in which it competes.

v. Changes and trends in the environment which may have a strategic impact on the corporate whole, or on any one of its parts. For example, firms operating in, or doing business with, some less developed countries (LDCs) need in place mechanisms which provide early warning of politically-related problems which could jeopardise company interests, including, say, the security of facilities or expatriate executives. In the defence business in many parts of the world intelligence about who really makes or influences decisions concerning the awarding of contracts is as important, and at times more important, than competitor intelligence.

Intelligence needs at corporate level also differ from those of business units, particularly in international companies where the parent firm retains considerable control and influence. Yet these needs are, ipso facto, complementary to those of the business units and must be formally integrated with them.

Competitive intelligence is employed by corporate managers and planners to help establish competitive strategies for each industry in which their firms participate, or may be planning to enter. In addition, competitive intelligence is used by corporate headquarters staff to better understand how competitors assess their businesses and how they intend to add value to them. Last, competitive intelligence at corporate level should be used not only to help establish corporate goals and performance measurements, but equally 'to develop methods and techniques to attain those goals'.[26]

Business unit

In practice it is managers responsible for competitive strategy at the business unit level who are mainly concerned with competitive intelligence. For it is at the business unit – or more precisely, at the served market – level where firms compete, where they win or lose their battles for growth, profit and position. The corollary of this is that in European firms competitive intelligence units are generally found in, or report to, business development or strategic planning groups.

We have said that competitive intelligence is tied to specific, usually, strategic decisions. We have also suggested that in firms that compete primarily through superior strategy 'management's focus needs to be more external than internal'.[27] American and European firms typically 'attempt to manage competition through strategic repositioning or by creating a more unique strategy.'[28] This contrasts with the style of Japanese firms which 'tend to compete against each other using very similar strategies',[29] emphasising superior implementation.

The overriding concern of competitive intelligence at the business unit level is that of the future plans and strategies of competitors. It is not macroeconomics assessments of the competitive environment, as important as this is. It is not market analysis. That is what market research departments and market research firms are for. It is not economic or environmental forecasting. Forecasts do not help business managers win this month's battles; nor, in practice, do they offer substantive support to the CEO and his top management team as they evaluate their strategic options.

To out-perform competitors senior managers require up-to-date intelligence that explains the competitor's capabilities, as well as what the competitor intends to do next month, next quarter, and maybe next year. The central aim of the competitive intelligence unit is to deliver to managers an intelligence product that provides analysis and assessments of what changes in key factors in the competitive environment mean for the firm and its future.

Nothing here is intended to suggest that an objective of competitor analysis is to formulate strategy which is reactive only. The idea of competitive intelligence is to know the enemy in order to defeat, not emulate, him.

Operational

It is of course at the operational level where strategy is truly tested. Managers must at all times be perfectly clear about the ability of competitors to actually achieve their strategic objectives, and therefore must be relentless in their pursuit of information that exposes functional and tactical weaknesses of competitors, and reveals fully their strengths.

How well do their sales and promotional tactics fit their stated marketing objectives? If service is an important element of their positioning strategy are they successful in meeting customer expectations (firms should become customers of their competitors)? How well do their delivery and distribution systems work? Do their discount practices match their official discount policies? What is behind the new engineering techniques which a competitor has reportedly introduced? New recruitment drives for managers, sales personnel and other specialists can alert firms to plans a competitor might have to gear up business activities, just as news of plant closures, or of major 're-organisation' or 'restructuring' are often symptoms of deeper problems.

Intelligence at the operational level can be particularly difficult to obtain, especially in areas such as costs and process. Finding gaps in the tactics, or in a key functional area of a competitor's operations, will often point the way to weaknesses which can be exploited at a strategic level.

THE APPLICATION AND USE OF INTELLIGENCE

How is competitive intelligence used? How should it be used?

Intelligence must contain two key elements if it is to be made actionable (i.e. action can be taken on it). First, it must include likely and relevant future developments. Second, there must be a direct link between the intelligence product, or output, and managers' responsibilities. There is much evidence to suggest that most managers of European-based MNCs have little, if any, experience with the intelligence process or product.

Recently the Society of Competitive Intelligence Professionals (SCIP) in the United States commissioned a landmark study on the role of competitive intelligence in corporate strategy and performance. The principal research approach involves a national survey of the packaged foods, pharmaceutical, and telecommunications industries. In their first progress report of the study's findings, the researchers, Professors Jaworski and Wee, offer solid evidence that suggests the extent of competitive intelligence activities leads directly to:

i. 'More positive relationships among the internal functional areas of the firm.'[30]
ii. 'Higher quality strategic plans.'[31]
iii. Increases in the SBU's [strategic business unit's] knowledge of their market/business environment.'[32]

Competitive intelligence, therefore, drives business performance – it enhances the bottom line – through intermediate consequences; 'by increasing market knowledge, internal relationships, and the quality of strategic plans'.[33] Indeed, competitive intelligence serves ultimately as the most powerful agent for change in the modern business organisation.

Figure 2.3 Competitive intelligence improves business performance

Source Presentation given at the SCIP 1993 Annual Conference by Bernard J. Jaworski.

The application and use of intelligence by firms will vary by company, by circumstance, by degree of organisational commitment, and over time. Managers can no longer rely upon favourite strategic recipes to nourish their companies' or their personal success. In a fast-changing, unpredictable environment, where 'surviving' in chaos rather than 'thriving' on it is the order of the day, competitive intelligence and competitive strategy must, in theory and in practice, be fully integrated, and managed as one and the same thing.

Dynamic strategies which endure feed upon continuous streams of intelligence. If, for example, a competitor is conducting test marketing of a new product now, it is now when that information must surface, and it is now when the strategic implications of that competitor's actions must be evaluated. Further probing will usually indicate offensive strategic response options that are appropriate. By moving fast enough the consequences of any success the competitor may ultimately enjoy at the expense of the firm (e.g. lost market share) can be mitigated, and sometimes eliminated altogether. In simple terms, a competitor may reach the conclusion that 'it just isn't worth it'.

Competitive intelligence facilitates the re-thinking and realignment of strategies, and the speed with which these are done. According to Alan Bergstrom, whose professional experience includes preparing a daily intelligence report for former President Reagan, this means:

i.   expanding market knowledge
ii. challenging assumptions
iii. reassessing objectives
iv. validating goals.

The application of competitive intelligence will of course differ at different levels of the firm.

At corporate headquarters detailed intelligence assessments of the competitors of an acquisition target can have a critical impact on decisions related to the take-over. Often the focus of interest in the acquisition process is too narrowly directed on the target company itself, and a complete picture of the relative competitive position of a recently acquired business is seen only in the course of time. In most cases the picture is an unhappy one.

On one occasion, I was asked by a pharmaceutical manufacturer to investigate the status of some 20 compounds thought to be under development by competitors for a therapeutic area – a market – approaching $1 billion in value. The client firm was itself in Phase II clinical trials, and had thus far invested millions of dollars in research and development. The company had not updated its competitive intelligence for 18 months. Development and marketing decisions concerning this product were being made in a vacuum. The surprise introduction of a competing 'blockbuster' drug, particularly one with similar therapeutic properties, could have resulted in the client writing off hundreds of millions of dollars in R&D and lost opportunity costs. In Europe episodes such as this are repeated time and time again.

Firms can also apply competitive intelligence in many different ways at the operational level. Salesforce personnel can sell more effectively if they are armed with detailed briefings informing them of exactly what they are competing against. They need to know the strengths and weaknesses, the positioning arguments, and the terms of sale and payment offered by competitors before they meet their clients. Product knowledge should extend beyond the firm's own offerings, to that of the competition's.

In the final analysis it is the responsibility of managers to act on competitive intelligence, creatively and decisively. Permanent competitive advantage does not exist because a stable competitive environment does not exist. The long-range plan of the past is a relic of business history. Today's competitive intelligence is tomorrow's column in the *FT*. For better or for worse firms survive in a sea of competition and in a world plagued by recession, uncertainty and increasing demands on human and physical resources. In this environment the power of information, of intelligence, becomes the ultimate power. With it managers have the chance to steer and maintain a course towards business success. If managers do not have intelligence, or if they wrongly apply it, the firm finally must perish.

NOTES

[1]George S. Yip, *Total Global Strategy* (Englewood Cliffs, NJ: Prentice Hall, 1992), p. 1.

[2]Barbara Blumenthal and Philippe Haspeslagh. 'Corporate Transformation: Amalgams and Distinctions'. Working paper 92/74/SM, INSEAD The European Institute of Business Administration, 1992, p. 4.

[3]Michael E. Porter, *Competitive Strategy: Techniques for Analysing Industries and Competitors* (New York, NY: The Free Press, 1980), p. 47.

[4]Herbert E. Meyer, *Real World Intelligence* (New York, NY: Grove Weidenfeld, 1987), p. 8.

[5]H. Norman Schwarzkopf, *It Doesn't Take a Hero*, (New York, NY: Bantam Books, 1992), p.384.

[6] ———— . *Factbook on Intelligence* (Washington, DC: Central Intelligence Agency, 1991), p. 13.

[7]Sherman Kent, *Strategic Intelligence for American World Policy* (Princeton, NJ: Princeton University Press, 1971), pp. 180-182.

[8]Kirk W.M. Tyson, *Competitor Intelligence Manual & Guide* (Englewood Cliffs, NJ: Prentice Hall, 1990), p. 10.

[9]Porter, *op. cit.* p. 3.

[10]Porter, *op. cit.* p. 7.

[11]Michael E. Porter. 'How Competitive Forces Shape Strategy', in *Readings in Strategic Management*, edited by David Asch and Cliff Bowman (Basingstoke, Hants: The Macmillan Press, 1989), p. 135.

[12]Michael E. Porter, *Competitive Strategy*, p. 24.

[13]Ibid. pp. 24–26.

[14]Ibid. p. 27.

[15]Michael E. Porter, *Competitive Advantage: Creating and Sustaining Superior Performance* (New York, NY: The Free Press, 1985), p. 11.

[16]Quoted by Michael K. Allio in 'The Argument Against Adopting a 'Process' Mentality', *Planning Review*, January/February 1993, p. 51.

[17]Ibid.

[18]Sumantra Ghoshal and Eleanor Westney. 'Organising Competitor Analysis Systems'. Working paper 90/63/SM, INSEAD The European Institute of Business Administration, 1990, pp. 3-4.

[19]Michael E. Porter, 'From Competitive Advantage to Corporate Strategy', *Michael E. Porter on Competition and Strategy* (Boston, MA: Harvard Business School Publishing Division, 1987), p. 15.

[20]Ibid.

[21]Gary Hamel and C.K. Prahalad. 'Strategic Intent', *The McKinsey Quarterly*, Spring 1990, p. 40.

[22]Gary Hamel and C.K. Prahalad. 'The Core Competence of the Corporation', *Harvard Business Review*, May–June 1990, p. 79.

[23]Ibid. p. 81.

[24]Ibid. p. 83.

[25]Ibid. p. 84.

[26]James R. Webb. 'Linking Competitive Intelligence to Corporate Strategy', *Competitive Intelligence Review*, Fall 1991, p. 21.

[27]William G. Egelhoff. 'Great Strategy or Great Strategy Implementation – Two Ways of Competing in Global Markets', Sloan Management Review, Winter 1993, p. 45.

[28]Ibid. p. 42.

[29]Ibid. p. 42.

[30]Bernard Jaworski and Liang Chee Wee. 'Competitive Intelligence and Bottom-Line Performance', *Competitive Intelligence Review*, Fall 92/Winter 93, p. 26.

[31]Ibid.

[32]Ibid.

[33]Ibid.

3 ANALYSIS AND INTERPRETATION

INTRODUCTION

Intelligence is information, or useful data, that has been 'enhanced, refined, shaped and distributed to meet the unique needs of one specific consumer . . . and no one else.'[1] It is information that has been analysed for a particular set of circumstances and from a particular perspective. Analysis and production are the fourth step in the intelligence cycle.

Analysis is the search for patterns. It 'entails sifting, screening, comparing with other data, and ultimately including it within a larger whole.'[2] It involves the transformation of information acquired in raw form into a usable intelligence product. Analysis is the value-added component of intelligence.

We can identify four specific types of analytical output:

i. The first category involves analysis that is predictive. It may, for example, 'consist of a comprehensive description and explanation'[3] of important trends in STEP, or industry- or market-specific factors, and the implications for the firm of one or more of these factors.

    An export company in the agricultural sector may need to know how a competitor has assessed the current (Uruguay) round of Gatt negotiations. In particular it would be important to know what the competitor believes will be the impact of each of several possible outcomes of the talks, both on its business and the industry, and how in each instance the competitor plans to respond.

ii. The second category involves analysis which aims to 'make data more meaningful, and . . . provide guidance to policymakers considering goals and alternative means of achieving them.'[4]

    In March 1993 Dr. Ernest Mario, chief executive and deputy chairman of Glaxo, Europe's biggest pharmaceuticals group, was ousted in a boardroom *coup*. At the time Glaxo's market value was £20 billion, and the company was sitting comfortably on a cash mountain of £1.5 billion. Glaxo had also enjoyed several years of double digit earnings growth fuelled by its ruthlessly efficient marketing organisation. Few CEOs in the pharmaceutical industry would have been unhappy to receive a quick analysis of what Dr. Mario's departure might mean for their companies. To what extent, for example, did this sudden changing of the guard at Glaxo reflect internal disagreements over the company's plans to enter the over-the-counter (OTC) drugs market, a segment in which it was not yet a player? What changes in strategic focus at Glaxo did this signal, and what influence would this have on the strategies of Glaxo's competitors?

iii. A third category of analysis provides 'warnings of major events, particularly attack, and . . . long-term estimates, trends and assessments of developments in major regions or important functional areas, based on empirical evidence.'[5]

A key purpose of competitive intelligence is to avoid surprises. Analysis which identifies potential threats of competitor plans to acquire, or perhaps enter into alliances with, other rivals is one example of this.

In 1992 Digital Equipment Corporation (DEC), once second only to IBM in computing, lost $2.8 billion. The company also lost money the year before. Nevertheless, under an ambitious new chairman and senior management team, DEC set a goal of becoming one of the top five global suppliers of personal computers (PCs) by 1995. DEC, the company that once failed to take PCs seriously, was positioning itself to make up for lost opportunities and lost time; it was going on the offensive. It is clear that firms competing against DEC may wish to gain a detailed understanding of the company's strategies for achieving its ambitions, and of the potential impact this is likely to have on the PC industry.

iv. The fourth category involves analysis comprised 'of pieces of current information on specialised . . . topics of concern to policy-makers.'[6]

For example, early in its strategy formulation process a business development group may need to know when and where a new competitive product will be launched long before the information becomes 'public'. Alternatively, in an effort to improve performance in one of its management or manufacturing processes, a firm may wish to benchmark companies both in and outside its industry known to be 'best in class'. Chapter 4 offers a comprehensive treatment of competitive benchmarking.

But whatever the type or types of analytical output, frequent and strong linkages to current strategic (and sometimes operational) needs of the firm must be established. Otherwise the competitive intelligence activity will lose credibility in the eyes of top management. In order to effect this linkage line managers should be directly involved in the analysis process.

The job of analysts, then, is to 'integrate various pieces of data into a coherent whole, put the evaluated information in context, and produce finished intelligence that includes assessments of events or developments and judgements about the implications of the information for the consumer.'[7] Senior managers, already suffering from information overload and tight agendas, need timely flows of analyses in order to develop and direct the implementation of strategy. Managers do not want to marinate in more facts.

On the other hand, managers must avoid the pitfall of what is sometimes called paralysis by analysis; where competitor analysis becomes virtually an end unto itself, or where managers and analysts become locked into an almost relentless pursuit of perfect, or excessively rational, competitive information. Competitor analysis is a process designed to provide actionable intelligence that decision makers can use to improve business performance. It has no other value. Actionable intelligence assessments:

- are future oriented
- help management develop better competitive strategies
- facilitate a better understanding than the competitor of change in the competitive environment
- will identify current and future competitors, and their strategies and plans.

Although perfect intelligence does not – cannot – exist, intelligence that alerts managers to information gaps, enables executives to develop better bases for financial and market forecasts, facilitates the assessment of market attractiveness, and helps managers anticipate the competitor's next move, does.

What managers analyse, and why, matters as much as how the information is analysed. For example, a comprehensive analysis of the competitor's 'knowledge assets' (institutional knowledge, management experience, and 'the way things are done here'), its investment decisions regarding these assets, and the effectiveness with which these assets are employed and integrated throughout the organisation will reveal far more about the competitor's capabilities and future direction than will a detailed assessment of the physical assets accounted for in the balance sheet. Equally, to know how and where a competitor adds value in each of its business activities will create more opportunities for gaining competitive advantage than will a cocktail of competitor financial ratios.

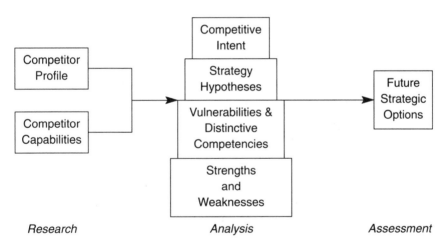

Figure 3.1 Inferring future strategies

Reprinted with the permission of The Futures Group from a presentation given at the SCIP 1993 Annual Conference by David Harkleroad. Copyright © by The Futures Group.

ALTERNATIVE APPROACHES

Three approaches to analysing competitor information are considered here:

1. Top-down analysis

The top-down approach to analysis involves concepts and techniques familiar to most business planners and senior managers. Traditionally it is the approach concerned with the corporate, and now global, view of things, the 'big picture'. That every company should explicitly identify, profile and systematically monitor its competitors goes without saying. At the same time, however, analysts and managers must remember that the objective of competitor analysis is not to understand competitors, the objective is to understand how to beat them.

The top-down approach involves higher level strategic questions about the competition. In particular: Who are our multipoint competitors (rivals with whom two or more of the firm's business units compete)? What is the fit between the competitor's resources and its strategies? What resource allocation decisions has the competitor made for its business and product portfolios? How effectively does the competitor leverage its resources? Does the competitor possess 'a strategic focal point, or . . . strategic intent, on which the efforts of individuals, functions, and businesses can converge over time'?[8] And what strategic weaknesses of our own, or what customer problems or unmet needs, could the competitor exploit?

The top-down approach is also appropriate for identifying and analysing strategic groups. Porter discusses strategic groups in *Competitive Strategy* (1980), and more recently Aaker offers his definition of a strategic group as a group of firms that:

- 'Over time pursue similar competitive strategies (e.g. the use of the same distribution channel and heavy advertising)'[9]
- 'Have similar characteristics (e.g. size, aggressiveness)'[10]
- 'Have similar assets and skills (e.g. quality image)'.[11]

The theoretical origins of the top-down approach are found in the notion of the product life cycle, the idea that at any point in time in a multi-business firm, or in a multi-product business, a number of businesses or products (or brands) are at different, identifiable stages in their life cycles. Each of these five stages – introductory, growth, maturity, saturation, decline – is related to the passage of time and to sales performance. Ultimately, according to this concept, the success with which a firm manages its business or product portfolio relative to its competitors is of fundamental strategic significance.

In essence, the top-down approach seeks to decipher the competitor's horizontal strategy – the goals and policies it has set to maximise synergy between business units for competitive advantage – and how likely it is to pursue them. Specifically, top-down analysis aims to highlight competitor vulnerabilities, or deficiencies, in areas such as corporate culture, finance, logistics, manufacturing, marketing, organisation and technology.

When in March 1993 IBM appointed as its new CEO Louis Gerstner, chairman and chief executive of food and tobacco group RJR Nabisco – a manager with no computer industry experience – competitors were quick to attack. As the head of Sun Microsystems observed: 'The customer is saying, holy mackerel, why should I buy any more from IBM until this guy figures out what he is doing?'

Of course public sabre rattling will not help Sun Microsystems or other IBM competitors win their battles with 'Big Blue'. They will need to monitor the computer giant closely, paying particularly close attention to how effectively and how fast Mr Gerstner and his team do five things:

i.   improve the organisation's customer orientation (satisfaction of customer needs, speed in anticipating market trends, etc.)
ii. create and articulate new technological vision
iii. develop and implement strategies that match this vision
iv. inspire and motivate the group's managers
v.   bring about change.

Mr Gerstner's track record at RJR Nabisco, and before that as president of American Express, suggests that IBM's competitors would be well advised to place the company under greater scrutiny, not less.

Top-down analysis examines the questions:

- to what competencies and markets has the competitor made strategic commitments?
- does the competitor pose a threat to our strategic position? what are the competitor's medium- and longer-term ambitions?
- what plans has the competitor explicitly made for new business development?
- does the competitor have the resources to put our own strategy at risk?
- will the competitor view our planned move as a strategic threat? if so, how will the competitor respond?
- do the actions of the competitor represent a strategic opportunity for us? if so, in what way can we gain advantage from the opportunity?

Porter, in his consideration of 'horizontal strategy' (how business unit strategies are co-ordinated), reminds us that 'there must be an overall firm game plan for dealing with each significant multipoint competitor and each competitor with a different pattern of interrelationships that could be threatening'.[12]

A few of the well-known analytical tools used in top-down analysis include the Boston Consulting Group's (BCG) Growth-Share Matrix, the GE/McKinsey Business Screen (or Product/Market Attractiveness-Competitive Position matrix), and the 12-cell Industry Maturity-Competitive Position Matrix developed by consultants Arthur D. Little.

2. Bottom-up analysis

This approach is appropriate at the business unit level and is typically used by managers with business development and planning responsibilities. Tyson discusses bottom-up, or micro-analysis, thus:

> The purpose . . . is to take a close look at the main competing forces in the industry. The goal is for [the] company to know its competitors as well as it knows itself. As a first step, a list of competitors for each existing or new product line is prepared. This list includes competitors making the same type of product or different products that accomplish the same function. Once competitors are listed, they are ranked by size and importance, and the major ones are selected for further study. The conclu-

sion of this examination ends with an assessment of key competitor issues.[13]

Bottom-up analysis is a key input to strategic planning, for it is at the business unit level that control is exercised over the firm's key strategic resources. Hence the function of bottom-up analysis is to enlighten managers on fundamental competitive issues: What is our competitor's strategy? At what point does their strategy intersect with ours? 'How does their strategy threaten our current and/or desired strategic position and goals?'[14] And what is 'the relative potency of the services undergirding [our] own and [our] competitors' product positions'?[15]

The US military refers to 'the analytical link between the commander's intelligence requirements and the collection effort'[16] as essential elements of information (EEIs). The concept of EEIs is important because it helps managers narrow the focus of the intelligence effort, thereby ensuring efficiency. EEIs are critical items of information regarding competitors and the external environment which managers need in order to answer their key strategic questions.

A white goods manufacturer profiling its competitors might use the following EEIs for a category Product Line Overview:

- washing machines
- dishwashers
- cookers
- dryers
- refrigerators.

For a category Pricing Policy the EEIs would include:

- types of sales incentives
- percentage of sales to top five customers
- strategies for increasing customer sales
- after-sales policies and conditions.

The answers, then, to questions of fundamental competitive (and therefore strategic) concern will emerge only from an analytical process that is focused, that is systematic, and that is user driven. And not until these questions are resolved can managers formulate strategy.

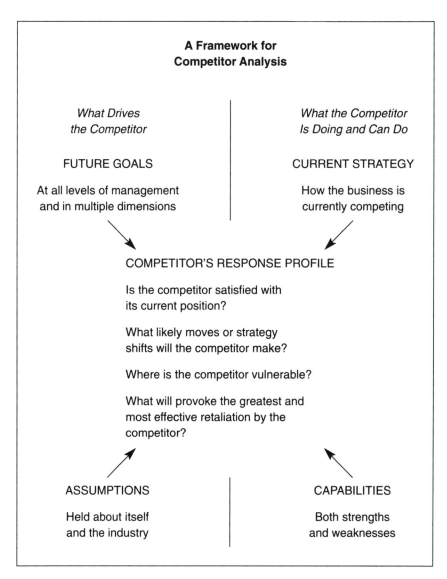

Figure 3.2 The components of a competitor analysis

Porter's model of competitor analysis – see Fig. 3.2 – provides managers with a tested framework in which to build the analytical process. Although Porter's explanations of the framework is, typically, descriptive, rather than prescriptive, its power lies in its conceptual simplicity. It is a framework managers can use to develop and shape their understanding of competitive forces.

Without knowledge of competitors' future goals, their current strategies, their capabilities, and their assumptions about themselves and the industry, competitors cannot be understood, and therefore cannot be beaten. Firms must continuously update their analyses of these issues in order to formulate and revise strategy. Strategy based on incomplete analysis is not strategy, it is 'muddling through'.

3. Time-based analysis

Today managers and workers alike are compelled to do more with less. Budgets and employee numbers are pruned, often severely, while the financial appetites, or expectations both of the firm and of its stakeholders continue to grow. Frequent and unpredictable change in the competitive environment creates pressures which cause even the most powerful of companies to re-assess what it is they are, or should, be doing (what business are we in? what are our objectives? what are our markets and market opportunities?), how efficiently and how effectively they are, or should be, doing it (how do we reduce development times? how do we reduce costs?) and, as many jobless managers can testify today, what is the minimum number of people we need in order to do it? The result is that the time and space available to the firm in which to respond to change 'in its markets, in customer demands, in technologies, in competitive boundaries, in products and processes, all at the same time',[17] is compressed. Time, timing, and competitive space emerge as fundamental strategic issues.

The notion of time-based competition has had enormous impact on managerial thinking and actions. Essentially, the idea, or objective, is to make organisations do things faster and more effectively. Stalk and Hout, both of BCG, argue that for a firm to become a time-based competitor its managers must accomplish three tasks. They must:

i. 'Make the value-delivery systems of the company two to three times more flexible and faster than the value-delivery systems of competitors.'[18]

ii. 'Determine how its customers value variety and responsiveness, focus on those customers with the greatest sensitivity, and price accordingly.'[19]

iii. 'Have a strategy for surprising its competitors with the company's time-based advantage.'[20]

Time-based analysis yields the greatest intelligence value to managers, particularly when based upon solid primary research. Time-based analysis is rooted in the theory of time-based competition, and stems from the investigation of competitor's 'marketing concepts, behaviour patterns, and systems in place, as well as performance measures.'[21] The analytical focus, in other words, is driven by, or structured around, the need to understand competitors from the perspective of certain key success factors (KSFs), and their relative importance.

KSFs, sometimes referred to as critical success factors, represent those things a firm must do better than its competitors in order to beat them. They are, as Aaker puts it, 'a set of assets and skills that provide the bases for competing successfully',[22] and they are of two types:

i. Strategic necessities, 'which do not necessarily provide an advantage because others have them, but their absence will create a substantial weakness.'[23]

ii. Strategic strengths, at which the firm excels, and which represent 'assets or skills that are superior to those of competitors and provide a base of advantage.'[24]

KSFs will (or certainly should) be identified, and described in the strategic plan of the company. KSFs may be company-, enterprise-, environmental- or industry-specific.

For example, KSFs for Volkswagen (VW), Europe's biggest car maker, would include price, quality, and technical development, all platforms upon which the company has successfully competed in the past. Another KSF for VW (and for other motor manufacturers) is costs. VW is one of the motor industry's highest cost producers, and in March 1993 the group's new chairman, Ferdinand Piëch, tackled the problem. In return for a five-year $20 million contract, he recruited GM's purchasing head, José Ignacio López de Arriortua, to run VW's worldwide production operations. López and his team had reportedly cut $1 billion a year from GM's North American parts costs, and at the time of his departure from Detroit he 'had already locked in two-thirds of his 1993 savings target of $2.3 billion with new contracts'.[25] In the face of shrinking demand, a strong mark and increasing competition, Piëch had little alternative but to initiate a radical and comprehensive cost-cutting programme. More importantly, in order for VW to maintain European market dominance, and restore waning competitiveness, it would have to move faster to slash costs than rivals Peugeot, GM, Fiat, Ford, Renault and the Japanese. And it would have to do so without sacrificing product quality.

KSFs drive the data and information requirements at the front end of the intelligence-gathering process, and they drive the analyses at the back end. This in turn leads to fast and efficient analysis of the strategic, tactical, and operational issues with which CI is concerned. Tyson emphasises that a time-based approach to competitive analysis involves answering the following questions:

i. does the information required relate to the current strategy of the competitor?
ii. does the information represent a change in strategy?
iii. does the information reflect long-term changes forthcoming in the market?
iv. does the information indicate changes in resources devoted to the market?
v. does the information describe personality or culture?
vi. does the information suggest changed assumptions about market conditions?
vii. does the information have an immediate impact on the company's future direction?

Competitive analysis has much to do with judgement. Similar to battlefield commanders, managers need to make decisions based upon the best information available today, not necessarily the best information. Competitors and the competitive environment as a whole are dynamic; they do not remain static while managers collect and assess perfect intelligence from which, ideally, perfect strategies might then be constructed. Time-based competitive analysis equips managers to make future oriented judgements about likely competitor moves (their strategies and plans), about changes in the competitive environment, about competitor intent, and about potential competitive threats in time to take action, and in time, therefore, to anticipate and outperform the competition.

THE LINK TO STRATEGY

We have said that competitive analysis is a user-driven process, and that its purpose is to generate an actionable intelligence product for policymakers. Aaker suggests four important benefits of understanding competitors and their behaviour: 'First, an understanding of the current strengths and weaknesses of a competitor can suggest opportunities and threats that will merit a response. Second, insights into future competitive strategy may allow the prediction of emerging threats and opportunities. Third, a decision about strategic alternatives might easily hinge on the ability to forecast the likely reaction of key competitors.'[26] Last, 'competitor analysis may result in the identification of some strategic questions, questions that will be worth monitoring over time.'[27]

Understanding the competitor's future direction involves understanding the extent to which it is striving for intellectual leadership. Does the competitor focus on gaining market share, or is it striving to create and shape the industry in which it will compete in the future? How, in other words, does the competitor plan to compete?

As I argued in Chapter 2, competitive analysis and competitive strategy are two inseparable parts of the same thing, whether that strategy is based on diversification, whether it is global, or whether it is based on leadership or niche (in growing or in declining markets).

Competitive analysis seeks to unravel the hidden complexities of competitor costs, of market dynamics, of competitor strategies, as well as the hows and whys of the ways competitors operate. Strategic planning and strategy implementation depend upon a focused and timely understanding of existing, emerging and potential competitors, and of the strategic groups operating in the marketplace.

WHAT USERS OF INTELLIGENCE REALLY WANT

Consumers of intelligence want information that enables them to gain competitive advantage. It's as simple as that. This is how Kevin Sharer, Executive Vice President of MCI Communications Corporation (1991 net sales $8.43 billion), put it to delegates at a recent conference of the Society of Competitive Intelligence Professionals (SCIP):

> You need to understand that I don't have enough time to do my job. I don't have time for academic stuff. My attention span is very short. Combine my lack of time and a feeling that I know it all and you have a tough sales call to make.
>
> So how do I like to get intelligence? I like to get it fast and I like to understand the facts. Facts can be lots of things. They can be analytic evaluation of cost structure, market research, or what the salesperson tells you. Every time I am listening to someone, I have one question going through my mind – so what? When you call on me, within one minute I am starting to form conclusions about whether I want to keep talking to you or not.
>
> So, I want it fast, I want it factual, I want it integrated. Please don't come out of a wheelbarrow and say, 'Hey, look what I got! I got all these jigsaw puzzle parts', and dump them down on my carpet and sit there and try to guess with me what sort of picture it makes. Please, put the puzzle together before you see me.[28]

The policymaker wants an intelligence product that offers insight, and serves as a guide to action. It must be relevant to the decisions he or she must make, and hence to the strategic needs of the organisation. Moreover it must represent a balance between 'what' and 'so what', it must be timely, it must be accurate (within acceptable margins of error), it must list sources and the reliability of those sources, it should offer alternative courses of action for managers to consider, and it should predict the implications of taking any one particular course. It should also be short and to the point.

SPECIAL ANALYTICAL TECHNIQUES

There is a wide and growing range of analytical tools available to managers. Many are well known, and all are used with varying degrees of success. But even the most sophisticated analytical methods and models are used only to support, not as proxies for, sound business judgement, or logical, interpretative thinking. Competitive analysts and managers must never stop asking the questions 'What does it mean'? or 'What's missing'?

There are many ways of finding clues to the competitor's future strategy. They include:

- analysis of environmental and industry change
- projections of changing market needs
- personality profiles of the competitor's top management
- new alliances, joint ventures, or takeovers
- accelerated, or new developments in manufacturing or technology
- changes in the way the company competes.

There are no 'best' analytical tools; each company must use (and many times develop) those tools which suits the project at hand. I have seen one reference book – *The Vest-Pocket CEO* (Prentice Hall 1990) – which alone describes 101 'decision-making tools for executives'.

Perhaps two tools of analysis and one analytical approach deserve mention:

BCG Growth-Share Matrix

This simple, two-dimensional model is used mostly for portfolio analysis of diversified companies, and will be familiar to all MBAs and planners. As a tool of competitive analysis it can help managers assess the position of different competitors. It is also used to plot competitor product portfolios, thereby indicating which competitors are in strong or weak positions, and which businesses or product areas they can be expected to defend to grow.

The BCG Matrix focuses on cash flow dynamics and uses the following variables:

- vertical axis: market growth rate, a proxy for the likely demand for cash from the business or product (or product group)
- horizontal axis: relative product share, a proxy for relative cost, or competitive, position.

The matrix is divided into four quadrants:

i. 'Stars' (high market share businesses in expanding markets . . . cash needs are heavy)
ii. 'Cash cows' (high market share business units in low-growth markets . . . relatively large amounts of cash generated)
iii. 'Dogs' (low market share business units in low-growth markets . . . profits are low and there may be net outflows of cash)
iv. 'Problem children' (low market share businesses in high-growth markets . . . heavy cash needs).

Each quadrant intrinsically suggests a different strategy for the business or product (or product group) positioned within it.

The BCG Matrix has a number of limitations, and should not alone be used as a guide to management action. For example, relative market share is not always a good surrogate for competitive position, and cash flow depends on many things other than market growth. Indeed, there are a large number of other factors that must be taken into account in competitor analysis.

Activity-based Growth-Share Matrix

Snyder and Ebeling have suggested 'that gaining a strong relative share in key value-added activities is more relevant to competitive position than gaining share of the related product market.'[29] Businesses, they insist, are as much a system of activities that must be managed and organised as they are a portfolio of products.

Snyder and Ebeling equate activities with the now more popular 'core competencies', and argue that by redefining 'the unit of analysis from product-centred business units to activities [it is possible to develop new] insights about how competitive advantage is created in the long run.'[30]

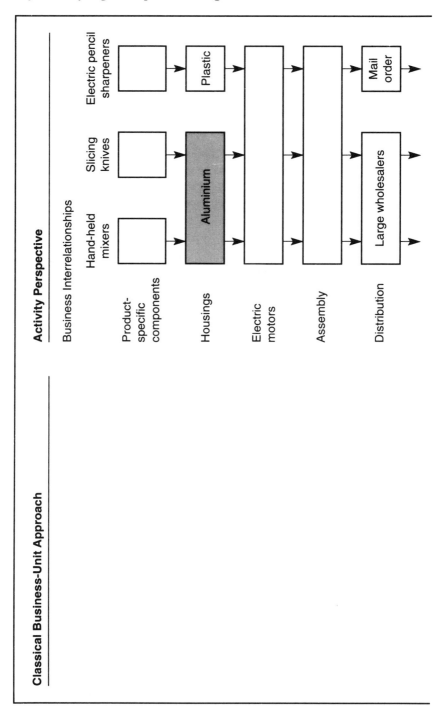

Figure 3.3 Slicing knife example

November/December 1992, *Journal of Business Strategy*, Faulkner & Gray Publishers, New York, NY. Reprinted with permission.

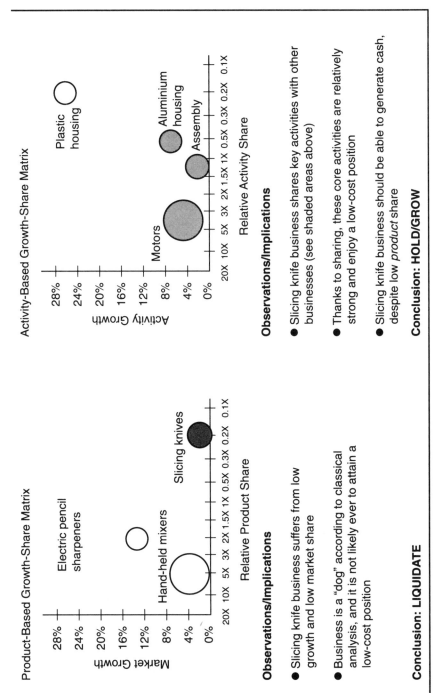

Product-Based Growth-Share Matrix

Market Growth

28% 24% 20% 16% 12% 8% 4% 0%

Electric pencil sharpeners

Hand-held mixers

Slicing knives

20X 10X 5X 3X 2X 1.5X 1X 0.5X 0.3X 0.2X 0.1X

Relative Product Share

Observations/Implications

● Slicing knife business suffers from low growth and low market share

● Business is a "dog" according to classical analysis, and it is not likely ever to attain a low-cost position

Conclusion: LIQUIDATE

Activity-Based Growth-Share Matrix

Activity Growth

28% 24% 20% 16% 12% 8% 4% 0%

Plastic housing

Aluminium housing

Assembly

Motors

20X 10X 5X 3X 2X 1.5X 1X 0.5X 0.3X 0.2X 0.1X

Relative Activity Share

Observations/Implications

● Slicing knife business shares key activities with other businesses (see shaded areas above)

● Thanks to sharing, these core activities are relatively strong and enjoy a low-cost position

● Slicing knife business should be able to generate cash, despite low *product* share

Conclusion: HOLD/GROW

They have developed the activity-based Growth-Share Matrix to support their analytical approach. The matrix variables are:

- vertical axis: activity growth
- horizontal axis: relative activity share.

Fig. 3.3 above illustrates the two very different conclusions suggested by both matrices, using the example of the slicing knife business.

PATENT CITATION ANALYSIS

The following section is contributed by Dr. Francis Narin and Vincent M. Smith, Jr., of Chi Research, Haddon Heights, New Jersey.

The threat of competitive technology enveloping an international company is constantly growing and constantly shifting in direction. In every business day worldwide there are more than 5,000 new scientific papers published, more than 1,000 new patent documents issued, and five US patents issued to the Japanese firm Hitachi. This stream of discoveries constantly challenges a company's products.

However, the science and technology buried in these papers and patents also provides a rich opportunity for competitive intelligence, and reveals much about the R&D activities of competitor companies and laboratories. The statistical properties of these patents and papers provide the data for technology indicators characterising a competitor company's research in great detail.

One technique for separating the technologically important innovations imbedded in patents from the large number of less significant, incremental advances is patent citation analysis, which has been developed most extensively within the US patent system. The basic idea behind patent citation analysis is that when a patent is cited in a large number of subsequent patents, then this earlier, 'highly cited' patent is likely to have been one of high impact.

More specifically, when a United States patent is issued it has, on average, five or six 'references cited by US patents' on its front page. These five or six citations identify the 'prior art' upon which the granted patent is based. The citations tend to be to recent patents, with a peak in referencing to patents that are four to five years old, in most active areas of technology.

These references are also highly concentrated. On average two-thirds of the patents issued in the United States are either never cited, or only cited one or two times, and a relatively small number of patents, just a few per cent, are cited 10 or more times. By identifying these few per cent of highly cited patents, one has a way of separating high impact inventions from ordinary, incremental advances, and thereby identifying companies and technologies that are likely to be of high interest.

In competitive intelligence these patterns of high citation can be used in two ways. First, they can indicate whether a company is likely to have important products which might evolve from its highly cited patents. Second, they establish links between companies, and can be used to identify the companies that are the central sources of new information and innovation in an industry or technology.

As an illustration of this first application, Fig. 3.4 shows the most highly cited patents for three pharmaceutical companies, SmithKline Beecham, Merck & Company and Takeda Chemical Industries, for the period 1975 to 1991, as cited through 1991. On those figures each line represents a single highly cited patent. The height of each line is the total number of citations the patent has received through 1991. Since it takes a number of years, typically four or five, for patents to accumulate large numbers of citations, one would not expect to find highly cited patents in the late 1980s. All three companies, therefore, do not yet show many highly cited patents for the recent years.

Nevertheless, the patterns for the three companies are strikingly different. SmithKline Beecham has a rather large number of highly cited patents in the mid- to late 1970s, many of which are associated with the discovery of cimetidine (Tagamet®) in the SmithKline and French laboratories in the United Kingdom.

Tagamet® was the first of the major designer drugs, and was one of the most successful pharmaceutical products of the last two decades. Note, however, that by the beginning of the 1980s SmithKline essentially ceased to have any highly cited patents.

In sharp contrast to this Merck has a pattern of steadily increasing numbers of highly cited patents, right through to the mid-1980s, the last years for which patents would have expected to accumulate more

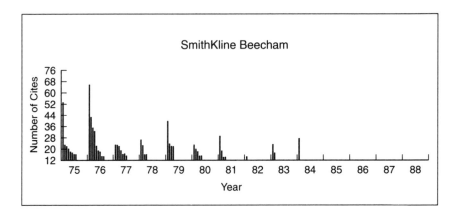

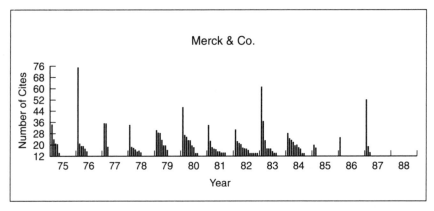

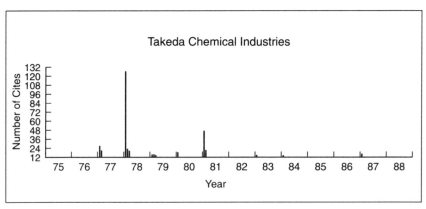

Each line is one patent.
All patents cited 15 times or more shown.
The scientific-technological decline of SmithKline Beecham and rise of Merck
is quite clear.

Figure 3.4 Highly cited patents for three companies

than 15 cites, and, in fact, Merck had a patent in 1987 that has already been cited 53 times, quite a remarkable number.

As a final contrast, Takeda Chemical Industries has one extremely highly cited patent for a broadly effective cephalosporin discovery, and relatively few since.

Looking at these figures one would conclude that the main technological impact of SmithKline Beecham in pharmaceuticals may have already passed, that Merck is a major innovative company in the pharmaceutical industry, and that Takeda had a few important discoveries some time ago, but is certainly not in the same innovative class as Merck or SmithKline Beecham.

This view of the centrality of Merck, and the peripheral position of SmithKline, is further illustrated by Fig. 3.5, which is an intercompany citation map for patents in the pharmaceutical industry. On this figure a solid line is drawn from each company to the company whose patents it cites most frequently, and a dotted line to the company whose patents are cited second most frequently. Note that on the main vertical axis there appear to be two central companies, Merck & Company and Bristol-Meyers Squibb, both large firms with highly cited patents, and by this measure in the centre of the pharmaceutical industry. On the left Johnson & Johnson (J&J) is also a highly cited company. Note that the cites to J&J's patents are from a distinctly different set of companies, and clearly reflect the much stronger emphasis of Johnson & Johnson on medical supplies and instrumentation, in contrast to the much higher emphasis on drugs in the patenting and sales of Merck and Bristol-Meyers Squibb. Note, too, that SmithKline Beecham, sitting below Bristol-Meyers Squibb on the diagram, is not cited first or second by any company, and therefore is certainly not a current source of innovative ideas for the rest of the industry.

Thus, these two figures clearly show how patent citation analysis can be used to focus competitor intelligence to identify the companies with high impact technology, technology that is likely to reflect itself into important products later on, and to crystallise the position of a company and its contributions within its industry. The techniques can be applied to broad areas like pharmaceuticals as shown here, or to very specialised technological areas, to assist in the technological assessment of competition.

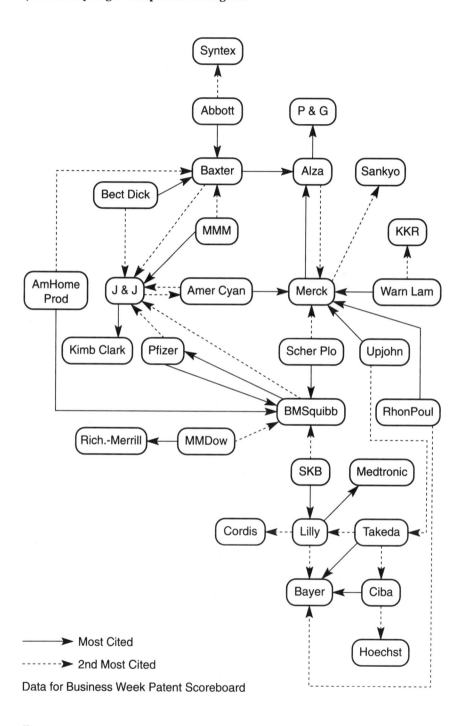

Figure 3.5 Inter-company citation map – pharmaceutical industry

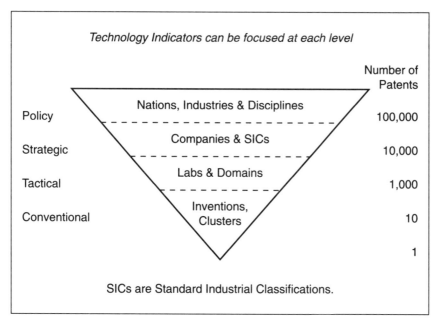

Figure 3.6 Levels of technology analysis

NOTES

[1]Herbert E. Meyer, *Real World Intelligence* (New York, NY: Grove Weidenfeld, 1987), p. 21.

[2]Roy Godson. 'Intelligence: an American View', *British and American Approaches to Intelligence,* p. 19. Edited by K.G. Robertson (London: The Macmillan Press for Royal United Services Institute, 1987).

[3]Ibid.

[4]Ibid.

[5]Ibid.

[6]Ibid.

[7]_____ . *Factbook on Intelligence* (Washington, DC: Central Intelligence Agency, 1991), p. 14.

[8]Gary Hamel and C.K. Prahalad. 'Strategy as Stretch and Leverage', *Harvard Business Review,* March-April 1993, p. 79.

[9]David A. Aaker, *Developing Business Strategies,* 3rd ed. (New York, NY: John Wiley & Sons, 1992), p. 65.

[10]Ibid.

[11]Ibid.

[12]Michael E. Porter, *Competitive Advantage: Creating and Sustaining Superior Performance* (New York, NY: The Free Press, 1985), p. 373.

[13]Kirk W.M. Tyson, *Competitor Intelligence Manual & Guide* (Englewood Cliffs, NJ: Prentice Hall, 1990), p. 162.

[14]William L. Sammon. 'Competitor Intelligence: An Analytical Approach', *Business Competitor Intelligence: Methods for Collecting, Organising and Using Information,* edited by William L. Sammon, Mark A. Kurland and Robert Spitalnic (New York, NY: John Wiley & Sons, 1984), p. 98.

[15]James Brian Quinn, Thomas L. Doorley, and Penny C. Paquette. 'Beyond Products: Services-Based Strategy', *Strategy: Seeking and Securing Competitive Advantage,* edited by Cynthia A. Montgomery and Michael E. Porter (Boston, MA: Harvard Business School Press, 1991), p. 306.

[16]Sammon, op. cit., p. 109.

[17]Andrew C. Boynton. 'Achieving Dynamic Stability through Information Technology', *California Management Review,* Winter 1993, p. 58.

[18]George Stalk, Jr. and Thomas M. Hout, *Competing Against Time: How Time-based Competition is Reshaping Global Markets* (New York, NY: The Free Press, 1990), p. 36.

[19]Ibid.

[20]Ibid.

[21]Ibid. p. 210.

[22]Aaker, op. cit. p. 99.

[23]Aaker, op. cit. p. 99.

[24]Aaker, op. cit. p. 99.

[25]Kathleen Kerwin and Zachary Schiller. 'GM Braces for Life after Lopez', *Business Week International,* 29 March 1993, p.26.

[26]Aaker, op. cit. pp. 68-69.

[27]Aaker, op. cit. p. 69.

[28]Kevin W. Sharer. From a speech given at the SCIP Fall Conference in Chicago, October 1990. *Competitive Intelligence Review,* Spring 1991, p. 5.

[29]Amy V. Snyder and H. William Ebeling, Jr. 'Targeting a Company's Real Core Competencies', *Journal of Business Strategy,* November/December 1992, p. 26.

[30]Ibid.

4 COMPETITIVE BENCHMARKING

This chapter is contributed by Clark D. Swain, Vice President of Kaiser Associates, Vienna, Virginia. Kaiser Associates is a management consulting firm specialising in competitive benchmarking, competitive analysis, industry and market analysis, and strategy development.

INTRODUCTION

Globalisation: for years business leaders have talked of the benefits of being competitive on a global basis. From London to New York, from Tokyo to Munich, corporations, big and small, have implemented global business strategies. But the rules of the game are quickly changing. New competitors are appearing on the horizon with the capabilities and resources of seasoned fighters. Consumers are flexing their muscles and forcing commodity status on many markets by insisting on both high quality and low prices. At the same time, the end of the Cold War has released enormous quantities of cheap labour and natural resources that have already changed the dynamics of a number of industries such as coal mining and steel.

In the midst of all of this change, a worldwide recession has sapped consumer demand. Markets that for years enjoyed profitability and growth find themselves with neither. Once legendary multi-national companies such as IBM and General Motors have fallen from grace and are engaged in battles for their very existence. Downsizing has emerged as the primary tool to cut costs and remain competitive. Yet downsizing is not a panacea. Cutting jobs without fundamentally changing how a company conducts business will not build a solid foundation for the future. To be competitive companies must re-examine both their strategies and operations to conquer the changing rules of engagement. Learning from those companies which are most successful at beating their competition is the most powerful method to learn how best to compete.

Competitive benchmarking is the tool that many companies are employing to accomplish this. It is a simple but effective way to benefit from others' experiences and avoid costly mistakes. This chapter will define competitive benchmarking, discuss its place in the strategic planning process, outline how to implement a competitive benchmarking programme, and provide a case study to illustrate its effectiveness. The primary objective is to present a pragmatic view, based on years of experience, of how competitive benchmarking can successfully be used to build global competitive advantage.

COMPETITIVE BENCHMARKING: A DEFINITION

Competitive benchmarking is the latest focus in the evolution of competitive analysis over the last couple of decades. It is an analytical process for rigorously measuring your company's strategies and operations versus the 'best-in-class' companies both in and outside of your industry, on a global basis. Insights generated by the benchmarking process allow you to identify and implement specific actions needed to close the gap between your company's performance and best-in-class performance. Simply put, competitive benchmarking helps companies make significant improvements without 're-inventing the wheel'.

A framework for strategic planning

To understanding benchmarking, it is important to grasp the role it plays in the strategic planning process. It is almost impossible to conduct successful benchmarking without relating it to the overall strategy of the company. Conversely, no meaningful strategic planning process is complete without a solid benchmarking analysis.

The starting point for any strategic planning process is a statement of the fundamental goal of the corporation. While a company strives to meet the needs of a variety of constituencies – employees, the local community, society at large – the most fundamental goal of the corporation is to maximise *shareholder* value.

The second tenet of any strategic process is the recognition that *profitability* is the basic driver of shareholder value. Market share, low costs and growth are all worthwhile objectives, but they're only means to an end. Unless those and other accomplishments lead to strong profits for the shareholders, they will not be translated into a high stock price and a maximisation of shareholder value.

The companies that have produced the strongest profitability and thus return to shareholders, on a sustained basis, tend to do three things very well.

First, they select the business in which to compete consciously and actively and on a continual basis. Well-run companies actively manage the business they're in through acquisitions, research and development, joint ventures, product-line extensions, divestitures, and so forth.

Second, well-run companies actively and discriminately allocate resources among their various businesses. Unstrategic companies often follow a resource allocation rule of 'everybody gets a little'. If they're in 10 businesses, and there is a certain amount of capital or discretionary resources to spend, those resources get spread around the businesses in an even or proportional manner. *Strategic* companies follow a very different pattern. While they may be in the same 10 businesses, they'll determine which of the businesses have strong profit prospects, which have mediocre profit prospects, and which have limited potential. They will funnel the bulk of their strategic resources to the high potential businesses, some capital to the mediocre businesses, and almost none to the weak ones. These companies succeed in maximising profitability by making sure they're not throwing good money after bad.

Third, successful corporations find synergies or linkages which cut across their various businesses. In other words, these companies develop skills which make the whole greater than the sum of its parts.

Conducting strategic analysis

In order to effectively *select businesses*, *allocate resources*, and *develop synergies*, a company needs to fully understand the strategic nature of its industry. That is why an *industry analysis* is normally the first step toward strategy development. Industry analysis is a systematic process for assessing the environment in which a business oper-

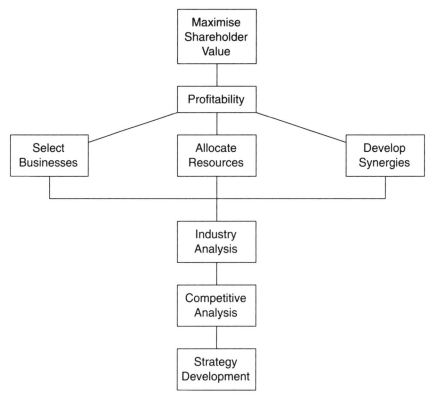

Figure 4.1 A framework for strategic analysis

ates. It includes fundamental analysis of the economic forces which shape an industry: the degree and nature of competitive rivalry, the power of customers and their purchasing behaviour, the power of customers and their purchasing behaviour, the power of suppliers, barriers to entry, threat of substitute products and services, industry economics, government regulation, and so forth.

Once an industry analysis is complete, it is time to proceed to *competitive analysis*. In fact, a solid industry analysis will make the competitive analysis process far more efficient. Rather than pursuing a lengthy, unfocused competitive analysis effort, industry analysis allows the strategist to concentrate on the relationship of the competitor to the key industry segments and the key success factors for competing in the industry.

Analysis of one's competitors should address and answer three fundamental questions. First, what level of emphasis will my competitor place on my business, i.e. what level of strategic resources is s/he likely to devote to the business? Answering this question requires an understanding of the overall financial strength of the competitor an the relative prioritisation of the line of business against which you compete within the competitor's portfolio of businesses. A price cut with the goal of gaining market share can be a very effective weapon against a financially weak competitor who does not place an emphasis on the business against which you compete. On the other hand, the exact same strategy will fail dramatically if the competitor is financially strong and if the business against which you compete is the competitor's highest priority for investment. That competitor will match your price cut to prevent you from gaining share, and you will both lose in the end.

Secondly, a competitive analysis should tell you *how* your competitor will compete in your business, or, in other words, how the competitor will spend the strategic resources it has at its disposal. This analysis should focus primarily on the areas where the key success factors lie, as identified in the industry analysis. In general, however, meaningful competitive analysis will predict how the competitor will compete in terms of three things: (a) how the competitor will come to market, i.e. with what product, price, sales and distribution, marketing effort, customer service, and so forth; (b) the competitor's cost position; and (c) the competitor's research and development efforts that will change its marketing or cost position over time. Product R&D may improve the competitor's future ability to market, while process R&D may improve the competitor's future cost position.

Finally, the third area of competitive analysis is an evaluation of the competitor's 'personality' or culture. Every company has a culture, and cultures aren't easy to change. In fact, company cultures are a lot like a person's personality. Even if an individual is aware that his or her personality is lacking in some way, it still isn't easy for the individual to actually change that personality. The same is true for companies: every company tends to 'like' to compete in certain ways, and just because top management or strategists decide to change the culture the company will not necessarily be *able* to change. A good evaluation of a company's culture will go a long way towards predicting the future actions of your competitor.

The last step in strategic analysis is strategy development, or the formulation of your company's strategy. Once again, good industry analysis and competitive analysis will make the strategy development process more efficient. If one understands – through industry analysis – what it takes to succeed in the business, and if the competitive analysis identifies how the competitors stack up relative to those key success factors, the strategy development effort is vastly simplified. It becomes the process of identifying how your company can out-perform competitors relative to those key success factors.

Strategy development translates into a series of functional strategies: strategies for product, pricing, sales, distribution, marketing, manufacturing or operations, research and development, and so forth. However, the major difference between successful and unsuccessful strategy development processes is very basic. Less effective strategy development processes tend to develop these functional strategies in a relative vacuum. These processes develop plans to build new plants, introduce new products, change prices, and so forth, but do not do a good job of demonstrating the relationship between those strategies and the industry and competitive analysis. They also do not demonstrate how those strategies will translate into superior profitability.

Effective strategy development, on the other hand, ties these functional strategies very closely to the conclusions of the industry and competitive analyses. In fact, until you can convince yourself that your various functional strategies will enable you to out-perform competitors relative to the key success factors, in attractive segments of the industry, you have not demonstrated how your company will earn superior profitability. Until you do so, the strategy development process is not really finished.

The role of benchmarking

Benchmarking is a rigorous process for tying strategy development to industry and competitive analysis. It is a method for: 1) measuring the performance of your 'best-in-class' competitors relative to your industry's key success factors; 2) determining *how* the best-in-class

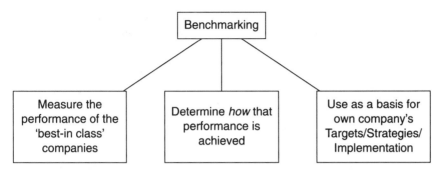

Figure 4.2 The role of benchmarking in companies

achieve those performance levels; and 3) using that data as a basis for your own company's targets, strategies, and implementation. A rigorous benchmarking process will ensure that the business strategy will attain a competitive position that will out-perform competitors relative to the key success factors.

Benchmarking can be carried out at two levels: strategic and operational. Strategic benchmarking is a process for ensuring that the company's fundamental strategy is consistent with the endustry key success factors and that it takes into account the impact of competitors' strategies. Operational benchmarking, far more detailed, is a process for ensuring that specific aspects of a company's functional operations – such as manufacturing cost, salesforce efficiency, research and development programmes, etc. – are sufficient to out-perform competitors in those specific operational areas.

A SEVEN-STEP PROCESS FOR BENCHMARKING

A successful benchmarking analysis includes seven steps:

i. determining which functional areas within your operation are to be benchmarked, i.e. those that will benefit most from the benchmarking process;

ii. identifying the key factors and variables with which to measure those functions;

iii. selecting the best-in-class companies for each area to be benchmarked – those companies that perform each function at the lowest cost, with the highest degree of customer satisfaction, etc. Best-in-class companies can be your direct competitors (domestic or foreign) or even companies from a different industry. For instance, any company seeking to improve the effectiveness of its customer service technicians might gain from analysing how Xerox achieves its superior service rating;

iv. measuring the performance of the best-in-class companies for each benchmark variable;

v. measuring your own performance for each variable and determining the gap between you and the best-in-class;

vi. specifying programmes and actions to meet and surpass the competition;

vii. implementing these programmes by setting specific improvement targets and deadlines, and by developing a monitoring process to review and update the analysis over time.

None of the steps listed above is completely new or 'revolutionary'. However, experience has shown that businesses which deliberately focus on benchmarking analysis are likely to achieve significantly greater improvement than companies which merely count on Steps 1 to 7 to happen by themselves.

Step 1: Determining which functions to benchmark

One of the surest ways for a benchmarking process to fail is to try to benchmark everything at once. Benchmarking analysis requires time, effort and management attention. This means that the various functions within a company must be prioritised: you must decide which functions should be benchmarked first, second and so forth, and which should not be benchmarked at all.

There are no set rules as to which function should be benchmarked first, but there are four key criteria which should be applied within your organisation in determining your priorities:

■ *Which functions represent the highest percentage of cost?* If your engineering function is found to be 20 per cent higher cost than the competition, and if engineering represents a large portion of your cost (say, 40 per cent of your total cost), then the potential reduction

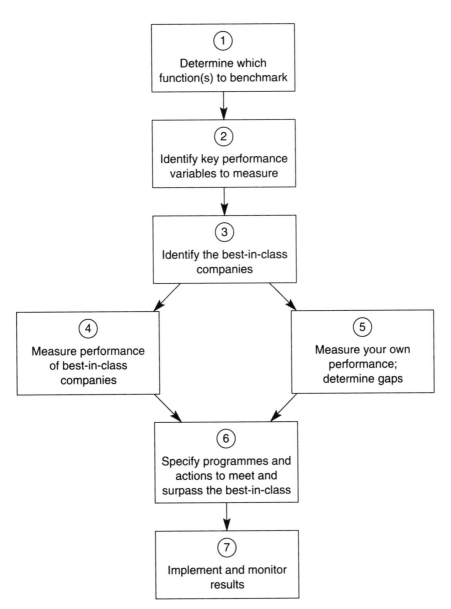

Figure 4.3 The benchmarking process

is 20% × 40%, or eight per cent of your total cost, which, in turn, will have an enormous impact on your margin. On the other hand, that same 20 per cent savings on engineering cost, if applied to an engineering function which represents only two per cent of cost, will have an impact of only 20% × 2%, or 0.4 per cent of total cost. Obviously, by focusing on those steps that constitute the greatest portion of cost, you are likely to identify the potential cost savings that could have the greatest impact on your overall organisation.

■ *Which functions play the greatest role in differentiating competitors in the marketplace?* Some functions may represent a small portion of cost, but may be absolutely crucial in determining who wins and loses in the fight to win customers. Functions like advertising, research and development, sales and specific portions of the manufacturing process may have competitive importance way out of proportion to their percentage of total cost. Such functions represent high priorities for benchmarking, since a gain in competitive position in those functions can have a major impact on the business.

■ *Which functions have the greatest room for improvement?* Even though you may be beginning a formal benchmarking process for the first time, you and your company have considerable experience of analysing your operations. You probably already have an intuitive sense as to which functions are top notch and which functions are not up to snuff. Those functions which you intuitively feel have greatest room for improvement represent higher benchmark priorities.

■ *Which functions are capable of improvement?* Because of politics, regulation, organisational constraints or other factors, some functions may yield more easily to improvement than others. If your company is high cost in a function, but in reality there's very little your company can do about it, then that function is not a priority for benchmarking.

None of these four criteria should be taken as an absolute. Instead, each should be considered and applied to each function in your organisation. Those functions for which the answers to these questions are, in general, the most positive should be the functions that are benchmarked first. The key point to remember is that benchmarking is not an end in itself, but a means to an end. The criteria are designed so as to select functions where you are likely to find potential improvements that are both important and achievable. There is nothing to be gained from benchmarking functions where the likely improvements are either very small or not very achievable.

Using these criteria, the functions that companies have benchmarked include manufacturing and various sub-segments of manufacturing (components manufacturing, sub-assembly, assembly, etc.), marketing, sales, distribution, research and development, engineering, human resources, data processing, purchasing, administration, finance, strategic planning, operations and numerous others. Most companies start with anywhere from one to three or four functions, and then proceed to the lower priority functions over time.

Step 2: Selecting the key performance variables
Benchmarking analysis measures a function in terms of specific variables of operations and performance – such as the number of accounts covered per salesperson, labour productivity, raw material yield in the manufacturing process, cycle time in the engineering process, etc. The specific variables to be benchmarked vary widely across different benchmarking analyses. However, the items to be benchmarked usually fall into several broad categories.

For *operational benchmarking* efforts, two broad categories of performance variables may be benchmarked. They are:

- cost variables, such as labour efficiency, compensation levels, overhead costs, etc.;
- 'differentiation' variables, i.e. variables that measure the degree of customer satisfaction with your offering in the marketplace. Differentiation variables include such factors as product line breadth and feature sets available, product quality, service levels and service quality, image and overall customer satisfaction.

Strategic benchmarking usually involves measurement of the best-in-class companies in terms of the following:

- financial performance, including market share, sales growth, profitability (as measured in a number of different ways) and so forth;

- company strategy, including overall strategy and strategy for each of the various functional areas. By correlating the different strategies with financial performance, the strategic benchmarking effort identifies those strategies which are the most successful in achieving the desired financial results.

Step 3: Identifying the best-in-class companies

The goal of any benchmarking analysis is to identify companies which are superior performers, so that their superior performance levels can be used as targets for your own company's operations.

The 'best-in-class' companies may be selected from four different categories:

- *Direct competitors*: for example, Ford has benchmarked itself against Honda, BMW, General Motors, Chrysler and dozens of other direct competitors.
- *Parallel competitors*: this category includes companies that are basically in the same business as your company, but that do not compete with your company directly. For example, a bank in London might successfully benchmark various aspects of its operation against banks in other parts of Europe. By looking beyond your direct competitors, you are more likely to uncover creative approaches which enable you to 'leapfrog' your competition.
- *Latent competitors*: in some cases, this can be the most important category of all. Latent competitors are companies with which you do not yet compete, but which loom as threats in the future. For decades, the auto companies in Detroit benchmarked their operations against each other. Ford watched General Motors and Chrysler, General Motors watched Ford and Chrysler, and so forth. Only when the Japanese and the Europeans had already succeeded in taking large amounts of market share did the American companies start benchmarking themselves against those competitors in a serious way. In retrospect, it is obvious that the Americans should have benchmarked themselves against foreign competitors long before those companies came to American shores. If they had done so, they might have repelled the threat, or at least limited the market share loss.

When latent competitors enter the market, they often re-define the accepted levels of performance by either lowering costs or offering a higher quality product or service. For precisely that reason, benchmarking against latent competitors *before* they compete with you can be the most valuable form of benchmarking in some instances.

- *Out-of-industry companies*: a particularly creative type of benchmarking involves measuring your performance against companies in completely different industries. For example, when Xerox wanted to improve the effectiveness and efficiency of its warehousing and order processing operation, they benchmarked themselves not against their direct competitors, but against L. L. Bean, the mail order company based in New England. Xerox believed that L. L. Bean represented a much more 'cutting edge' warehouse and order processing operation than any of the other copier companies, and that it could learn much more by going outside its industry for this particular benchmarking effort.

  Benchmarking against out-of-industry competitors can be a key way to leapfrog your competition. If you are trying to improve your operations only by measuring what competitors are doing, you are constantly in a catch-up mode. If you can bring in new techniques and processes from outside the industry, you have the opportunity to get ahead of your competition.

Once you have generated a list of potential companies against which to benchmark, how do you narrow the list down and decide exactly which companies to use? Again, there are no hard and fast rules, and each of the following guidelines has exceptions. Nonetheless, the guidelines which follow apply to most situations and should be used as a starting point:

- In general, you should limit your list of benchmark companies to between four and six companies. In some cases eight or ten companies are necessary, and in some cases two to three will suffice. In general, however, less than four does not provide enough variety and good data, and more than six produces diminishing returns. Companies that benchmark against ten competitors often find they learn little from the seventh to tenth competitors that they didn't learn from the first six, particularly if the first six were chosen carefully.

- try to use as diverse a set of companies as reasonably possible. For example, if you have half-a-dozen low-cost Far Eastern competitors and half-a-dozen speciality competitors in Europe, use some of each. The reason for this is again that benchmarking is a means to an end, not an end in itself. If you choose six similar competitors, the data on the last few of them will be 'nice to know', but will tell you little about your own operations that you didn't learn from the first three competitors that you studied. The more diverse the set of competitors, the more insights you're likely to generate for your own operations.

- try in general to pick companies with the best bottom line performance, i.e. the best market share, sales growth, profitability or whatever. In general, the companies doing best are the ones that you're going to learn the most from, and there's less to learn from the marketplace losers. In particular, if there are one or two competitors in your market that really stand out as being the most successful, they definitely should be included in your benchmarking effort.

- finally, also pick any companies that have a particularly creative or effective strategy in the specific functional area you are benchmarking. If you're benchmarking a distribution function, for example, you may be aware of a competitor that, despite mediocre overall results, has come up with a superior way to approach distribution. By including these creative and 'different' companies in your search, you are likely to uncover the greatest amount of insight about how to improve your own operations.

Step 4: Measuring the performance of the best-in-class companies
Once you have decided which functions to benchmark, which performance variables to measure those functions by, and which companies to benchmark against, it is time to go out and gather the data for the best-in-class companies.

Data for benchmarking analyses usually comes from three types of sources: published sources, data sharing and interviews.

PUBLISHED SOURCES
Published sources are the best place to start a benchmarking effort.

However, rarely can all the information needed be found in published sources alone. There are several different categories of published sources of information, and their relative strengths and weaknesses are outlined below.

- *Securities and Exchange Commission Filings* must be submitted by all public companies in the United States. These include yearly and quarterly financial reports and special reports such as a Prospectus or Proxy, which are filed when companies issue new securities or become involved in mergers and acquisitions. These sources provide both financial and qualitative information on companies and are typically more useful in strategic benchmarking. However, a careful combing of the filings of small- and medium-sized companies can provide useful data for operational benchmarking as well.
- *Company Published Documents* include annual reports, product brochures, periodic news releases, recruiting brochures and other documents. While much of this information is general, more often than not, there will be a few 'gems' of key data buried in these documents. This type of information can be collected by contacting the investor relations and/or sales offices of the benchmark company.
- *General Business and Trade Articles* are valuable information sources in many benchmarking projects. General business magazines (e.g. *Business Week*, *The Economist*) and trade magazines (e.g. *Chemical Week*, *Advertising Age*) can provide data and insights beyond that available in other sources. Most published articles are indexed in a variety of published and on-line directories.
- *Local Newspaper Articles* are the most often overlooked source of competitive benchmarking information. Many successful benchmarking efforts obtain data from local newspapers located near a competitor's headquarters, plant or major office. These articles often contain information on hirings, layoffs, wages, key personnel changes, new products, business strategies and so forth. In one manufacturing benchmarking analysis, a local library's files contained 20 years of articles on a particular plant and allowed the analyst to develop a detailed history of plant expansions and modifications. Some companies monitor local newspapers regularly, not only for articles, but also to review competitors' want-ad placements.

- *Analyst Reports* are documents produced by investment houses (e.g. BZW, Goldman Sachs) as they evaluate investment opportunities for their clients. In general, all public companies are followed by at least one Wall Street or City analyst and, in most cases, by several. Analyst reports include both financial and strategic information. To accommodate the analysts, companies often release detailed data through these documents. Analyst reports are available directly from the brokerage houses or from various on-line databases.

- *Credit Reports*, available from companies like Dun & Bradstreet, are sources for information on private companies. These reports provide both financial and management data, and while they are not the best source for detailed benchmarking information, they can provide some critical pieces of data.

- *Multi-Client Market Reports* typically focus on a particular market and its major competitors. These reports rarely provide the detailed data needed for operational cost benchmarking, but they often provide the basic market share and product information needed for strategic benchmarking.

- *Trade Associations* often provide competitors within an industry with surveys of overall industry trends and industry average cost and performance benchmarks. In addition, within these associations, there are often particular individuals with specific areas of expertise; if they don't have the information you need, they will often refer you to someone who does.

- *Government Agencies* responsible for regulating industries generate a diverse array of published documents. For example, in the US most manufacturing companies must file plant information with either the Environmental Protection Agency (EPA) or the Occupational Safety and Health Administration (OSHA). Information on the number of employees, the types of machines used and major raw materials can often be gleaned from these filings. The various Directorates of the EC in Brussels also require companies to file information about how they do business. It often takes creativity and persistence to identify the appropriate government agencies and individuals that have this data, but the payoff can be significant.

In sum, there is an abundance of published information that should be tapped when performing a benchmarking analysis. While published sources are typically more valuable in strategic benchmarking, they also are the starting point for operational benchmarking. Successful benchmarking requires a complete review of all sources of published data.

DATA SHARING

Some firms have very successfully shared data with other companies in order to enhance their benchmarking efforts. Various types of data sharing are legal and others are not; it is crucial that you consult your corporate counsel if you have any doubt as to whether what you are doing is appropriate. However, some types of data sharing (e.g. with out-of-industry companies) are clearly legal. Other types of data sharing go on all the time, with some corporations considering them proper and legal, and other corporations thinking otherwise. Your own company rules and the advice of your corporate counsel should be your guideline. Types of data sharing include:

- *professional conferences*, where industry players get together to share ideas on the latest state-of-the-art techniques in the industry;
- *direct information sharing* with out-of-industry companies. For example, in benchmarking a function such as data processing or engineering, it is quite common to find that superior companies in other industries are willing to share their successes and approaches with you in return for learning some of your state-of-the-art techniques. As these companies don't compete with you directly, you may find that you can get excellent insights and data from them without jeopardising your own competitive position;
- *informal sharing*. In many companies, the managers of your manufacturing plant have been to competitors' plants; your salespeople come across competitors' salespeople all the time; and your engineers know the engineers at your competitors. Often there is a wealth of information shared informally through these channels. What is appropriate to know and use and what isn't must be approached cautiously, and once again the guidance of your internal counsel should set the standards. However, the reality is that most companies regularly use such information, many of them considering it appropriate to do so.

EXTERNAL INTERVIEWS

Depending upon the level of detail of the data you are seeking, published sources and information sharing will get you anywhere from 30 per cent to 100 per cent of what you need. When they are not sufficient, there is a wealth of external sources that can be interviewed to fill the gap. These sources include customers, distributors, suppliers, industry experts, regulators and government officials and the benchmark companies themselves. Different companies have different guidelines about the appropriateness of contacting competitors themselves as part of the benchmarking effort. Some companies have absolute prohibitions against talking to competitors. others prohibit employees from doing so, but allow the hiring of third parties to contact competitors. Still other companies allow the contact but limit the types of questions that may be asked. In this area, it is absolutely essential that you consult with your company's guidelines and your corporate counsel to determine what is considered appropriate in your organisation. Again, the reality is that the vast majority of companies do this sort of interviewing, often through third parties, as part of their competitive and benchmarking analysis.

The good news is that regardless of the prohibitions that apply in your organisation, there are almost always enough outside sources to contact which, coupled with published sources and information sharing, yield the data necessary for benchmarking analysis. This does not mean that you can always get every piece of data that you want on every competitor. However, you can always get enough information to put together an analysis which tells you where, how, and how much your organisation needs to improve.

Step 5: Measuring your own performance

Most companies conducting benchmarking analyses are able to get data on their own organisations and are able to get a large amount of good data on best-in-class companies. The problem usually is that these two sets of data are not consistent. For example, if it is cost data, it may be based on different accounting systems or spread over different organisational entities.

The trickiest and most crucial part of the benchmarking process is to get the internal data and the external data on an 'apples-to-apples' basis. In fact, organisations doing benchmarking for the first time often misunderstand the process and focus on the difficulty of getting outside data. However, the reason they are having that difficulty is because they think they have to get the outside data in exactly the same form as their internal data, which is often impossible. The companies that do benchmarking well get outside data and inside data in different forms, but develop creative ways to translate the two into a common ground for comparison. In particular, there are some clever but relatively simple ways to take disparate cost information and still produce 'apples-to-apples' comparisons of internal costs and best-in-class company costs.

There is one other factor to keep in mind when gathering data on internal operations and external competitors. Benchmarking – and competitive analysis in general – is a field in which the ability and willingness to estimate are crucial. It is an area where directional accuracy, not accounting accuracy, is the goal. In other words, the goal is not to get information precise to the third decimal place, but to get information precise enough to identify areas where improvement is needed and to identify how that improvement can be achieved. If you are not sure whether further accuracy is needed in gathering a certain piece of data, ask yourself this question: 'If I had another level of accuracy, would I do anything different based on it, or does the level of accuracy I have already tell me enough to know what to do?' Often you'll find that the final level of accuracy which could be pursued would provide you with relatively little additional information about what you need to do. For example, good cost benchmarking analyses usually identify areas where you are high cost by five or 20 per cent. Knowing whether you are high cost by 5.2 per cent or 5.8 per cent has little bearing on what future actions your organisation should take.

Step 6: Specify programmes and actions to close the gap

The programmes and action steps that come out of successful benchmarking analyses usually fall into four categories:

- *'Try harder'*: in this category, the company identifies that it is high cost, has a poor quality salesforce, or whatever, and concludes that it simply must buckle down and try harder to close the gap. While trying harder is a positive step, one should be sceptical of a plan that includes *only* this step. Usually your organisation is already trying pretty hard, and unless there is a fundamental change in systems, people, strategy or something else, you won't accomplish your objectives merely by telling everyone to try harder than they're trying already.

- *Emulate the competition*: some of the actions recommended by benchmarking analysis are based on emulating the successful actions of the competition. While this is sometimes the best you can do, if an entire strategy is based purely on emulation, it usually has little chance of success. If all you're doing is copying the things that other competitors are doing, you have little chance to get ahead, especially since they'll probably be moving ahead while you're catching up.

- *Leapfrog the competition*: a successful strategy based on a benchmarking analysis should include some functional elements that actually 'leapfrog' or get ahead of the competition. You are most likely to find these by opportunities studying companies outside your industry or companies in other segments of the market that may be further ahead in certain functional areas than your existing competitors.

- *Change the rules*: sometimes, a realistic benchmarking assessment concludes that there is no way that you can catch up or get ahead of the competition given the current rules of the game in your industry. For example, if labour cost is the whole key to success, and your average cost of labour is $24/hour while you're competing against Korean competitors with an average labour cost of $2/hour, no realistic strategy is going to close that gap unless you are willing to become a Korean competitor yourself. However, companies that have been faced with this situation have often used the benchmarking process to come up with a strategy to change the basis for success. Thus they avoid gaps that just cannot be closed. For example, one competitor that manufactured a wide range of components sold to OEMs found that they were higher cost than the Far Eastern competition and lower quality in terms of engineering know-how than the European competition. They were boxed in from both sides. However, they successfully designed a strategy, patterned after benchmark companies from *outside* their industry, that enabled them to connect their various component products into a unique *system* which offered a variety of advantages to the OEMs. By changing the rules of the game, they carved out a successful niche for themselves in the marketplace and have enjoyed superior financial results ever since.

Obviously, any benchmarking analysis that does not translate into programmes and actions that are implemented successfully has not been worthwhile. All of the following are needed in order for successful implementation to take place:

- *Translation of the analysis into recommendations*: some benchmarking analyses have failed because the analysts saw it as an interesting exercise to gather some good comparison data, yet failed to complete the process by developing recommendations to close gaps between the best-in-class and their own companies.
- *Support from above*: a benchmarking analysis either must be sponsored at the outset by top management in the company or business, or must win top level endorsement once it is conducted. Otherwise, it has relatively little chance of being successfully implemented.
- *Involvement of the right individuals*: it is generally bad practice to conduct a benchmarking analysis of a function without having a variety of individuals from that function – both those with political power and those with the technical and competitive knowledge – involved in the process from the start. An outsider may be the catalyst and may conduct a lot of the analysis, but unless he or she has 'buy-in' from the key functional managers, those managers are likely to pick apart the analysis at the end rather than support it. Any benchmarking analysis is going to have lots of data which will be questioned by people in the function under study. However, the key is to give them an opportunity to question that data as the process goes along. That way, when the effort is complete, they can focus on the implications of the analysis, rather than question the data.

Step 7: Monitor progress and recalibrate over time
To gain the greatest value from your benchmarking efforts, it is crucial to update and monitor the results of the analysis over time. Has your company met the targets that you set for it? Why or why not?

One Japanese competitor has carried this to the extreme. The company has a manufacturing plant which produces over 500 different parts. At one end of the manufacturing plant is a huge bulletin board with a graph for each part indicating targeted cost reductions for each month over a three-year period, as well as actual cost performance. Underneath each of those charts is the name and picture of the individual in the plant who has been assigned responsibility for making sure that the particular part's costs actually come down. This system has proved to be a great motivator to ensure that the results of the company's benchmarking effort are in fact carried out. This approach may be too extreme for many companies, but it illustrates the accountability and follow-through that is characteristic of all good benchmarking processes.

Successful benchmarking analyses are often 'recalibrated' approximately one year later. At that point, any number of things may have changed:

- Industry dynamics may have changed in such a way that key success factors have been altered. The performance variables you considered most crucial a year ago may therefore need to be amended.
- New competitors may have entered or may be looming as latent competitors. These competitors need to be added to the analysis. Similarly, you may want to drop some of the other competitors from a year ago, particularly if you found there was little to learn from them by benchmarking their operations.
- Competitors may have progressed more than you thought they would, so that their costs or other aspects of their performance are better (or worse) than you have projected. You need to update your own targets accordingly.
- You also need to measure your own progress relative to your objectives. Have you accomplished in the last year what you said you would, and if not, how should the analysis be amended?
- If your own progress has not been up to snuff, you need to identify the cause of the shortfall: were the strategies and actions you recommended the wrong ones, or was the basic strategy correct but there were problems with the execution?

As you conduct benchmarking analyses on an on-going basis, there is one common pitfall that must be avoided. Companies often forget that while they are improving their operations, competitors are improving as well. This type of mistake may seem obvious, but it is often made. Companies are so intent on focusing on their own progress that they forget that competitors are moving targets.

COMPETITIVE BENCHMARKING CASE STUDY

In the example below, an electronics manufacturer recognised the difficulty of benchmarking manufacturing cost for a product with over 200 components. As a result, the company focused on the competitors' assembly operations within manufacturing and developed some broad yet insightful benchmarks to determine its own competitive position. Competitive manufacturing strengths and weaknesses were apparent at the conclusion of this analysis and were used to determine future manufacturing strategy. (Both the industry and the company have been disguised.)

Data Systems, a major player in the electronics industry, had recently entered the market for 'compugraphs', a computer system for specialised graphics applications. While the company had a less than two per cent share of this rapidly growing market, it was considering a major capital investment in plant and equipment to become a market leader. The market was currently dominated by two mid-size companies, Custom Electronics and Innovation Technology. In addition, Data Systems' largest competitor, National Electronics, had recently entered and captured a nine per cent share.

Data Systems determined that, in order to develop a winning manufacturing strategy, it needed to benchmark the manufacturing capabilities of the three most successful players in the market. The primary goal of the benchmarking effort was to establish the appropriate level of plant automation that Data Systems would need to establish a long-term competitive advantage. The critical issue was how to manage the apparent trade-off between automating to achieve long production runs and low cost, and the need to incorporate line flexibility for product customisation.

Benchmark \ Company	Custom Electronics	Innovative Technology	National Electronics
Unit Market Share	35%	30%	9%
Units Produced/Month	4,000	3,500	1,000
Marketing Strategy	● Offer broad product line ● Build-to-order, customise ● Sell direct	● Narrow product line ● Build-to-inventory ● Sell through third party	● Recently entered market with single product ● Target existing market segments ● Focus on gaining share
Manufacturing Strategy	● Buy most components on open market ● Labour-intensive assembly ● Investing in some limited proprietary technology	● Increasingly make more components in-house ● Investing in automation ● Limited proprietary technology	● Source most components from in-house plants ● 90% automated assembly ● Proprietary technology

Figure 4.4 Overview of 'compugraph' competitors' market position and strategy

Analysis

To meet these objectives and better understand the manufacturing strengths and weaknesses of its competitors, Data Systems set up three categories of benchmarks:

- overall market and manufacturing strategy benchmarks;
- labour cost and productivity benchmarks;
- non-labour cost benchmarks.

The first chart above compares the markedly different strategies of each of the three competitors. Custom Electronics, the current market leader, has developed marketing and manufacturing strategies targeted at customised built-to-order compugraphs. Its ability to customise and to reduce new product development cycles to under 18

	Average Units Per shift	Direct Assembly Labourers			Indirect Labourers			Management/Supervisor			Total Labour Cost Per Unit
		Headcount Per Shift	Wage/ Hour	Labour $/Unit	Headcount Per Shift	Wage/ Hour	Labour $/Unit	Headcount Per Shift	Wage	Labour $/Unit	
Custom Electronics	80	370	$8.50	$315	150	$8.50	$128	75	$32K	$120	$563
Innovative Technology	72	180	$11.00	$220	150	$11.00	$183	60	$31K	$103	$506
National Electronics	27	54	$12.25	$196	32	$12.25	$116	20	$37K	$109	$421

Figure 4.5 'Compugraph' manufacturing labour benchmarks

months were the clear reasons for he company's success in the early stages of market development. Innovation Technology, on the other hand, had decided to move away from customisation and to begin to standardise its product line; as a result, it had recently invested in capital equipment which reduced the need for direct labour. Finally, National Electronics had recently entered the market with a strong bias towards high volume, highly automated production, but its plant was currently believed to be at low utilisation levels.

To compare the level of automation within each company's plant, Data Systems collected information such as volume of production, labour headcount, and wage rates for each competitor. The next chart summarises these results and illustrates that while total labour cost per compugraph produced was comparable across all three competitors, there were significant differences in the wage rates and man-hours per unit. Custom Electronics had a very labour-intensive assembly process but managed to reduce overall labour costs by hiring low paid, relatively unskilled workers. Innovation Technology managed to put fewer labour hours into each unit but paid higher wage rates than Custom Electronics. Finally, National Electronics exhibited the highest wage rates and the lowest labour hours per unit – as a result of a higher proportion of management in its labour mix.

Finally, the next chart includes key non-labour benchmarks. Customer Electronics exhibited low levels of automation and, due to its build-to-order strategy, high levels of raw materials and work-in-process. Additionally, Custom had some other problems, including a lower product yield and long order-to-ship cycles. Innovation and National, with greater automation and higher inventory turns, benefited from better production quality and an ability to ship the product faster.

Results

Upon completion of a customer survey, Data Systems found that customer needs in the compugraph market were changing rapidly. Product customisation was becoming less important than product quality, reliability and availability. In addition, the customer survey found that as the market grew, customer price sensitivity was increasing. By coupling these results with the manufacturing benchmarking analysis, Data Systems concluded that:

	Gross Property Plant and Equipment Per Direct Labourer	Inventory	Estimated Automated Hours of Assembly	Product Yield End of Line	Product Order-To-Receipt Cycle
Custom Electronics	$160K	Turnover 3.3x Mix: Raw Mat 55% W-I-P 25% Finished Goods 20%	30%	95%	30-40 Days
Innovative Technology	$320K	Turnover 3.5x Mix: Raw Mat 30% W-I-P 20% Finished Goods 50%	50%	97%	5-10 Days
National Electronics	$390K	Turnover 4.5x Mix: Raw Mat N/A W-I-P N/A Finished Goods N/A	80%	98%	15-25 Days

Figure 4.6 Selected 'compugraph' non-labour manufacturing benchmarks

- Custom Electronics was not the competitor with the best manufacturing strategy, despite its leading market share;
- Innovation and National had developed a manufacturing strategy that was better suited to a maturing, higher-volume compugraph market;
- Data Systems should establish its new plant operations targets based primarily on the performance levels and processes of Innovation and National;
- Data Systems should use the manufacturing benchmarking results in its marketing efforts in order to highlight the quality and delivery weaknesses of Custom Electronics.

SUMMARY

Competitive benchmarking is an enormously powerful tool that helps companies become more competitive without 're-inventing the wheel'. The opportunities for improvement are almost endless. The seven-step process for conducting a benchmarking analysis can apply to almost any function. However, benchmarking analyses vary widely, based on the company, the industry and the specifics of the situation. The best benchmarking efforts will deliberately weigh the various criteria and rules described above and tailor the analyses to the particular problems being addressed.

5 THE PACKAGING AND DISSEMINATION OF INTELLIGENCE

This chapter is contributed by Kirk Tyson, founder and Chairman of Kirk Tyson International, Oak Brook, Illinois

INTRODUCTION

Packaging of intelligence can many times make or break a key strategic or tactical decision. As such, we can never assume that good analysis stands on its own. We cannot simply gather information, analyse it, and disseminate it in its raw form. The intelligence co-ordinator must add value to the raw information.

This value can be in the form of further synthesis for different audiences. The information in raw form can be disseminated without synthesis to other knowledge workers requiring unstructured detail. However, that same information must be further synthesised for managers and directors, depending on their level and function.

In this chapter I will discuss the need for understanding your audience through the use of an intelligence hierarchy. I will illustrate specific types of reports that can be prepared at each level of the hierarchy. Finally, I will discuss at length a particular style of writing (the inverted pyramid) that works best for competitive intelligence.

Writing intelligence reports is a most difficult task for company managers. They find it very difficult to synthesise the 'truckloads of information' into brief action-oriented reports.

Two problems arise at this point in the intelligence process:

- you have a truckload of information in various stages of completion
- senior management has neither the time nor the desire to read a truckload of information.

The task is to convert the information you have gathered into succinct 'intelligence'.

RELATING INTELLIGENCE TO STRATEGIC PLANS

When dealing with large volumes of competitive titbits, it is helpful to pull yourself up out of the detail and re-examine your overall objective. Your objective is to identify the information that may have a potential impact on your own strategic plans. Notice the word 'potential'. Any one competitive titbit may be relevant today or it may not. If it is not relevant today, it may be tomorrow. Certainly, it is necessary to develop a process for storing all the titbits for future access.

The task is to focus on the information that may be relevant today. This is the information that you want to analyse and report. This is the intelligence you want to surface for senior management review.

The intelligence should therefore be actionable and be related directly to the strategic plans of your organisation. In addition, the intelligence should be developed on a team basis so that a better chance exists for management to 'buy in' to a recommended change in strategy.

Intelligence gathering is a collective effort and not the effort of one individual. Therefore, your first task is to abandon any pride of authorship you might have. A team approach to the intelligence process is a must.

The team approach will help you focus on the value of the information being presented rather than your tenacity in finding it or your clarity of prose. Several other guidelines should be followed when reporting intelligence. They include the following:

- identify the essential elements of information (EEIs)
- determine the primary users of the intelligence
- use a bullet-point format
- use graphs and charts
- avoid the use of numbers
- state conclusions and supporting information in a concise manner
- develop a hierarchical approach to reporting.

IDENTIFYING THE ESSENTIAL INFORMATION

A client once led me into a 370 square metre room, filled with published material on his competitors – collected over the last 50 years! The first step was to separate anything of potential intelligence value and perform the laborious task of extracting the intelligence. This was accomplished quickly, however, using a dictaphone and a matrix worksheet. Rough rule of thumb: 'Probably less than 10 important bits of intelligence are found in any large stack of information.'

I recommend that you stick to the intelligence and leave the raw data in the file cabinet. You may find the synthesis process to be difficult in the early going, especially if you have 370 square metres of material. However, a few months of practice will be all you need to become an expert at concentrating on the essentials.

DETERMINING THE PRIMARY USERS OF INTELLIGENCE

Every user of information wants their intelligence reported according to their specifications. They are not always able to articulate their needs, however. There are those individuals who want lots of detail; their response is usually, 'tell me everything you can about every competitor'. Then there are users who are not sure of what they want, but you are expected to guess correctly and provide it to them . . . quickly!

In designing intelligence reports, you will need to take into account those that want detail, and those that want summary information. You will also need to tailor the information depending on their level and their location in the organisation. This can be a very time-consuming effort but it is absolutely necessary for the success of the overall process.

WHY BULLETS PROVIDE MAXIMUM PUNCH

How many times have you received a report that is multiple pages and all words? Usually, it sits in your in-tray until you have some spare time . . . which means you never read it!

Intelligence should be clear and concise. Intelligence should not be a thick book. A bullet-point format can convey much information in an easily digestible format.

THE IMPORTANCE OF GRAPHS AND CHARTS

How many times have you received a report that is multiple pages and all numbers? Like the report with all words, it sits in your in-tray.

It takes a few minutes just to figure out the format in which the information is presented. Once the format is digested, it takes more time to extract the important information.

In most instances, you can express numerical data with charts and graphs. Whenever possible, try to avoid lists of numbers. Graphs and charts can convey important intelligence quickly and concisely. Presenting intelligence in a digestible format greatly aids strategic and tactical decision-making. Each well-thought out report will also help in gaining support for the overall intelligence function.

WHY A HIERARCHICAL APPROACH IS ESSENTIAL

Fig. 5.1 illustrates the intelligence hierarchy. It begins at the lowest level with a database of raw information. From this database, monthly news bulletins are produced and distributed widely to knowledge workers within the organisation. The next level is represented by competitor profiles which are prepared in either summary or detailed form. The next layer consists of strategic impact worksheets where value starts to be added to the information. It is at this level that intelligence begins to be formed. Even more value is added at the next level which consists of more comprehensive situation analyses. The hierarchy is capped with monthly intelligence briefings and special intelligence briefings targeted towards senior management.

Chances are that you have some of these reports if your company is already conducting intelligence activities. Many companies consider competitor profiles as the primary end result of the information they gather. Unfortunately, those companies go no further up the information hierarchy.

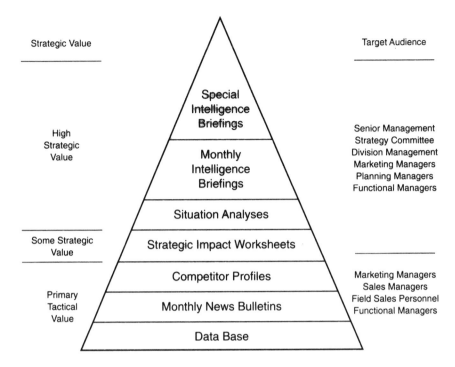

Figure 5.1 Intelligence hierarchy

Competitor profiles are of no strategic value in and of themselves! Before information can have strategic value, analysis must be performed to determine the impact of the information on your organisation. In essence, you must move up the hierarchy to provide the kind of intelligence which will have an impact on the strategic plans of your organisation.

Each layer of the hierarchy is described in Exhibit 5.1. Exhibits 5.2 to 5.7 illustrate each report in the hierarchy. The database of raw information is used to generate the monthly news bulletin and is then cross-checked against the competitor profiles so they can be updated if necessary.

It is on the strategic impact worksheet where strategic value begins to be added. The monthly news bulletin is first sorted, then summarised, and finally an initial pass at determining the strategic or tactical significance of each item is added.

Exhibit 5.1

SUMMARY OF INTELLIGENCE REPORTS				
Report Type	*Description*	*Level of Strategic Value*	*Target Audience*	*Frequency of Reporting*
Monthly News Bulletins	Contains both strategic and tactical information from both internal and external sources.	None	Field Sales Personnel Marketing/Sales Management	Monthly
Competitor Profiles	Contains general information about a competitor, usually maintained in a 3-ring binder. Updates on a continuous basis.	None	Marketing/Sales Management Field Sales Personnel	As required
Strategic Impact Worksheets	Similar to monthly news bulletin but the initial attempt at identifying as items of strategic/tactical impact is added.	Low	Marketing/Sales Management Other Functional Managers	Monthly
Monthly Intelligence Briefings	Includes key strategic and news items. Is a bound report. Articles and interview notes are summarized and presented in bullet format for management and included in detail in book.	Medium	Division Management Functional Managers	Monthly or quarterly
Situation Analysis	Summarizes key strategic issues and includes the detailed analyses which support the summary.	Medium	Division Management Senior Management Functional Managers	As required
Special Intelligence Summary	A one to two page report which identifies an issue, summarizes the key supporting analyses and prepares a recommended course of action.	High	Senior Management	As required

Next, the monthly intelligence briefing combines strategic and tactical information in a bullet-point format suitable for senior management consumption. The briefing is supported by detailed articles or interview notes in the back.

Situation analyses and special intelligence briefings are designed to address specific strategic issues which might arise. Of the two reports, the situation analysis contains much more detailed analyses than does the special intelligence briefing. The target audience and purpose of the two reports are the reasons for the difference. Special intelligence briefings are designed for senior management consumption and are only one to two pages long. Situation analysis reports are designed for middle management and can contain a number of pages.

Exhibit 5.2

MONTHLY NEWS BULLETINS

Monthly news bulletins usually contain both strategic and tactical information. The information is obtained during the month from both internal and external sources. News bulletins are simply listings of information; no value is added. They are used primarily as a tool to promote field input and to communicate across regions. The contents of a news bulletin normally include:

- The information itself
- Information source
- Date the information was received
- An indication of which products, services, markets or functional areas are affected
- Reliability index
  - Rumour
  - Fact
  - Hard fact

The users of this report tend to be marketing managers, sales managers and field sales personnel. This report should be prepared monthly in a bullet-point format.

Example

Date	Competitive Information	Source	Reliability Index
October, 1986	Corporate headquarters has heard a rumour that J.R. Industries has a new plastic bottle in test market. Specifically, the new bottle is a two litre, tamper-proof beverage container that is being test marketed at convenience stores in the Dallas area. In addition, J.R. Industries anticipates introducing the new bottle within 90 days.	Sam Houston (Salesperson)	Confirmed Rumour

---

Exhibit 5.3

COMPETITOR PROFILE

The competitor profile contains general information about all aspects of the competition, from plant locations to sales and marketing strategies. Information should be collected in a three-ring binder that can accommodate basic data and will easily lend itself to the periodic updating of the profiles as new information becomes available. The competitor profile should be updated on an ongoing basis and distributed to marketing managers, sales managers, field sales personnel, and other selected functional managers.

Example

Company Locations

XYZ Incorporated
Division of ABC International
516 S. East Street
Denver, Colorado

ABC International
11211 Highway B
Calgary, Alberta

Competitor Profile
October, 1986

Key Management Personnel*

–E. Thompson: Chairman and CEO
–G. Wilder: Vice Chairman and President
–L. Wilson: Vice President of Marketing
–K. Cagney: Vice President and Controller
–C. Donnelley: Vice President of R & D
–M. McCauley: Vice President of Sales

*This section would include background information on the key management personnel.

Plant Locations		Number of Employees	Square Footage
Unites States:	Denver, Colorado	550	320,000
	Dallas, Texas	125	75,000
	Milwaukee, Wisconsin	350	280,000
Canada:	Calgary, Alberta	80	60,000

*This section would include other statistics such as total capacity, capacity utilization, equipment used, etc.

Sales and Sales Trends

			Market Share
United States:	$206 million	Growing	38%
Canada:	$98 million	Stable	45%

Distribution and Field Sales*

– 23 Unites States Distributors
– 9 Canadian Distributors
– Western Region Sales: 17 salespeople in three districts
– Midwest Region Sales: 25 salespeople in four districts
– Southern Region Sales: 12 salespeople in three districts
– International Sales: 10 salespeople

Sales Mix

– Retail: 25%
– Institutional: 75%

*This section would include reporting responsibilities, distributor locations, key customer information, etc.

Product Lines	Percent of Sales
– Mixers	36%
– Slicers	49%
– Blenders	15%

Marketing Strategies:

■ Position products as high quality at competitive prices
■ Expand market share by acquiring smaller competitors

Exhibit 5.4

STRATEGIC IMPACT WORKSHEET

It is in a strategic impact worksheet that strategic value is added to the information that has been gathered. The worksheet is similar to the monthly news bulletin, but one level of value is added – a 'guess' as to the strategic impact or tactical significance of the information. Contents of a strategic impact worksheet include:

- Date and source of information
- Functional impact
- Division affected
- Geographical significance
- Type of information and reliability index

This worksheet format shows qualitive information and the potential strategic impact of each piece of information. It is usually targeted toward marketing managers, sales managers, and other selected functional managers.

Example

Date	Competitive Information	Strategic Impact	Source	Reliability Index
October, 1986	Corporate headquarters has heard a rumour that J.R. Industries has a new plastic bottle in test market. Specifically, the new bottle is a two-litre, tamper-proof beverage container that is being test marketed at convenience stores in the Dallas area. In addition, J.R. Industries anticipates introducing the new bottle within 90 days.	J.R. Industries is a new company that has made a large investment into r&d and new product introduction. Because of this, J.R. has been gaining market share rapidly. In the past year, its market share has increased seven percent overall. In addition, it has a very strong hold in the Texas area where it holds close to 30 percent market share. J.R.'s introduction of another new product will definitely have a negative affect on our market share, both overall and in Texas.	Sam Houston (Salesperson)	Confirmed

Exhibit 5.5

SITUATION ANALYSIS

This is the most valuable of the analyses prepared in the hierarchy. It is a written report supported by charts, graphs, static numerical information and results of modelling/statistical analyses. It is the detailed support for the special intelligence briefings and should contain the following:

- Strategic issue

- Supporting information
  - Product/service
  - Sales/marketing activities
  - Strengths and weaknesses
  - Future plans and strategies

- Alternative source of action

- Recommended course of action

This report is usually targeted toward senior management, division management, marketing managers, sales managers and other selected functional managers.

Example

Recent Key Events

- Convenience stores in Dallas, Texas are test marketing the new bottle produced by J.R. Industries.

- J.R. expects to introduce the bottle within 90 days.

- J.R. has gained seven percent in overall market share in the past year.

- J.R. already possesses a commanding 30 percent share of the Texas market.

Strategies

- Identify how J.R. is producing the new bottle and what it would take for us to do the same.

- Increase research and development efforts to keep up with the competition.

- Step up marketing efforts of current product lines, especially in the Texas market.

Exhibit 5.5 continued

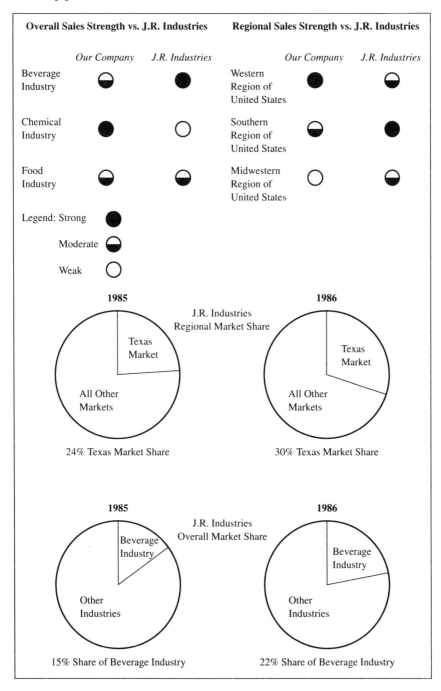

Exhibit 5.6

MONTHLY INTELLIGENCE BRIEFINGS

Monthly intelligence briefings can include both strategic and tactical information. This is a bound report which would have a few pages of intelligence bullet points followed by copies of articles and interview notes from the month. Depending upon the amount of collected information, this report may optionally be produced on a quarterly basis. Monthly intelligence briefings are usually targeted toward senior management, division management, marketing managers and other selected functional managers.

Example

Monthly Intelligence Briefing
November, 1986

Page 1

■ Altek's business is gradually improving and the company is currently operating at 75 percent of its capacity. In addition, order backlog for Altek's headsets continues to grow. It now seems that Altek's fear of severe price competition at the low end of the market was premature.
(The Daily Journal)

■ Per a source at Altek, the company was operating at 75 percent of its capacity in September. In October, however, the company operated at approximately 80 percent of its capacity. In addition, Altek anticipates operating at close to 100 percent capacity by January of 1987.
(Altek Plant Manager)

Subsequent Pages

■ Articles

■ Database searches

Exhibit 5.7

SPECIAL INTELLIGENCE BRIEFINGS

Special intelligence briefings are the highest form of intelligence. They are reports that are produced only on demand. They are prepared only when there is a strategic or tactical decision to be made by senior management. They should only be one to two pages in length and should contain the following kinds of information:

- Strategic issue

- Supporting information

- Alternative courses of action

- Recommended course of action

Special intelligence briefings are targeted toward senior management.

Example

Special Intelligence Briefing
October 10, 1986

Strategic Issue	Supporting Information	Recommended Strategy	Alternative Strategies
■ J.R. Industries is introducing a two-litre tamper-proof beverage container.	■ Convenience stores in Dallas, Texas are test marketing the new bottle. ■ J.R. expects to introduce the bottle within 90 days. ■ J.R. has gained 7% overall market share in the past year. ■ J.R. already possesses a commanding 30 percent share of the Texas market.	■ Identify how J.R. is producing the new bottle and what it would take for us to do the same.	■ Increase research and development efforts to keep up with the competition. ■ Step up marketing efforts of current product lines, especially in the Texas market.

WHERE TO PUT THE EMPHASIS FOR MAXIMUM RESULTS

Competitor Intelligence systems must deal with two types of information about companies: static and dynamic. Static information, by definition, changes infrequently. Company locations, plant sizes and production capabilities are examples of static information.

Static information, once known, need not be reported to management. Management has neither the time or the inclination to re-read old information. Static information must be stored and used only to assist in the analysis of new dynamic information. Again, competitor profiles, because of the nature of the information they contain, have little or no strategic value.

Conversely, dynamic information changes daily. The reporting needs and the strategic importance of the two types of information differ drastically. Dynamic information describes what is changing about a competitor and is, therefore, information which must be analysed and reported frequently. Dynamic information, taken by itself, may not tell a strategic story. However, groups of dynamic information can outline a company's entire strategic plan!

As you move up the hierarchy, the dynamic information is sorted by its level of strategic importance. Various analyses are performed so that the impact of the information on the company can be determined.

KEYS TO SUCCESSFUL REPORTING

To summarise, emphasis should be placed on the following when creating intelligence reports:

- strategic versus tactical information
- decision-oriented information
- inclusion of supporting data only if relevant
- multiple reports versus one large report for levels below senior management
- distribution to individuals on a need-to-know basis.

Assuming you can accomplish the above, your next task is to develop a systematic process for producing the intelligence on a routine basis. This can initially be a very difficult undertaking. However, once the process is established, you will find out how much easier it is to deal with small amounts of monthly information rather than 'truckloads'.

THE SYSTEMS APPROACH TO REPORTING

Most companies choose to mechanise the reporting process. While this can be initially accomplished through word processing, it can also be done with database or spreadsheet software. No matter what method is chosen, three generic reporting formats will produce just about any of the reports you will need for competitor intelligence purposes. These reports are illustrated in Exhibits 5.8 to 5.10.

Exhibit 5.8 shows the first generic format. This format can be used for either the monthly news bulletin, strategic impact worksheet, or the monthly intelligence briefing.

Exhibit 5.9 shows the second generic report. This format lends itself to any information where historical and/or future perspective is needed. The report can be used for quantitative information (i.e. revenues, profit margins, prices) or qualitative information (i.e. selling methods, strategies).

Exhibit 5.10 illustrates the third format. This format is used when you want to see competitor information side-by-side with your own information. Again, the information itself can be either quantitative or qualitative.

The Inverted Pyramid

I continue to be amazed at the number of successful business people that cannot write well. For this reason, I want to discuss a writing technique that works particularly well for intelligence reports. I refer to it as the inverted pyramid.

The inverted pyramid is a time-based approach to writing. It is a practical approach to formulating a clear, concise, and logically structured document in less time. This approach to writing focuses on

Exhibit 5.8

GENERIC REPORTING FORMAT # 1

DATE	SOURCE	RELIABILITY*	INTELLIGENCE	IMPACT
2/8/89	Public Relations Manager/ABC Chemical Co.	Hard fact	Ten fully operational engineered products divisions in Europe	Intent to Steal Market Share Away From Us
2/12/89	Manager/Chemical Purchasing Dept. XYZ Tire Co.	Rumour	ABC Chemical Co. talking with global competitor about joint venture for polyester production	Don't Know Need More Information
2/15/89	Plant Manager ABC Chemical Co.	Fact	ABC's Texas plant increasing equipment by 35 percent	They Will be Able to Ship Product Faster Than We Can
2/22/89	Sales Rep. XYZ Tire Co.	Confirmed Rumour	ABC Chemical Co. and XYZ Tire Co. setting up joint venture for product development	Don't Know Need More Information

*Rumour, Confirmed, Fact, Hard Fact

Exhibit 5.9

GENERIC REPORTING FORMAT # 2

	HISTORICAL				INFORMATION TYPE	PROJECTED			
	YEAR 1	YEAR 2	YEAR 3	CG%		YEAR 1	YEAR 2	YEAR 3	CG%
					ABC COMPANY				
	$20	$26	$28	14.5	Price of polyester per Unit	$30	$32	$33	4.5
	$11	$15	$16	15.5	Cost of polyester per Unit	$19	$20	£21	7
	500	700	600	8.5	Number of employees Marketing	600	600	600	0
	600	900	1000	20	Number of employees Sales	1300	1500	1800	14
	600	500	400	–16.5	Number of employees Finance	400	300	300	–12.5
	2600	2300	2100	–9.5	Number of employees Operations	2000	1800	1700	–7.5
					XYZ COMPANY				
	$32	$38	$43	13	Price of Super Tire	$47	$51	$45	6.5
	$19.20	$24.50	$31	19	Cost of Super Tire	$33	$37.50	$40.50	9.5
	$24	$30	$34	14.5	Price of Econo Tire	$37	$39	$40	3.5
	$14.40	$18.90	$24.90	21	Cost of Econo Tire	$27	$30.50	$32.50	8.5
	Emphasis on revolutionary compound	Emphasis on durability and handling	Promoted as 'racing tires for street driving'		Sales methods of SuperTire	Competition grows emphasis on quality	50,000 miles unconditional warranty implemented	Heavy marketing to professional racing organizations	
	Promoted as 'best selling, multi-use tire'	Increased competition Increased marketing to urban areas	Installed '800' customer service number for questions		Sales methods of Econo Tire	Marketing to 'common man' increases	30,000 miles unconditional warranty implemented	Emphasis on quality 'no-hassle' service	

Exhibit 5.10

GENERIC REPORTING FORMAT #3

INFORMATION TYPE	YOUR COMPANY	OTHER COMPANIES						
		ABC	XYZ	PDQ	CCD	ORR	FGH	IJK
Price of polyester per unit	$27.50	$30	$32	$29.5	$28	$33	$26	$30
Cost of polyester per unit	$16.50	$18	$19	$18	$20	$22	$15.5	$19
Number of employees Marketing	520	600	480	650	575	700	685	550
Number of employees Sales	1100	1300	850	1400	1250	900	1175	975
Number of employees Finance	360	400	295	475	390	505	350	420
Number of employees Operations	1820	2000	1480	1690	1960	2200	1930	1895

organising ideas from the top down. This process is designed to make an entire message remarkably easy for a reader to absorb.

It is essential that there be a precise sequence of thoughts in any written report. Otherwise, confusion arises. The inverted pyramid suggests that you provide the 'bottom line' thought, followed by the supporting thoughts.

Unfortunately, most of us learned a very different style of writing in school. We learned a more scientific approach to writing that was deductive in nature. We were taught to gather and write our facts in a building block approach. This building block approach then would lead to a logical conclusion, one that the reader would hopefully agree with.

Deductive reasoning is considered a useful way to think, but it results in laborious writing that is often boring to the reader. Most business reports use deductive reasoning to make an elaborate story out of what should be a straightforward point. One should always present a message inductively, primarily because it is easier on the reader.

Most journalists use an inductive, or inverted pyramid, style of writing. When you read the daily newspaper, most articles hit you with the bottom line of the story in the first few paragraphs. As the story goes on, each succeeding paragraph is of less interest, and the final paragraph is usually quite insignificant. The reason journalists use this style of writing is so that the editor can cut the story at any point, and it is still a full story for publication. This style works remarkably well for intelligence reports as well.

Here are the basic concepts of the inverted pyramid approach:

i.   each intelligence report represents a large inverted pyramid with several individual inverted pyramids contained within;
ii. thoughts at the top of the main pyramid must always be a synthesis of the subsequent thoughts;
iii. thoughts at the top of the individual pyramids must always be a synthesis of subsequent thoughts;
iv. Each individual pyramid must always contain similar kinds of information, and they should be written in a logical order.

Most people do not read an intelligence report for the information that they already know. They read to find out the things they do not know. The inverted pyramid style of writing provides the reader with a structure which allows the reader to focus on the new information, while scanning the old.

As the intelligence report is written, the writer must raise and answer questions until there are no questions left. The writer must also ensure that there are no unanswered questions in the text. For example, your manager heard that your primary competitor is going to launch a new product. Your top-of-the-pyramid statement is, 'We have confirmed that XYZ Company will launch their new product.' Then, much like a journalist, you would answer the questions you have raised with this statement. You would apply the journalist's standard list of questions: Who, what, when, where, and why. The result may look like this:

> We have confirmed that XYZ Company will launch their new product. It will be launched in France in June 1994 just after the annual industry show. It will initially be priced at ECU4,000 and will be sold through a direct sales force of 25 people. The company will spend approximately ECU10 million on advertising and promotion related to the launch. XYZ is hoping that this new product will enable the company to become number one in this market segment within two years.

As you can see, this is clearly an inductive style of writing using the inverted pyramid style. To illustrate how this story should not have been written, consider the following written in a deductive style:

> XYZ has been a major competitor to us for many years. Back in 1887 they pioneered the original technology for our industry. They have always been an innovative company. In the past, they have introduced a major new product about every 10 years. Their last major product launch was in 1984. They always seem to launch their product in France, and our sources confirm that this will be the launch location if they choose to bring out their new product in 1994. Their direct salesforce now numbers approximately 25 people. We believe that pricing for this possible new product would be approximately ECU4,000 based on expected features and their current cost structures. Their advertising and promotional budget is usually extensive for a new product, and we expect that they would spend approximately ECU10 million if they launch their new

product at this time is because they have dropped from the number one share position to number three. Historically, they have been able to move up one or more positions after launching a new product. Therefore, in conclusion, we believe XYZ will launch another major product in 1994.

If you had a choice of reading either version, I'm sure you would pick the first one. It is much easier and faster to read reports written in the inverted pyramid style. Exhibit 5.11 provides a more in-depth sample of an incorrect approach for intelligence purposes.

Notice that paragraph 1 summarises the answer clearly, but it raises additional questions in the reader's mind which are not immediately answered. These questions must be answered to completely satisfy the reader. The reference to government privatisation initiatives is not specific enough. The reference to 'projects' is too vague and is not supported.

The sentences in paragraph 2 should be reversed. The second sentence is actually the top-of-the-pyramid point. Paragraph 3 again refers to 'initiatives', but does not say what they are. Paragraphs 5 and 6 should be reversed; paragraph 6 sets the tone for the thoughts. Paragraph 12 mentions 'one' of the differentiating points. This begs the question, 'what are the others?' Paragraph 16 finally provides the 'initiatives' that the reader should have seen much earlier in the report.

Now that we have looked at an example of how not to write a report, let's look at a better writing sample. Exhibit 5.12 provides a sample of the inverted pyramid approach.

Notice that the bottom line thought is presented first and is then followed by the supporting thoughts. This is true for the overall pyramid as well as the individual pyramids within the overall one. There is a logical flow of the information, a logical ordering, and an emphasis throughout on inductive reasoning.

In this chapter, I have attempted to provide some overall guidelines for writing intelligence reports and disseminating them to various levels within the organisation. Again, the packaging of intelligence is extremely important. Good packaging will augment good analysis, and provide the added value that will make or break a strategic or tactical decision.

Exhibit 5.11

INTELLIGENCE BRIEFING – INCORRECT APPROACH

ABC Consulting Company

[1] ABC sources state the firm's goals in Mexico are:

- to support government privatisation initiatives
- to conduct projects to streamline government organisations and reduce costs
- to provide business systems consulting to help company managers obtain fast, reliable information
- to provide operational consulting services, and other special services keyed to the needs of Mexico's recovering economy
- to provide tax planning to aid client companies in dealing with increasing government efforts to generate higher revenues.

[2] According to sources, ABC is looking at Mexico as the 'new' Korea, due to Mexico's economic reforms. ABC's plans for the next five years include expanding ABC by opening three new branches – two in Northern Mexico near the border, and one in Southern Mexico.

[3] High-ranking sources state that most of ABC's business in Mexico is in the area of manufacturing. Sources also state they would like to move strategically into more financial consulting because of the recent government initiatives mentioned above, and the greater market opportunities as a result of these initiatives.

[4] Sources in both Mexico and Canada also mentioned the Canadian–US Free Trade Act as a key factor in increasing the number of companies from Canada which are moving their manufacturing operations to Mexico. Sources anticipate that this trend will increase over time. If a Free Trade Act is instituted with Mexico, 'the growth in Mexican manufacturing will become an amazement', states one ABC Consulting source.

[5] The interaction between the consulting branch and the accounting side of ABC is of special importance in the Mexican practice. While a partner from either side may provide the initial contact and on-going follow-up with a client, he or she will draw liberally upon resources from all areas of the firm. In other words, if an audit highlights areas of concern, the partner in charge will call in help from the consulting side quickly, in order to help the client get on track, and to sell additional services.

[6] An overall objective of the firm is to provide a high level of service in all areas, so that clients feel no need to go outside of Andersen for any of their accounting or consulting needs. This includes being able to draw on worldwide resources when necessary.

[7] Jose Hablas is the managing partner of all ABC operations in Mexico. Hablas is a Mexican chartered accountant, working primarily in audit, and has been with ABC for over 30 years. He has been managing partner for seven years, and has been a partner for nine years.

[8] Jose Madrigal is the managing partner for ABC Consulting. He was born in Mexico in 1948, and gradu-

Exhibit 5.11 continued

ated from National University of Mexico in 1972 with a mathematics degree. Madrigal joined ABC in 1972. He is married, has five chidren, and enjoys playing golf.

[9] Most of the partners of ABC in Mexico have backgrounds in business administration, industrial engineering, systems engineering, and/or accounting. Accounting is the most common background due to the nature of the firm's business, states an inside source.

[10] ABC recruits recent graduates, and advances them internally through the ABC ranks. One inside source states the average time it takes a staff member to become a partner is 13 to 14 years.

[11] The major Mexican universities the firm predominantly recruits from are University of Ibero Americana, University of Anahuac, Atonomis Institute of Mexico, and the Monterrey Institute of Technology.

[12] Sources state one of the differentiating points for ABC is the number of Mexican nationals that are partners within the firm. Sources state this enhances the firm's business relationships as well as government and community relationships.

[13] 25 per cent of their business in Mexico is with US firms, and 75 per cent is with Mexican firms that may or may not have American relations.

[14] Company sources stated that in the 1970s, the firm had approximately 200 personnel in Mexico, and in 10 years that number increased to over 500.

[15] Inside sources state ABC established its Mexico practice in 1955. Sources also state that the Mexico practice has the potential to become North America's newest growth centre.

[16] According to ABC sources, Mexico's economy grew by only three per cent in 1989, but there are indications that the country's economic growth may increase sharply over the next few years. According to these sources, the primary reasons for Mexico's economic resurgence are linked to government initiatives, such as:

- reducing the top marginal tax rate to 35 per cent
- removing restrictions on foreign investment
- deregulating transportation
- lifting protection of the state petrochemical monopoly
- eliminating most non-tariff barriers to trade
- undertaking free trade talks with the US.

Exhibit 5.12

INTELLIGENCE BRIEFING – INVERTED PYRAMID APPROACH

[1] Greenfield Regional Medical Centre will primarily focus its efforts on:

1. the expansion of its 'Wellness' or general health improvement programme
2. cancer treatment.

The Wellness programme is currently only a 'no smoking' programme that assists people in kicking the smoking habit. Soon to be added to the no smoking programme are a weight-loss programme and a physical fitness programme. The Wellness programme is administered at the hospital's Wellness Centre, which is located at a site separate from Greenfield Regional Medical Centre. Sources acknowledge that the Wellness Centre has been in existence for approximately five years.

Greenfield recently added a cancer treatment facility because the hospital administration felt that the Greenfield area would experience a growing need for cancer treatment.

[2] Sources believe Greenfield's primary strengths include the following:

– cancer treatment centre
– outstanding surgeons and physicians
– strong management
– satisfying the community's medical care needs
– a member of HealthNet.

Greenfield added the cancer treatment centre approximately two years ago. Sources report that the centre possesses state of the art equipment, such as a linear accelerator.

The centre is considered a 'treatment area' and is not a dedicated cancer unit. That is, there are no actual beds in the centre for cancer patients to stay. Sources state that the oncology physicians did not want a separate unit for cancer patients. Rather, they preferred that the cancer patients be intermingled, to a limited extent, with other patients in the 265-bed hospital.

The seriously ill cancer patients are placed in a wing of the intensive care unit (ICU). The ICU currently occupies one entire floor of the hospital. The 'non-critical' cancer patients are placed among three nursing areas, with other non-cancer patients, covering two floors.

Sources state that Greenfield utilises a 'competent, dedicated, and loyal staff of surgeons and physicians'. The hospital has approximately 150 physicians on staff.

Sources claim that another strength of Greenfield is its strong management. Greenfield management aims at providing the best possible service to the Greenfield community.

The strength of management lies in the fact that the hospital directors are advanced and promoted from within their departments; adding to the already established loyalty and dedication they exemplify at Greenfield, as well as within the community. The loyalty exists because of the strong family heritage the top managers possess in Greenfield. Sources also state that turnover of directors and medical personnel is very low.

Exhibit 5.12 continued

As a small community-based hospital, Greenfield keeps up-to-date with medical technology. This allows the hospital to offer services that satisfy the needs of the community so that the residents do not have to travel long distances to receive the proper medical attention.

[3] Three weaknesses were cited:

i. obstetrics
ii. cardiology
iii. psychiatric services.

Sources state that the number one weakness of Greenfield is obstetrics. This is primarily because there is a lack of obstetricians living in the Greenfield area. Local laws encourage large malpractice suits against obstetricians. Although there have not been a large number of malpractice law suits, sources assert that the cases involved a significant monetary award.

Cardiology is also weak. Although heart services are considered the hospital's second most notable service, the hospital does not perform open-heart surgery.

Psychiatric services are non-existent because of the absence of qualified psychiatrists.

[4] Sources state that there are three products over the next three years that Greenfield is most likely to push. These include cancer treatment services, Wellness programmes, and preventive disease programmes (which are centred around the Wellness programmes).

[5] Sources report that the marketing strategy of Greenfield is currently consumer oriented. In implementing the consumer marketing strategy, Greenfield uses the following methods of advertising:

– local radio
– local television
– local newspapers and journals
– telephone interviews
– flyers and questionnaires given to patients when they are discharged.

Greenfield spends between ECU 500,000 and ECU 600,000 on consumer advertising per year.

Sources believe that Greenfield is becoming more physician oriented in its marketing strategy, as evidenced by the fact that the hospital is contemplating the hiring of a physician recruiter to recruit physicians for the hospital and to market directly to area physicians.

The physician recruiter would play a very important role for Greenfield in acquiring top of the line, qualified physicians to work for the hospital in addition to selling the hospital to area physicians.

The marketing strategy the physician recruiter will utilise to market the hospital's services to area physicians includes the following:

– one-on-one interviews
– sending literature to physicians
– telephone interviews
– trade journal advertising
– site visits.

Exhibit 5.12 continued

[6] Private practice physicians admit approximately 65 per cent of the hospital's patients, while the emergency room, primarily due to the area's high percentage of elderly persons, admits 35 per cent of the patients.

6 CASE EXAMPLES

The original version of the following case study appeared in Planning Review (May/June 1991), and is reprinted with permission from The Planning Forum, the International Society for Strategic Management and Planning. The authors are Robert A. Margulies, formerly Manager, Competitive Assessment, Douglas Aircraft Company, and André G. Gib, formerly Senior Specialist, also at Douglas Aircraft's Competitive Assessment unit.

AN AEROSPACE MANUFACTURER

Introduction

In 1984 the Douglas Aircraft Company, the commercial transport division of McDonnell Douglas Corporation, had been in business for 65 years. In that time the company had made over 40,000 commercial and military aircraft. These included: the ubiquitous DC-3; the DC-9 twin-jet airliner; the short- to medium-range, narrow-bodied MD-80 series; the KC-10 military tanker, and the long-range, wide-bodied DC-10. Along with Boeing and Europe's new entrant in the aerospace business, Airbus Industrie (created in 1970), Douglas Aircraft dominated the world market for passenger jets.

But life was not easy. At the time, Douglas Aircraft had only recently reversed ten years of losses, and many of the world's airlines were in trouble. Indeed, Sanford McDonnell, Chairman and Chief Executive of McDonnell Douglas, cautioned in his report for 1984 that if the company did not receive 'new orders or a solid assurance of future orders before the end of 1985, it could become necessary to decide that the tri-jet line must be closed in 1987, when all aircraft now on order will have been completed.' There was enormous pressure on Douglas Aircraft to keep their family of passenger jets up to date, and to boost competitiveness.

In late summer of the same year, Douglas Aircraft unveiled plans at the Farnborough Air Show for the MD-11 long-range, three-engined jet airliner, the twin-engined MD-89, and the shorter-fuselage MD-87. The company was forecasting that from 1984 to 1998 the airlines of the non-communist world would take delivery of 4,700 aeroplanes (worth US$210 billion in 1984 money), and Douglas Aircraft was determined to have its share of the market. But competition was intensifying.

In October 1984, the Chairman and CEO of the McDonnell Douglas Corporation in St. Louis, Missouri, directed that each of the company's major components establish a competitive intelligence organisation to improve its understanding of the competition. One premise behind this directive was that an assessment of the competition in the marketplace was essential, and that the company's current informal methods of competitive-intelligence gathering were inadequate. Another premise was that only ethical and legal data-gathering techniques were to be used, especially since there was so much information available from a wide variety of public sources. The directive specified that the overall process must be action oriented with a focus on analysis, assessment and communication.

The company's major subsidiaries and divisions, which we call the company units, responded by establishing formal competitive intelligence as an extension of the strategic management process. Its assignment was to survey three external elements:

- the business environment
- the customer's needs
- the competitor's activities.

Organisation and process definition

Each unit of McDonnell Douglas was to focus its competitive intelligence efforts directly on management's needs. For example, at the Douglas Aircraft Company in Long Beach, California, the Competitive Assessment Department was created within the Division and Program Office organisations to oversee all competitive intelligence activities. The group directed the staff involved in competitive assessment, and co-ordinated and integrated their data collection, processing, and dissemination activities in a four-step process.

Step 1: Survey management to determine the subject and purpose of information needed

This survey increased the probability that information would be collected in a systematic fashion with priorities being set by the end users of the data and not by the producers. Management's advice aimed competitive intelligence efforts toward what the customers and competitors were doing now, as well as what they were likely to do in the future. These forecasts were based on an analysis of the competitor's past behaviour, present operations, resource capabilities and current strategies.

Step 2: Collect the data

Each functional area was surveyed to determine what kinds of competitive information were already gathered. Then a centralised function was set up to co-ordinate the compiling and cataloguing of this information.

Step 3: Analyse, assess and interpret the information collected

For the process to be effective, it was necessary to enlist the personnel with the necessary skills for the tasks at hand.

Step 4: Disseminate the intelligence

Communication at the management level was by briefing and written report. The audience for the distribution efforts was determined by the project content. The purpose of the overall effort was to make certain that appropriate steps were being taken to improve the current and future competitive posture of the company in technology, management and productivity.

Competitive assessment start-up

The initial task of the Competitive Assessment Department was to identify the competing product lines of our major customers. Next, we identified likely sources of information and established ethical ground rules for gaining access to the data. We developed a format for analysis reports that would be responsive to management needs. And, lastly, we conducted a preliminary competitor analysis of our major competitors to 'test' the abilities and teamwork of the department members. Management was briefed on both the results of the study and the effectiveness of the group effort.

The first broad-approach applications of competitive intelligence

Two parallel studies were undertaken by different teams to develop comprehensive databases on the major competitors and their product lines. Each study used a different approach to accomplish its objective. Team members from each of the functional divisions participated in these studies.

Competitive Assessment Team 'A' built an extensive database but did little analysis and no assessment on the set of competitors it identified. The major thrust of its study was collecting, collating and comp-iling data at the responsible function. Several areas were comparatively analysed. No implications or alternatives were presented.

Competitive Assessment Team 'B' presented a balance of data collection, analysis and assessment on a second set of competitors. The data was collected, collated and compiled at a central location. Where possible, a comparative analysis was conducted to indicate whether Douglas Aircraft was behind, on par, or ahead of its competitors in the functions examined. Two detailed analyses were used to develop implications: SWOT (strengths, weaknesses, opportunities and threats), and SPOT (strengths, problems, opportunities and threats).

When senior management was briefed by both groups, the approach of CA Team 'A' was poorly received. Surprisingly, however, the approach of CA Team 'B' was received with mixed reactions. The lack of total positive response triggered a self-examination of the role of competitive intelligence within the company. The consensus was that rather than providing useful intelligence, the process inundated management with an excess of information with little specificity or relevance to their needs.

Applying analytical tools to the study results

An internal study was undertaken on ways to improve the competitive intelligence function, and discussions were held with management to solicit their suggestions. The results indicated that it was critical for management to know how the company's strengths and weaknesses compared with its competition, and to identify critical opportunities and threats. Wherever possible, competitive intelligence needed to articulate the implications identified by the opportunities and threats analysis, and recommend strategic alternatives. Use of analytical techniques such as a SWOT and SPOT analysis, and the TOWS (threats, opportunities, weaknesses and strengths) Matrix added value to the analysis and assessment. By providing management with implications and strategic alternatives, competitive intelligence could be effectively integrated into the strategic management process. The use of these tools in a follow-up Team 'B' Competitive Assessment effort was at the beginning of an analytical approach to the competitive intelligence activity that would be accepted by line managers.

The need to fine-tune the competitive intelligence capability

One of the steps taken to improve the contribution of competitive intelligence was the development of a competitive assessment workshop to provide participants with the techniques and methods needed for effective competitive-intelligence-gathering activities. One objective of the workshop was to provide an understanding of methodology and to present the foundation and techniques necessary to collect competitive intelligence data legally and ethically. The workshop material was developed in-house by the Competitive Assessment Department and was customised for the Commercial Products Division.

A 'focused' project-oriented approach to competitive intelligence

While management considered the use of the detailed SWOT and SPOT analyses and the TOWS Matrix a step in the right direction, they felt that the analysis still fell short of the specific, relevant and actionable intelligence they needed for effective strategic management.

The Competitive Assessment Guidance Committee (CAGC) held discussions on ways to make the results of their intelligence gathering more specific and actionable. Management's interest was fired by the focused or project-oriented technique. Nicknamed the 'rifle approach', this process brought in information and intelligence that was relevant, timely and feasible. It also improved the responsiveness of the Competitive Assessment Department.

The rifle approach first identified the critical key issues management would need to focus on over the next 12 months (with data to be updated on a regular basis). This was accomplished by forming a steering committee to brainstorm a list of key issues. This list was then ranked and reviewed with management, and the issue they considered the most important then became the target for the first focused, project-oriented competitive intelligence effort.

At the next meeting the CAGC assessed the project and selected a team leader. They defined the project and established such constraints as boundary, scope, scheduling and budget. The duration of the focused project was eight weeks, during which its key goal was to generate specific competitive assessment tasks as a framework for the effort.

A competitor capability forecast

The competitor capability forecast which follows is based on an actual study co-ordinated by the Competitive Assessment Department, although it has been disguised. The project involved looking at the probability of competitor X launching product Y during time frame Z, and attaining key design and technology objectives A, B and C.

Getting under way

As a first step, a CAGC discussed the relevant importance of the various issues senior management considered critical, and the focus was narrowed to a specific product of one competitor. The CAGC then expanded its team to include other individuals with the critical expertise needed to guide the project.

When the CAGC next met to discuss the selected project, it developed a task statement, set the scope and boundary of the project, and drew up a time schedule. Critical success factors[1] were identified, and two competitive assessment teams were developed – one to collect data (participants chosen by functional area), and the other to analyse data (participants chosen both by functional area and by name).

Before the next meeting, the project team leader conducted a competitive assessment audit and developed a list of specific questions to be answered by the data-collecting team. The basic framework for the competitive assessment audit was adapted from work by Kotler, Gregor and Rogers on the 'marketing audit',[2] and William Rothschild's 'strategy worksheets'.[3]

The main reasons for using the audit were to assist the project leader in evaluating the competitive environment, and to determine what areas had already been investigated and to what degree. The intent was to concentrate on critical areas where the Douglas Aircraft Company was not knowledgeable. The specific questions reflected the focused project-oriented competitive assessment data requirement established by the CAGC to provide management with the intelligence they required. The questions were distributed to the CAGC for comments and then discussed at the next meeting, where they were changed if necessary and annotated for assignment to the proper functions.

Once the project was precisely delineated, the database manager was briefed on the types of information required. The manager's job was then to access various on-line databases, assemble a bibliography, compile clippings and retrieve data from the firm's Market Information Centre in preparation for the initial meeting.

Finally, both of the Competitive Assessment teams were briefed on the project. At the kick-off meeting, a representative of senior management participated to emphasise the importance of the project. The project team leader discussed the background of the study, the methodology, the time schedule and the assignments. The database manager informed the team members of the resources available and distributed copies of the bibliography that had been assembled. Personnel who were new to the competitive assessment team were identified and scheduled for an in-house workshop on collecting data for competitive assessment.

Data-collecting phase

Although data collection is conducted throughout the competitive assessment cycle, in the focused approach the major collection effort was intensified in view of the need to complete this step within two weeks of the kick-off meeting. Data was collected on both Douglas Aircraft and the competitor. Two joint meetings of the teams were held to monitor results and provide feedback. Additionally, two sets of one-to-one sessions were conducted. These sessions enlisted members of related areas, their managers or supervisors, and the project team leader to brainstorm the interrelations and implications of the data being collected. Also, the data was evaluated for reliability of source and accuracy of information.

Analysis and assessment phase

This phase was the heart of the competitive assessment process. The analysis team was composed of experienced, knowledgeable individuals who, in most cases, had decision-making authority. The information was compiled in the Competitive Assessment Department, catalogued, and evaluated. Small teams from related functions then analysed the data.

The analysis portion was divided into three phases (adapted from William Rothschild's framework):[4]

- Phase 1 explored the competitor's past experiences and accomplishments – such as what did they achieve, how was it achieved, and what was the degree of success?
- Phase 2 involved reconstructing the competitor's past strategies – such as strategies followed to achieve present competitive position, SWOT, and Company Capability Profile.
- Phase 3 required conducting a resource audit of the competitor and the product – such as available resources, how they were being employed, and how might they be employed.

Still using the Rothschild techniques, the analysis team developed an enterprise profile of the competitor and the new product. The assumptions and information on which the profile was based were divided into internal factors (strengths and weaknesses), and external factors (opportunities and threats).

Key External Factor	Weight	Rating	Weighted Score
1. Growing Market for Aircraft in Market Segment SR/MR XXX.	1. .25	1. 4	1. 1.00
2. Strategic Alliances or Joint Ventures to Maintain or Strengthen Market Share.	2. .10	2. 3	2. 0.30
3. Competitor Y Launched New Aircraft in Market Segment SR/MR XXX.	3. .20	3. 1	3. 0.20
4. Low Fuel Costs Do Not Justify New Engine.	4. .25	4. 1	4. 0.25
5. Reluctance of Airlines to Pay for New Technology.	5. .20	5. 1	5. 0.20
Total:	1.00	N/A	1.95

Constructing the External Factor Evaluation Matrix
1. List the Key Opportunities and Threats Facing the Organization.
2. Assign a weight (relative importance of each factor to success in the industry) ranging from 0.0 (not important) to 1.0 (very important) for each opportunity or threat. Total value to equal 1.0.
3. Assign a rating ranging from 1.0 to 4.0:
   ● 1 = Major Threat
   ● 2 = Minor Threat
   ● 3 = Minor Opportunity
   ● 4 = Major Opportunity
4. Multiply each factor's weight by its rating to determine a weighted score for each factor.
5. Add up the weighted scores for all factors to determine a total weighted score for the organization.

"The Quantitative Strategic Planning Matrix", Fred R. David. *Handbook of Business Strategy, 1985-1986 Yearbook,* William D. Guth, editor. Boston, MA: Warren, Gorham & Lamont, Inc., 1985, pp. 21-14.

Figure 6.1 External factor evaluation matrix

Internal Environment / External Environment	Strengths (S) 1. Broad Product Line 2. Financial Strength 3. Etc.	Weaknesses (W) 1. Capacity Constraints 2. Derivative Aircraft Competing Against New Aircraft in SR/MR XXX 3. Etc.
Opportunities (O) 1. Market Segment SR/MR XXX Growing by X% by 1995 2. Competitor Z-Weak Position & Vulnerable 3. Etc.	**SO Implications** 1.1. Need New Product to Maintain Market Share into 1990s 1.2. Limit Competitor Z to Niche Player 2.2. Pursue Aggressive Pricing	**WO Implications** 1.1. Unable to Meet Forecast Demand with Current Capacity 2.1. Opportunity for Other Competitors to Gain Market Share
Threats (T) 1. Competitor Y Has Launched New Aircraft in Market Segment SR/MR XXX 2. Reluctance of Airlines to Pay for New Technology 3. Etc.	**ST Implications** 1.1. Emphasize Family of Aircraft Strategy 2.1. Airlines May Not Buy New Airplane 2.2. Earnings May Not Reach Goals	**WT Implications** 1.1. Competition May Increase Market Share at Our Expense 1.2. Possible Loss of Market Share in Mid-1990s

To read Implications, the first number is the external environmental situation, the second number is the internal environmental situation.

Adapted from "The TOWS Matrix–A Tool for Situational Analysis", Heinz Weihrich. *Long Range Planning*, Vol. 15, No 2, April 1982, pp. 54-66.

Figure 6.2 threats-opportunities-weaknesses-strength matrix – competitor X

Next, using Fred David's 'internal factor evaluation matrix',[5] the internal factors were ranked and reduced to a list of key factors relating to the competitor's strengths and weaknesses. Then the factors were assigned a weighted score to indicate their relative importance to the critical success factors of the aerospace industry. A rating was assessed to indicate whether the key factor was a major or minor weakness, or a major or minor strength. Then the weighting and rating were combined to provide a weighted score that would indicate whether the competitor's strategic position was strong or weak.

A similar process was used on the external factors (see Fig. 6.1).

The key strengths, weaknesses, opportunities, and threats were listed. After considerable discussion, the competitor's internal strengths and weaknesses were matched up with the external opportunities and threats on Heinz Weihrich's TOWS Matrix (see Fig. 6.2).

This information provided clues to strategic alternatives that the competitor might use. These strategies were then ranked and weighted based on the intelligence that had been developed. Then, using the information from the internal audit conducted on our organisation, we repeated the same process with our own business.

Next, we combined the information from the competitor (representing the external environment) and our organisation (representing the internal environment) and created a second TOWS matrix. This information suggested the feasible strategic alternatives available to management for meeting the challenge of this particular competitive product.

We next tested our strategies and assumptions using Richard Mason and Ian Mitroff's Strategic Assumption-making and Testing System (SATS).7 Using the information gleaned from the assessment, the analysis team listed all assumptions and strategies. The assumptions for each strategy were then ranked by how they related to the overall competitor strategy. The top-rated assumptions were then ranked a second time according to their degree of certainty. Then the strategies were analysed to determine how they contradicted each assumption. After the information was processed, the project team leader and several of the key analysis team members assessed the relative probability of the competitor's future strategic moves for the product being studied.

At the meeting between the CAGC and the analysis team, different tools were used to present the data: the Key Success Factor grid, the External Factor Evaluation Matrix/Internal Factor Evaluation Matrix (EFEM-IFEM), the TOWS Matrix, the Quantitative Strategic Planning Matrix (QPSM – see Fig. 6.3), the Company Capability Profile, and comparative analysis charts.

	Ratings	Strategic Alt #1[3]	Strategic Alt #2[3]
● **Internal Strength & Weakness Statements:**[1]			
■ Strong Financial Position	4	12[3]	12[3]
■ Market Share Leader	4	16[4]	8[2]
■ Capacity Problems. . .but Modernizing & Automating Factories	2	4[2]	4[2]
■ Technical Excellence. . .but Conservative in New Technology Application	3	9[3]	9[3]
■ Manpower Shortages in Critical Skills	1	1[1]	3[3]
● **External Opportunity & Threat Statements:**[2]			
■ Growing Market for Aircraft in Market Segment SR/MR XXX.	4	16[4]	12[3]
■ Strategic Alliances/Joint Ventures to Maintain or Strengthen Market Share	3	9[3]	9[3]
■ Competitor Y Launched New Aircraft & Competitor Z Planning on Launching Derivative Aircraft in Market Segment SR/MR XXX.	1	4[4]	2[2]
■ Low Fuel Costs Do Not Justify New Type of Engine	1	1[1]	4[4]
■ Reluctance of Airlines to Pay for New Technology	1	1[1]	4[4]
● **Sum Total Attractiveness Score:**[4]		**73**	**67**

Notes:
1. Internal "S & W" Ratings: 1 = Major Weakness; 2 = Minor Weakness; 3 = Minor Strength; 4 = Major Strength.
2. External "O & T" Ratings: 1 = Major Threat; 2 = Minor Threat; 3 = Minor Opportunity; 4 = Major Opportunity.
3. Attractiveness Scores: (Located in Half Columns Under Strategic Alt.): 1 = Not Acceptable; 2 = Possibly Acceptable; 3 = Probably Acceptable; 4 = Most Acceptable.
4. Total Attractiveness Scores (Located in Half Boxes): Computed by Multiplying Ratings by Attractiveness Scores.

"The Quantitative Strategic Planning Matrix", Fred R. David. *Handbook of Business Strategy, 1985-1986 Yearbook*, William D. Guth, editor. Boston, MA: Warren, Gorham, & Lamont, Inc., 1985, pp. 21-14.

Figure 6.3 Quantative strategic planning matrix question: 'will competitor X launch all new aircraft program?'

Based on this meeting, we revised sections of the project report to ensure that the intelligence and the presentation format met the needs of the customer – in this case, senior management. To raise management's confidence level, all charts were annotated with the source of the information. The findings of the final project report represented a consensus of all members of the CAGC.

An initial presentation of the project report was made to the CAGC and to both Competitive Assessment teams to check on the accuracy, specificity, and relevance of the intelligence.

DISSEMINATION PHASE

In this phase, the CAGC and key members of the Analysis Competitive Assessment team made a presentation to management that attempted to answer the question initially posed by the study – the probability of competitor X launching product Y during time frame Z, which met key design and technology objectives A, B and C. In addition, the project identified both the competitor's and Douglas Aircraft's strengths, weaknesses, opportunities, and threats, and offered implications that were directly related to the strategic alternatives being considered. In the end, this competitive assessment formed a key part of a strategic analysis presentation that led to a major strategic decision.

Copies of the presentation were distributed to key managers and technical experts in other divisions and corporate components. Presentations were also made to appropriate departments and divisions. The CAGC then convened a final time to assess how well the project had met senior management's objectives, and to recommend changes in the process for the next project.

THUMBS UP FROM MANAGEMENT

Project-based competitive assessment was favourably received by senior managers because they felt it was responsive to their specific needs. The bottom line was that this approach gave them specific,

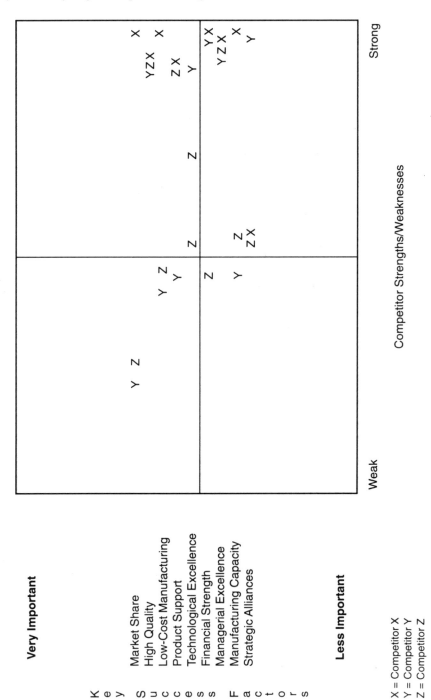

Figure 6.4 KSF/Competitor strength grid

Source 'How to select a Business Strategy', David A. Aaker, *California Management Review*, Vol. 26, No. 3, pp 167–175'

accurate, relevant, actionable and timely intelligence that had a positive impact on their decision-making. The process also improved management's insight into the strategic business unit's competitive environment.

A PHARMACEUTICAL COMPANY

Note: This example is based on real events. Some details have been changed in order to protect the identities of the companies concerned.

In early 1993 managers in one business development group of a large European pharmaceutical manufacturer were raising questions about one of the company's key 'pipeline' compounds. There was concern that more than 20 competitive substances worldwide had been identified as being under development, of which seven were thought to have gone beyond the pre-clinical development phase. Important strategic issues were at stake. Top management would soon be deciding whether to continue or suspend the development programme.

Several million dollars had already been invested in research and development and, not surprisingly, scientists in the development team were keen to continue with the project. The company was also intent on the product entering the market as a leading contender in a key therapeutic area. The sales potential for the drug in Europe and the United States in its first five years of product life was conservatively estimated at close to $400 million, so the financial carrot was an appetising one.

What was especially worrying for the business development team was the possibility that one of their most powerful competitors would launch a product two years ahead of the company's own offering. It was public knowledge that the competitive compound was already somewhere in Phase III clinical trial development. But there were still many unanswered questions.

The firm's Competitive Intelligence unit was tasked by the head of Strategic Planning to carry out a review. The competitive intelligence staff proceeded to evaluate information already in hand from market research, the development team scientists and from published sources.

From this analysis, the Competitive Intelligence unit was able to determine specifically what information top management would need before taking action. They would, for example, need to know:

- effects of generic drugs on pricing
- up-to-date profiles on the competitive compounds, covering such issues as efficacy and side effects
- the exact position of the leading competitive compound within Phase III trials, and the results to date of the trials
- details about the competitor's plans for marketing the drug, including an understanding of how the product was to be positioned.

The first steps in putting the information puzzle together involved collecting, processing and analysing considerable amounts of data and information from in-house and published sources. My own firm was then asked to conduct intensive research, focusing on primary sources in three continents.

In one month the puzzle was nearly complete. Enough information had been gathered and analysed to give the company an accurate and timely understanding of the status of practically every competitive compound in development. The competitors themselves, clinicians at trial centres, pharmaceutical industry analysts, and some regulatory agencies had told us everything the client wanted to know.

The decisions subsequently taken by top management with respect to the company's compound, and its development, were based upon facts; not rumours, not guesses, not interpretations of published material, and not 'gut feel'.

NOTES

[1] J.K. Leidecker and A.V. Bruno. 'Identifying and Using Critical Success Factors', *Long Range Planning*, Vol. 17, No. 1, February 1984, pp. 23-32.

[2] Philip Kotler, William Gregor, and William Rogers. 'The Marketing Audit Comes of Age', *Sloan Management Review*, Winter, 1977.

[3] William E. Rothschild, *How to Gain (and Maintain) the Competitive Advantage in Business* (New York, NY: McGraw-Hill Book Company, 1984), pp. 115-141.

[4] William E. Rothschild, *Putting It All Together: A Guide to Strategic Thinking* (New York, NY: AMACOM, 1976), pp. 103-121.

5Fred R. David. 'The Quantitative Strategic Planning Matrix', in *Handbook of Business Strategy, 1985–1986 Yearbook*, edited by William D. Guth (Boston, MA: Warren, Gorham & Lamont, Inc., 1985), pp. 21-1 to 21-19.

6Heinz Weihrich. 'The TOWS Matrix – A Tool for Situational Analysis', *Long Range Planning*, Vol. 15, No. 2, April 1982, pp. 54-66.

7Richard O. Mason and Ian Mitroff, *Challenging Strategic Planning Assumptions* (New York, NY: John Wiley & Sons, 1981).

7 ORGANISATION AND MANAGEMENT

This chapter is contributed by Kirk Tyson, founder and Chairman of Kirk Tyson International, Oak Brook, Illinois

INTRODUCTION

The development of a competitive intelligence process is a complex effort requiring the support of management and key line personnel throughout the organisation. Department managers also can make large contributions by supplying information. And all of the above play instrumental roles in designing a process that is workable and efficient.

In this chapter, I will discuss how to develop, organise, and manage a competitive intelligence process. I will also discuss how to link the intelligence process with an ongoing strategic management process.

A high-level process flowchart (Fig. 7.1) depicts in summary form all of the process elements. The inputs consist of published and non-published information, and the outputs are the reports discussed in Chapter 5. The competitive intelligence process itself is what stands between the inputs and outputs. Standing in the middle, it can be a bottleneck or it can be a finely-tuned machine.

Unfortunately, most people look at process flowcharts such as this one and assume that a computer sifts through all the information and sorts it out. Let me suggest that in most cases it is people, and not machines, that analyse and arrange incoming competitor information.

At some undetermined time in the future when artificial intelligence systems are in place to analyse competitor data and suggest alternative strategies, the process box may, in fact, be a computer. Today, however, the computer can only aid in manipulating data for reporting purposes. The critical ingredients in competitive intelligence systems are people, including line personnel and the intelligence co-ordinator.

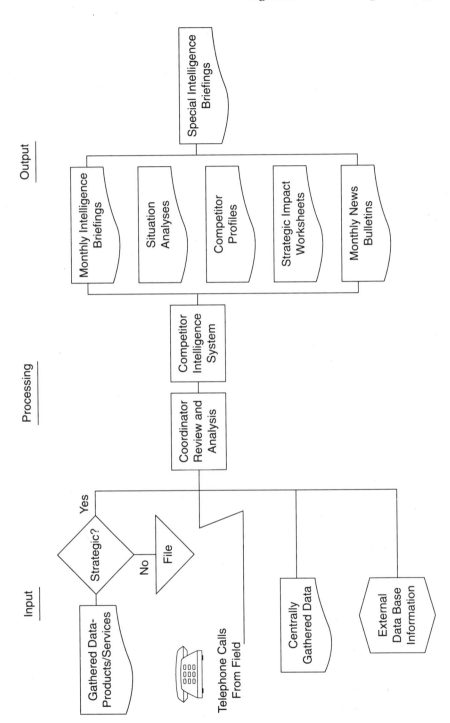

Figure 7.1 High level system flowchart

All too frequently companies err by trying to design and install the ideal competitive intelligence system, one covering all competitors, all markets, and all technology. This approach assuredly leads to failure. It is much better to focus on one situation at a time and string together a series of small successes. This helps to accomplish the strategic change within an organisation that is necessary for overall success.

Bringing about strategic change is an on-going activity that necessitates the creation of an on-going process for gathering and analysing intelligence. The recommended approach to developing such a process is illustrated in Exhibit 7.1.

Exhibit 7.1

SYSTEM DEVELOPMENT APPROACH

1 Establish the need for an intelligence function and gain the co-operation of others.
2 Identify reporting requirements.
3 Identify data requirements and sources.
4 Gather data and prepare prototype reports.
5 Determine an approach to mechanisation.
6 Design and install the mechanised system.

ESTABLISHING THE NEED FOR THE INTELLIGENCE FUNCTION

Start by reviewing your company's strategic plans, organisation charts and monthly management reports. The purpose of this exercise is to identify major strategies and areas of emphasis. It also identifies potential providers and users of intelligence.

Next, identify your key direct competitors. If the initial list is over five in length, 'sharpen the pencil'. There have been many times that company managers have said to me, 'We have 100 to 200 key competitors.' This is impossible! In any one served market, there will probably be no more than five key competitors.

Use the 80/20 rule if you are having problems. Identify the 20 per cent of the companies that provide 80 per cent of the competition, and then focus on one or a few competitors as you develop your intelligence process. As you are assessing the relative strengths and weaknesses of your main competitors, you should then identify the one that represents the biggest threat.

The next step should be to outline your overall approach to developing a process. A major part of this should include estimating the cost of developing this function as well as its on-going costs. The development costs represent the cost of designing the system, including any software, hardware and database subscriptions. On-going costs include the payroll cost of the intelligence co-ordinator(s), database charges, clipping charges, software development costs, and outside research and consulting services.

GAINING THE CO-OPERATION OF OTHERS

After completing these planning steps, meet with potential 'champions' to pre-sell the concept. Look for key managers in the organisation who have the necessary clout to provide support for a competitive intelligence plan. The intelligence function has been seen in sales, marketing, planning, research and development, and even quality assurance. The specific functional area which you approach is of little importance as long as your audience is comprised of 'champions'.

Senior management approval may not always be necessary. After all, most senior managers believe that intelligence gathering is already established within the organisation. They assume that someone in the sales and marketing function is co-ordinating this effort. If they only knew . . .

IDENTIFYING REPORTING REQUIREMENTS

Intelligence gathering should focus on key success factors (KSFs). Ideally, these factors should be translated into measurable key control indicators so that competitive activity can be measured in a quantitative as well as a qualitative way. Some key success factors lend themselves to quantitative analysis much more directly than others. For example, if high market share is a key success factor, it is easy to identify a key control indicator. However, measuring a key success factor such as image is harder because subjective factors are more difficult to quantify.

The next step is to determine the basis upon which your company competes in the marketplace. Do you compete on price, differentiation, focus, or some other factor? Your intelligence reports should relate to the basis upon which you compete. For example, if your company does not compete on price, don't focus the data gathering and reporting effort on the prices of competitors' products and services.

After thinking about the information you want your intelligence process to produce, define the types, levels of detail, and frequencies of reports. Monthly reporting is generally best. Quarterly reporting may have very little value because it may lag behind current conditions. Much of the value of intelligence is in its timeliness.

The next step is to develop preliminary report formats with 'live' data from one key competitor. Again, it is much easier to sell the concept if you have something tangible to offer. Take your ideas and sample reports to potential users. Discuss the reports with the users and solicit suggestions for enhancement.

IDENTIFYING DATA REQUIREMENTS AND SOURCES

This step of the process requires identifying potential data requirements and the alternative sources for each bit of information. Any one piece of information is probably obtainable from both internal and external sources and in published and non-published form. For example, if you require information about a company's annual sales, potential sources are available, including:

- an annual report from the company
- ex-employees
- on-line data bases
- SEC reports
- competitor employees
- your employees

● distributors of competitor products
● common suppliers.

Once you have listed the potential sources of information, you can prioritise each source and build your network for collecting each piece of information. This process has been discussed in detail in other chapters.

GATHERING DATA AND PREPARING PROTOTYPE REPORTS

Start by gathering data for one key competitor. Sort the data as it is received and develop a filing system. As one file gets too big, break it down into smaller files. It is best to let your filing system evolve so that it reflects your needs as you progress. Then when you are ready to build a mechanised database, the conceptual design will already be complete.

After the initial data gathering is complete, prepare a set of prototype reports, and issue these reports regularly for a period of two to three months. During this time, discuss the reported information with the users to determine their overall satisfaction level.

Repeat this cycle on a monthly basis so that the prototype system continues to provide the needed information. When you are comfortable that you can produce intelligence on one competitor, start with another while you continue with the first. Using this evolutionary process, rather than striving for instantaneous generation of a complete process, significantly reduces the risk of failure.

DETERMINING THE BEST APPROACH TO MECHANISATION

This should be the last step in developing a competitive intelligence process. Many companies try to go to a computerised system too early in the process. Until you have a good set of manual procedures and files in place, mechanisation is not advised. Most of the successful intelligence groups have not started out by building computerised databases. Those that have tend to keep them very simple with only high-level profile information.

When you start to move towards mechanisation, you also have to change your mind-set as it relates to computer systems. Decision-support systems are flexible tools that enable data to be manipulated in an unstructured manner. They are very different from transaction systems, such as payroll, billing or order entry. Competitive intelligence systems are decision support systems.

Decision support systems consist of fourth and fifth generation software tools that allow users to program with a minimum of technical support. They are used in highly unstructured ways and are developed in an evolutionary fashion to meet the changing needs of decision makers.

DEVELOPING AN EVOLUTIONARY APPROACH

Start simple and keep it simple! Begin by using personal computers with word processing, data base, and spread sheet capability. Always use the 80/20 rule when considering mechanisation. Implement only the 20 per cent of the system that provides 80 per cent of the benefit.

Again, don't try to build the ideal mechanised system that stores everything you want to know about every competitor. This is an impossible task. Companies that have taken this approach end up two years later without a system in place and no interim successes along the way.

DESIGNING AND INSTALLING THE MECHANISED SYSTEM

The specific design and installation tasks you must follow depend on your software and hardware selection. Remember: you're not finished when the first set of reports is produced. This is a decision support system. Continually re-evaluate the reports and the overall system design.

Again, a word of caution. Don't try to mechanise too soon. Too many people become enamoured of potential software and hardware solutions to the point that they lose sight of their objective of producing timely and relevant intelligence for decision-making. In very simple terms, there are four stages in the development of a competitive intelligence process.

I would characterise Stage I in the process of organising intelligence information as 'The Mess' or 'The Current Situation', with Stage IV being the 'Ideal Process'. I have seen far too many companies immediately attempt to leap from Stage I to Stage IV. By doing so, they have already failed. Let me suggest two additional stages that you should pass through. Stage II should include the development of a good manual process; any mechanisation at this point should only consist of word processing. Stage III should be the point at which you begin to experiment with software tools such as spreadsheets, databases, graphics and so on. In this stage, you should develop dozens of prototypes with live data.

The methods described in this chapter will allow you to migrate towards an 'ideal system' over a period of three to five years, and they will help to guarantee you some intelligence successes along the way. Even with this evolutionary approach, however, the biggest challenges you face are not systems issues, but organisational issues.

ORGANISING THE PROCESS

Organising a competitive intelligence process can be difficult to accomplish. The first constraint is usually one of cost. Most companies prefer not to devote resources to a function until it can be proved that the function is necessary and will succeed.

The next problem is one of finding a 'champion' who has enough clout to bring about change in the organisation. This is usually the 'fast tracker' within management at the corporate or business unit level.

Finally, the concept of competitive intelligence must be sold to those in the organisation who will be providing information to the process.

SETTING OBJECTIVES

Begin by establishing the overall objectives for competitive intelligence activities over a period of three to five years. Most intelligence groups find it takes this long for the process to evolve.

Don't set first year objectives so lofty that they cannot be achieved. Remember, it is better to start small and build on success. Some typical first year objectives might include:

- to begin active solicitation of intelligence from both internal and external sources
- to monitor two to three key competitors on a continuous basis
- to establish the intelligence co-ordinator role
- to develop a manual data base for competitors
- to issue news bulletins, strategic impact worksheets and intelligence briefings on companies being monitored.

The evolving nature of the process suggests that in later years the objectives must be broadened. For example, you should continue to add additional companies at a rate that can be supported by the staffing levels you select. As the intelligence staff and network become more efficient, they will be able to support the addition of more companies without increasing the staff.

ANALYSING STAFFING NEEDS

Based on the objectives you have outlined for the intelligence function, determine the primary tasks to be performed and the amount of time required to perform each task. The tasks usually include some combination of those listed in Exhibit 7.2.

Once the tasks are identified, determine the necessary mix of part-time and full-time personnel. The mix is substantially different in the initial stages. Initial data gathering is usually done with part-time resources assembled as a task force or project team. On-going activities require at least one full-time co-ordinator.

Based on the tasks and resources, determine the background that full-time candidates should have. A marketing or planning employee who understands the markets in which you compete would be an ideal

Exhibit 7.2

TASKS REQUIRED OF INTELLIGENCE PERSONNEL

- gathering information via telephone from internal company personnel
- gathering information via telephone from external company personnel
- reading and summarising clippings
- performing on-line database searches
- interacting with internal company personnel
- analysing information for strategic and/or tactical significance
- preparing periodic reports
- presenting findings to management
- responding to ad-hoc inquiries

---

candidate. However, the most important characteristics of a candidate are communication skills, motivation, enthusiasm and curiosity.

Although industry experience is sometimes a plus, it is not always necessary. The functional skills of data gathering, organising and communicating far outweigh the benefits industry experience might offer. In fact, in most telephone interviews, it is better if you are not an expert.

SMALL COMPANIES VERSUS LARGE

Intelligence gathering is not any different for small companies than for large organisations. However, the functional organisation needed to collect intelligence in large companies is more complex.

Small companies

Small companies can often achieve success by assigning the co-ordinator role to the vice president or director of marketing who actively co-ordinates the gathering and analysis of information. Fig. 7.2 illustrates the intelligence function in a small organisation. With only one co-ordinating point, a great amount of control can be exercised over the function.

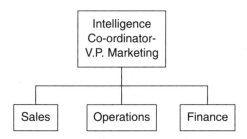

Figure 7.2 Intelligence function – small organisation

The vice president or director of marketing utilises part-time resources to accomplish the gathering and analysing of competitive information. This person actively solicits input from employees in sales, operations and financial areas of the organisation. His or her budget usually does not include full-time personnel. The only incremental budget consideration is the cost of third-party research and clipping services.

Large companies

In the case of the large organisation, the actual level in the organisation for the intelligence co-ordinator should coincide with strategic planning efforts. For example, if the organisation does its strategic planning using a large centralised strategic planning function, the competitive intelligence function would probably work best if centralised. Most firms have moved away from the large central organisation for planning and now prefer to develop plans at the level in the organisation where they must be implemented. If this is the case in your organisation, this approach should be used for the competitive intelligence function as well.

The large organisation presents a more difficult co-ordinating role. The organisation chart is similar to the small organisation but is multiplied by the number of distinct business units comprising the total organisation. This in turn necessitates a central co-ordinating point. This is illustrated in Figure 7.3.

In the first year, it is best if each of the intelligence unit co-ordinators works independently. The central intelligence co-ordinator's role becomes more important when the gathering performed at the lower levels becomes more broadly based.

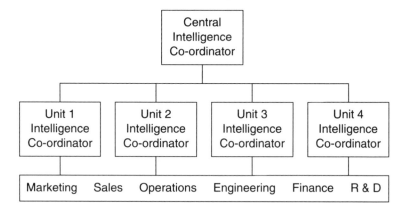

Figure 7.3 Intelligence function – large organisation

Hundreds of observations over the years suggest to me that the intelligence function tends to bring business units together and sometimes dissolves the rivalries that exist. This happens because everyone realises the importance of ongoing competitive intelligence, and they realise that much can be gained by sharing their resources to achieve a common end.

The recommended approach in large organisations is initially to develop a 'quiet, private network' of individuals who want to participate in the intelligence function.

Forget about such fanfare as a formal announcement by the CEO that the intelligence function is being established. Don't include this function in each manager's objectives. Don't include intelligence responsibilities in the job descriptions of employees. You initially want to develop an informal team of employees who participate because they want to and not because they have to.

Developing the 'quiet, private' intelligence network takes time and essentially requires figuratively re-drawing the organisational charts of the company. For example, you want to find those individuals in each business unit who are enthusiastic, aggressive, curious, and want to participate in the network. These individuals may be as many as ten levels below top management. The managers of each of these ten levels may not want their subordinates participating in the network unless the manager is controlling it. You can begin to see the potential political problems. This is the primary reason for the 'quiet, private' approach, at least in the initial stages.

The best intelligence comes directly from the source. Ten layers of review usually results in good intelligence being watered down or filtered out. Decision makers need information directly from the source so that it can be analysed for intelligence purposes.

To the greatest extent possible, the intelligence co-ordinator should be a full-time resource. In large organisations, an intelligence function with all part-timers seldom works. It is recommended that one full-time unit co-ordinator be selected in the initial stages to be followed by others as the function evolves.

A typical start-up budget for a large organisation is illustrated in Exhibit 7.3.

Exhibit 7.3

START-UP BUDGET FOR A LARGE ORGANISATION	
Salaries and benefits	$100,000
Microcomputer and Software	20,000
External Database Charges	20,000
External Clipping Charges	10,000
External Research and Consulting	50,000
	$200,00

HOW BEST TO USE THIRD PARTIES FOR RESEARCH

The use of third parties is recommended to further maximise the time of the co-ordinator. For example, clipping services can clip articles on a more cost-effective basis than can be achieved by trying to perform this task internally.

Intelligence firms also can be helpful in accelerating the process of information gathering and analysis. They can assist in synthesising monthly intelligence, performing the more difficult information gathering tasks, assisting in the design of an intelligence system, and training employees.

The third-party status of intelligence consultants also helps to break down any political barriers that may exist within an organisation. In this way, they serve as a catalyst in the process and help to ensure the success of the intelligence function. External firms also serve as something of a buffer between the firm at target primary sources, thereby adding confidentiality to the research effort.

Third parties are best used during the initial development or for fine-tuning the intelligence process. The participation of consultants should be substantial during the first six to 12 months of operation, and their tasks should be divided into system development and network development. Their participation should include a phased shifting of responsibilities so that you are self-supporting after the six to 12- month period. After the initial period, their participation should be limited to research efforts during which they conduct interviews to find hard-to-obtain information.

SELLING THE CONCEPT WITHIN YOUR ORGANISATION

Many advantages become apparent in a co-ordinated competitive intelligence process:

- It brings about a more efficient use of limited resources. The concept of one co-ordinator better utilising his or her time by involving others in the process is a major selling point.
- An intelligence process leads a company to act rather than react to events in the marketplace and helps it to capitalise on opportunities.
- It helps business unit managers increase their overall understanding of the business and the ways in which the company can achieve a competitive advantage.

However, even with all of these advantages, support is difficult to obtain until management has seen results or understands what can be reasonably expected from a competitive intelligence system.

The selling of the competitive intelligence concept should be done in steps as the process evolves. It is difficult, if not impossible, to sell the entire concept in the beginning. Many managers believe this function is already being accomplished somewhere in the organisation. These managers usually don't see the value of a more co-ordinated competitive intelligence function.

The best way to sell the concept is to produce a series of successes. Steady, positive results over a period of time enable you to string together a series of small successes. This illustrates the importance of the function to managers who may not initially appreciate the value of a co-ordinated approach. It is during this time that they will have a better chance of buying in to the process.

The ultimate selling point is demonstrating that the process has enabled your organisation to stay one step ahead of the competition.

ORGANISING FOR THE FUTURE: ONE SCENARIO

I have been in the information business for almost 20 years. During that time, I have seen great strides in technology, which allow users of information to manipulate data in a myriad of ways. What I have not seen is a conscious effort to co-ordinate and cultivate information as a major corporate asset.

Information exists in many forms in many places. Unfortunately, it exists in bits and pieces, and only a small fraction of it is organised in a way that benefits the overall organisation. For example, in one area of an organisation, sales information is gathered and summarised. In another area, operations information is gathered and summarised. In yet a third area, accounting and financial information is gathered and summarised. What has happened historically is that information has been co-ordinated on a functional basis or a product/market basis, and there has been little, if any, cross-fertilisation.

As discussed in the beginning of this book, the overall process of strategic management must become an ongoing activity as opposed to a once-a-year exercise.

In order for strategic management to become a routine effort, continuous streams of information are required. Information on the competition represents one of these continuous streams. The others can be classed as internal (marketing, operations, financial) and external (market, environment, technology, customer, supplier).

Certainly the technology exists to handle these streams. The capability already exists within most organisations to develop a mechanised approach to the process of competitive intelligence. Consequently, the technology/systems issues do not represent the major stumbling block to the development of a competitive intelligence process. The problems are primarily organisational.

Unfortunately, most organisations were initially established on a functional basis. The three usual functions were marketing, operations and finance. Over time, more and more companies adopted a product/market approach and perhaps even established strategic business units. However, even under these approaches, the marketing, operations and financial areas still persisted. I call this the 'tricycle approach' to organisational management.

And just as the tricycle has one large wheel, so does each company have a dominant culture. Some are controlled by the marketing/sales group. Others are dominated by the financial guys. I submit that the tricycle approach will not work as it becomes critical to make more timely strategic and tactical decisions. It will take an organisation that can move more quickly. I submit that the tricycle is 'out', and the car is 'in'.

Obviously, it takes four wheels to run a car, and not three as with a tricycle. So what is the fourth wheel? I believe the fourth wheel is the wheel of information. The information wheel is needed to co-ordinate the gathering and disseminating of information so that all areas of the organisation will benefit. Companies can no longer afford to have most of their information not being used. They can no longer afford to have information in private file cabinets, desk drawers, and in the heads of employees who ultimately leave the organisation. Information is an asset, and it needs to be better co-ordinated.

Many intelligence co-ordinators whom I have spoken with over the years have sometimes felt like a fifth wheel. They feel they are beating their heads against the wall trying to gather and disseminate information. Again, the system mechanics are not the problem; it is people. Let me suggest that intelligence co-ordinators are not a fifth wheel, but rather the critical fourth wheel that will propel their organisations to greater competitive advantage.

For those pioneering the trail of competitive intelligence, you are blazing a path that ultimately will unlock the buried treasure of information in your organisation. If you are a persistent and successful change agent, you also will help others as they too attempt to feed critical streams of information into the strategic management process.

KEYS TO SUCCESSFUL INTELLIGENCE

Over time it has become evident that there are certain key factors for success in any intelligence effort, such as establishing the need for competitive intelligence, ensuring management support and involvement, and developing a disciplined but flexible approach.

Exhibit 7.4 outlines a plan for implementing an intelligence activity, one that you can tailor to your specific situation. Using this plan should help to ensure a successful start-up or refinement of your intelligence function.

Exhibit 7.4

SUMMARY ACTION PLAN

  i develop prototype system and begin gathering information
 ii further establish your information needs and develop a network
iii refine reporting requirements
 iv refine data requirements and narrow down your sources
  v continue gathering data and preparing prototype reports
 vi determine staffing requirements for on-going activities
vii determine an approach to mechanisation
viii design and install a mechanised system

THE SINGLE MOST IMPORTANT FACTOR

After working with hundreds of organisations, including over 70 of the Fortune 100, it has become apparent to me that most organisations are looking for an easy solution to developing a competitive intelligence function. It also has become apparent that all of the current literature on the subject does not provide a clear enough explanation of what is required for a simplified approach.

Exhibit 7.5

SYSTEM AND NETWORK COMPONENTS	
System Components	*Network Components*
Gathering published information – Searching databases – Examining clippings Synthesising information – Abstracting information – Entering and storing data Analysing information – Manipulating data – Modelling Reporting information 　　　　　Preparing: – Monthly news bulletins – Competitor profiles – Strategic impact worksheets – Situation analyses – Monthly intelligence briefings – Special intelligence briefings Developing a mechanised system	Identifying primary providers and users of information Selling the intelligence concept to management Selling the intelligence concept to other managers and staff Soliciting on-going system input from information providers Soliciting on-going system feedback from system users Selling strategy recommendations to network users Continually expanding the network

Part of the problem is that most managers approach tasks consecutively rather than concurrently. The most successful intelligence systems I have seen are those that approach the development of a system concurrently with the development of a network. System and network components are illustrated in Exhibit 7.5.

I previously alluded to the fact that the biggest problems encountered in the development of a competitive intelligence programme are people-related, not system related. Therefore, a greater effort should be expended on network development as opposed to system development. However, it is difficult to develop the network until a basic system is in place, and vice versa. The best method is to approach the two tasks concurrently.

A concurrent approach, shown in Fig. 7.4, will yield a functioning intelligence process in a much shorter period of time than would otherwise be the case. Companies find it takes three to five years to develop an effective intelligence process. However, companies that have

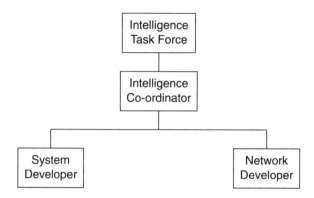

Figure 7.4 The concurrent approach

approached network and system development concurrently have been able to accomplish an effective function in less than half the time.

This can be explained when considering the typical approach most companies take in designing a process, which is to start as if using a blank piece of paper. Interviews are conducted with individuals at various levels throughout the organisation to obtain a better understanding of business functions (products, services, delivery mechanisms) and management processes (strategic planning, budgeting, management reporting). During this interviewing process, information needs relative to the competitive intelligence function are also sought. Reports are then designed, input requirements determined, and process mechanics defined. Assignments are then issued to individuals enlisted to support the network.

What is wrong with this approach? Basically, it works well for developing more traditional transaction systems such as payroll, accounts payable, sales analysis, general ledger, and financial reporting. However, as I mentioned earlier, a competitive intelligence system is a decision-support system which does not lend itself to a traditional development approach. A decision-support system is one that is in constant change, adapting to current business conditions and organisational structures. The traditional approach yields a system that is out of date before it is completed.

Consequently, I recommend that the traditional approach not be used so that front-end development time can be reduced, and implementation time maximised.

I use the word 'prototype'. Decision-support systems should be thought of as constantly changing. An initial prototype system can be developed in one day, or certainly in less than one week. I recommend developing this prototype and using it as the starting point in developing the intelligence network. Then, when the interviews are conducted with potential users and providers of information, you are not starting with a blank piece of paper. In addition, the system will evolve the way the users want it to and not the way the designers have specified. Network development is the most important factor that will make or break the intelligence function.

A great deal of time needs to be spent with users and providers to get them to buy in to the process. As a facilitator of change, you must sell them on the concept, sell them on the process, sell them on the network and their participation, and sell them through a series of successes along the way. This can only be accomplished with a concurrent approach.

A WORK PROGRAMME GUARANTEED TO WORK

Using the approach described above and illustrated in Fig. 7.4, it is recommended that the task force and the co-ordinator spend the majority of their time on network development. Exhibit 6 at the end of this chapter is a detailed action plan guaranteed to work assuming the concurrent approach.

TOWARDS PERPETUAL STRATEGY

As of this writing, many intelligence groups within companies are doing a good job of gathering and analysing intelligence. The vast majority have some type of process in place for gathering and analysing intelligence, but most have encountered major difficulty in linking the intelligence activity with the strategic and tactical decision-making process. One reason for this difficulty is that intelligence co-ordinators have made the assumption that decision makers know what to do with the intelligence they are given.

Planning and decision-making are probably the two most important tasks of business leaders throughout the world. Yet most business leaders do not really understand how to perform these tasks. No one has ever taught them. Almost no formal training exists at the university level. The vast majority of company training programmes do not cover these subjects. Few books exist and the few in existence are usually more conceptual than how-to. So how do leaders learn how to plan and make decisions? In three ways:

i. by discussing these topics with their peers
ii. by reading snippets about other companies in newspapers, magazines and trade journals
iii. through trial and error (most common).

What is even more frightening is that the remaining 99 per cent of company employees learn about planning and decision-making in the same way.

What employees do learn through their formal and on-the-job training is how to analyse. Many have turned analysis into a complex art form. Dozens of university courses, scores of books, hundreds of articles, and thousands of conference conversations have led many an employee to conclude that analysis is the end rather than the means.

To link the intelligence function with the strategic management function, the intelligence professional must become much more than a gatherer and analyser of information. The intelligence professional must become a perpetual strategist, a very special breed of change agent. The perpetual strategist educates management on the front end of the intelligence process, and facilitates strategic and tactical decisions on the back end of the process. The effective perpetual strategist is also a process engineer who develops a structured decision-making process to link intelligence with strategic management.

Competitive intelligence is here to stay. While virtually unheard of in the 1970s, it is today considered a necessary tool for surviving in the marketplace. A competitive intelligence process and network, if organised properly, will provide one of the vital streams of information that is absolutely necessary in making routine strategic decisions.

Those companies able to integrate competitive intelligence into their strategic decision-making will be winners, and the employees responsible for organising the intelligence effort will be applauded for the major roles they have played in making their companies victorious.

Exhibit 7.6

DETAILED ACTION PLAN

Task	Responsibility	Date
1. Develop prototype system and begin information gathering.		
A. Review the company's strategic plans, organisational charts and monthly management reports. Identify major strategies and areas of emphasis.		
B. Identify primary users and providers of information. Develop initial internal and external networks.	_____	_____
C. Identify key competitors (current and potential), products/services, customers, markets, and technology.	_____	_____
D. Assess relative competitive strengths and weaknesses.	_____	_____
E. Identify the competitor that represents the biggest threat.	_____	_____
F. Design initial reports.	_____	_____
G. Determine initial data requirements and begin gathering data. Subscribe to clipping services and data bases.	_____	_____
H. Gather data and prepare first sets of reports with 'live' data.	_____	_____
2. Further establish the need for function and develop network.		
A. Answer the question, 'Why competitor intelligence?' Define competitor intelligence and its relationship to the overall strategic management function of the company.	_____	_____
B. List the potential benefits of a more co-ordinated approach to the intelligence function.	_____	_____
C. Outline the overall approach to the development of the function.	_____	_____
D. Approximate the incremental cost of initially developing this function, as well as the ongoing costs.	_____	_____
E. Meet with potential 'champions' within the organisation to sell the concept.	_____	_____
F. Determine if senior management approval is necessary.	_____	_____
G. Establish task force(s) and identify intelligence co-ordinator(s).	_____	_____
H. Begin to conduct ongoing interviews with potential users and providers of information in the network.	_____	_____

Exhibit 7.6 continued

Task	Responsibility	Date
3. Refine reporting requirements.		
A. Determine industry success factors.		
B. Translate industry success factors into key control indicators.	_____	_____
C. Determine the bases upon which your company competes in the market place.	_____	_____
1. Price		
2. Differentiation		
3. Focus		
4. Other		
D. Further define types and levels of reporting.	_____	_____
1. News bulletins		
2. Competitor profiles		
3. Strategic impact worksheets		
4. Executive intelligence briefings		
5. Situation analyses		
6. Special intelligence briefings		
7. Other		
E. Refine frequency of reporting.	_____	_____
1. Daily		
2. Weekly		
3. Monthly		
4. Quarterly		
5. As required		
F. Refine the list of key users of intelligence.	_____	_____
1. Senior management		
2. Line management		
3. Staff management		
4. Salespeople		
5. Other		
G. Continue to develop prototype report formats with "live" data from key competitors.	_____	_____
H. Continually discuss reports with users and providers in the network and solicit suggestions for enhancement	_____	_____
I. Refine report formats based on discussions.	_____	_____
4. Refine data requirements and sources of information.		
A. Review reporting requirements and refine the list of required data.	_____	_____
B. Further develop internal network of individuals who provide intelligence. Continue to sell the concept to individuals already in the network.	_____	_____

Exhibit 7.6 continued

Task	Responsibility	Date
C. Identify knowledgeable industry sources for your external network.	_____	_____
D. Develop a call sheet (consisting of name, affiliation, and phone number) for the internal and external networks.	_____	_____
E. Call each name on the call sheets and ask each person for their ideas on sources of information.	_____	_____
F. Review directories of on-line data bases to determine any additional ones that may suit your purposes.	_____	_____
1. 'Supermarkets'		
a) Dialog™		
b) Nexis™		
c) Newsnet™		
d) DataStar™		
e) Other		
2. Industry specific data bases		
3. Financial data bases		
4. Dun & Bradstreet		
5. Compustat		
6. Other		
G. Continue to review directories of business information.	_____	_____
H. Continue to contact trade associations.	_____	_____
I. Continually discuss findings with library personnel and augment your list of sources.	_____	_____
5. Continue gathering data and preparing prototype reports.		
A. Continue gathering data for one key competitor or a few key competitors by using the following.	_____	_____
1. Clipping services		
2. On-line data bases		
3. Internal and external networks		
4. Other		
B. Begin to develop a manual filing system.	_____	_____
C. Prepare a complete set of reports for one key competitor and issue regularly for a period of two to three months.	_____	_____
D. Discuss reports with users to determine satisfaction level and then determine changes to be implemented.	_____	_____

Exhibit 7.6 continued

Task	Responsibility	Date
E. Implement changes and review with users after a two- to three-month period.	_____	_____
F. Begin to gather data about other competitors.	_____	_____
6. Determine staffing requirements for the ongoing function.		
A. Determine primary tasks to be performed.	_____	_____
1. Gathering information via telephone from internal company personnel	_____	_____
2. Gathering information via telephone from external company personnel	_____	_____
3. Reading and summarising clippings		
4. Performing on-line data base searches	_____	_____
5. Interacting with internal company personnel in the interpretation of information	_____	_____
6. Analysing information for strategic and/or tactical significance	_____	_____
7. Preparing periodic reports		
8. Presenting findings to management		
9. Responding to ad hoc inquiries		
B. Estimate time required to perform each task for each competitor.	_____	_____
C. Estimate time frame in which the intelligence functions will be developed.	_____	_____
D. Determine mix of part-time and full-time required personnel.	_____	_____
1. Initial data gathering and analysis		
2. On-going activities		
E. Determine qualifications needed by full-time candidates based on the percentages of time required for each intelligence task.	_____	_____
1. Business or technical degree		
2. Company experience		
3. Planning experience		
4. Marketing experience		
5. Financial experience		
6. Systems experience		
7. Research experience		
8. Communications skills, written and oral		
9. Motivation, enthusiasm, and other factors		
F. Estimate number and type of personnel required and associated costs.	_____	_____
G. Review staffing requirement with management.	_____	_____

Exhibit 7.6 continued

Task	Responsibility	Date
H. Screen internal candidates.	_____	_____
I. Screen external candidates.	_____	_____
7. Determine an approach to mechanization.		
A. Develop an evolutionary approach to mechanization.	_____	_____
1. Word processing.		
2. PC data base		
3. PC spread sheet		
4. Interface to mainframe computer		
5. More sophisticated fourth and fifth generation approaches		
B. Review reports previously designed.	_____	_____
C. Review manual filing system.	_____	_____
D. Develop tentative data base design:	_____	_____
1. Top down		
2. Bottom up		
E. Develop checklist of software requirements.	_____	_____
8. Design and install the mechanized system.		
A. Review software alternatives.	_____	_____
B. Select software and hardware.	_____	_____
C. Finalize report design based on software capabilities.	_____	_____
D. Finalize data base design.	_____	_____
E. Code, test, and de-bug the system.	_____	_____
F. Build the data base.	_____	_____
G. Develop procedures.	_____	_____
H. Produce first set of mechanized reports.	_____	_____

8 THE COLLECTION AND PROCESSING OF INTELLIGENCE

INTRODUCTION

Collection and processing are, respectively, the second and third steps in the intelligence cycle. Collection 'involves the gathering of the raw information from which finished intelligence will be produced.'[1] Processing is concerned with 'the conversion of the vast amount of information coming into the system to a form more suitable for producing finished intelligence.'[2] In many firms the collection and processing of intelligence is referred to as the research phase.

Sources of data and information fall into two categories: open (i.e. secondary) sources, and primary (usually human) sources. Sources in both categories are found inside and outside the organisation. However, it is primary sources that yield the most intelligence value. If a product manager in a pharmaceutical company wants to know the trial design, or findings to date for a competitor compound now in clinical trials, the obvious choice of information sources would include investigators at the trial centres, medical advisers, executives at the competitor firm itself, and, possibly, other competitors. Secondary sources are unlikely to shed much light on what the product manager wants to know.

Collection is linked dynamically with analysis and, like analysis, it is user driven. The output of collection and processing is the input to the analysis function. Hence it is essential that the goals and scope of the collection activity are defined precisely. The wrong, or too much, data and information can soon become overwhelming, and render useless even the best attempt at analysis.

It is important that the firm's competitive intelligence unit does not assume principal responsibility for the collection of raw data. The competitive intelligence unit is a strategic 'knowledge asset' of the firm – comparatively small in number – whose value will soon depreciate if demands are placed upon it which are rightfully the province of the corporate library or market research department.

Intelligence personnel must leverage their resources, especially their time, by drawing upon the resources of other elements of the organisation. If the finance department has already collected (and possibly analysed) relevant information about the competition, then the CI unit should use it. If pieces of the intelligence puzzle are available from customer services, human resources, operations, marketing, purchasing, or R&D, CI staff must make it their business to locate it, get it, and use it. CI does not add value to the strategy formulation process by 're-inventing the wheel'.

Collection is an iterative process: users establish their intelligence requirements; information is then gathered; it is processed (which includes testing for reliability); it is analysed; the plans or actions which then spring from the analysis prompt new requirements; and these requirements, in turn, lead to the refinement of existing, and to the setting of new, collection tasks.

Once the 'problem', or intelligence needs, have been formulated, the collection process can be thought of in terms of the following sequence:

- determine the research design
- determine the data – and information-collection methods
- design researcher's collection forms, and if possible agree these with the intelligence consumer
- collect the data and information.

The issues of focus and needs determinants have been discussed in Chapter 3 – Analysis. Therefore I will concentrate here on presenting a broad overview of how and where information is gathered for intelligence purposes.

HOW DO YOU GET IT? WHO GETS IT? WHERE DO YOU GET IT?

Internal sources

In big organisations most of the information required for CI purposes already exists internally. Usually 80 per cent or more of the intelligence a manager needs in a firm like Alcatel, BASF or Compaq is available from sources inside the company. The challenge lies in finding it, and finding it in time for analysis and decision-making purposes.

Periodic intelligence audits can be of help in uncovering the company's hidden information resources. Fuld defines the intelligence audit as:

> . . . an inventory of your company's intelligence assets. These assets include private competitor files, individually constructed databases, scattered market studies purchased outside the library, as well as names of industry and competitor experts within your company.[3]

Firms cannot successfully collect and process (much less analyse or use) information for intelligence purposes without a formal competitive intelligence programme in place. In most cases the complexity of the intelligence needs, as well as the knowledge, skills and effort associated with meeting these needs, is too great. The problem, quite simply, is that there is too much data and information available – much of it clutter – relative to the abilities and time managers have to digest it. Competitive intelligence exists to relieve managers of information overload, not add to the dilemma. The intelligence mission is not to acquire detailed knowledge of every element of the competitor's business; rather it is to remain up-to-date on competitor plans and actions likely to have a strategic impact on the business of the firm.

Once intelligence needs have been specified by the consumer (ideally in consultation with the senior CI co-ordinator or manager), the objective is to collect selectively the most useful – not the largest quantity of! – information needed as cost effectively, as efficiently, and as quickly as possible. It is the quality of intelligence, and the speed with which it is gathered which determine the degree of success of the collection effort. The firm must avoid late discovery of competitor intentions and plans, or precious resources are wasted just trying to catch up.

Although academics and consultants are quick to exhort firms to build the CI function around a programme of continuous monitoring of competitors, in practice this seldom occurs. Continuous monitoring is sometimes practical (but not often), and on occasion will be useful (but not always). According to the European Association of Information Services (EUSIDIC), reporting in their recent study of competitive information programmes at 15 major US based firms with global activities:

> . . . it is probably still more effective to concentrate on extensive and in-depth information on one particular company with a specific goal in mind, even long term. Project orientation will be effective because it will satisfy top management and end in recognisable results.[4]

The rigorous monitoring of competitors is an ideal companies should strive for. But as managers will know, the reality at present is somewhat different. CI activity is project-driven activity because today's firms are themselves essentially project-driven. Managing the large-scale enterprise means 'Living on the fault line where intensifying competition and calls for more transparent accountability collide, [and executives] must deliver more business performance than ever before – and in less time.'[5] Managers therefore want intelligence that will contribute directly to the specific strategic and tactical decisions that must be made today. Tomorrow is too late.

So while it is often necessary to monitor continuously one or more competitors for a certain length of time, most firms do not, nor can they afford to allocate the resources that would be required to place all major competitors under intense surveillance.

Intelligence collection requirements, and therefore the approach and focus of the collection effort are a function of the specific information needs of managers, and vary considerably from project to project.

Examples of internal sources of competitive information, and the types of information available from these sources, are shown below:

Finance managers and accounting personnel
- borrowing capacity
- comparative financial indicators
- details about historical performance.

Human resources staff
- management development programmes
- organisation
- recruitment policies and practices, and recent recruitment campaigns
- training
- unions (contracts, problems, etc.).

Marketing managers and sales executives
- compensation of sales representatives
- details of distribution channels
- market and customer development activities
- pricing and discount practices
- product differentiation
- promotion mix
- sales practices
- size of competitor sales, or field force
- training programmes.

Operations managers and staff
- capacity and utilisation (plant, distribution and warehouse centres, etc.)
- cost trends
- employee mix
- facilities information
- research & development (R&D) activities
- specific nature of operations
- status of automation/mechanisation.

Competitive information is also found in other areas of the firm. These include advertising, customer service and support, information systems, legal, purchasing, training, licensing, etc. The key lesson is that the greatest resource the firm possesses for competitive information is its own employees.

The CEO, too, the most important consumer of intelligence, often is the best intelligence source. CEOs of big corporations are privy to valuable information which may not be available elsewhere. CEOs spend much of their business and leisure time talking to their counterparts in industry, to leading academics, to investment bankers, to senior government officials, to consultants, and to representatives of special interest groups. In effect CEOs spend much of their lives collecting (and disseminating) information of strategic significance. The CEO is as much a supplier as he is a customer of intelligence, and must not be overlooked in the collection process. It is not unusual for middle-level managers to devote many hours or days researching information already known by their chief executive.

So what is the best approach to gathering competitive information already collected and stored by the firm? Following the intelligence audit, the CI co-ordinator or manager must:

i. Develop an informal network of information sources in the organisation. The network should not be structured around functional, political, or other organisational barriers or so-called lines of communication. CI managers must have unrestricted access to anyone in the organisation, of any rank, and at any time. This implies change, which in turn means resistance. If, however, the intelligence effort is to make a material difference to the bottom line performance of the firm, CI managers or co-ordinators cannot be constrained by executives' agendas or protocol.

ii. Set, and 'religiously' adhere to, a policy of providing value-added feedback to sources. Internal sources cannot be expected to support the intelligence function simply for the greater good of the company. It might be nice if this was the case, but in real life things do not happen this way. Moreover, many of the most important internal sources of intelligence may be geographically or organisationally remote from the intelligence manager or unit, and will therefore have little 'natural' incentive to co-operate. By offering sources something in return for their contribution to the intelligence function, their pro-active participation is encouraged. For example, providing intelligence about the strengths and weaknesses of competitor's product offerings to the company's sales force helps them do their jobs better (sell more and sell smarter), and thereby serves to motivate support for CI. Intelligence itself is the return on investment that internal information sources value most.

Open sources

The range of open – mainly published – sources is infinite. Some, obviously, are better than others, but most, even collectively, provide little in the way of real intelligence value. This is not to suggest that open sources play a small, or unimportant role in the intelligence gathering process – open sources are vital – but, from an intelligence perspective, their qualitative value (relative to primary sources) is low. Open sources can be compared to the foundations of a house; one would not wish to construct the dwelling without the appropriate foundations, but they are only the starting point. For the most part, CI researchers and analysts have deadlines to meet, and do not have time to scrutinise the vast quantity of secondary information to which they have access. There is no real option but to go to human sources to collect and validate intelligence.

Strategy decisions require knowledge about what the competitor is capable of doing (this is where open sources are especially helpful), about new developments in the competitor's competencies, on what the competitor intends to do, and when, where and how the competitor intends to do it. Competitive intelligence is concerned with what is likely to happen, with the future; it is not concerned with yesterday's report in the *Financial Times*.

Where a company attributes the failure to make profits or gain market share to 'increased competition' (other euphemisms are 'price wars', 'cheap imports', 'unfair practices', and 'government subsidsed', etc.) it is, in fact, admitting its own failures of strategy and intelligence. In plain language it got it wrong.

Sweden's SKF, the world's leading roller bearing manufacturer, blamed losses of SKr355 million for the first quarter of 1992 mainly on weak demand in the European car industry. What a surprise!

SKF's no doubt perfectly drafted script (the strategic plan) appears to have been formulated on the assumption that the competition would lie down and play dead in the first act, or, possibly, that the

European car industry would suddenly, miraculously, recover from its deep troubles of the past few years. Thus a company which loses the competitive war deserves the consequences of defeat, however severe these may be.

To avoid failure, to gain competitive advantage, and to win in the marketplace, the firm must base its strategic assessments of its competitors, its markets, and its environment on continuous streams of intelligence. It must also develop an organisation-wide culture that promotes strategic, and therefore competitive, thinking. Employees throughout the organisation must be enlisted to contribute to the collection effort by raising their 'awareness of the competition and of management's needs for competitor information'.[6]

It is not an aim of this work to examine in detail data collection techniques, or open information sources. A number of excellent texts have already been written on the subjects,[7] and they are of little practical interest to senior managers. It is not their job to pore over business directories, print-outs from electronic (on-line) databases, stacks of 'clippings', trade journals, government publications, or any of the scores of other sources available in the public domain. This is the role of market researchers, of corporate librarians, and, to a lesser extent, of competitive analysts. In short, the concern of CEOs and other senior managers is, first, how to define their intelligence needs, and, second, how to interpret and use it once it is in their hands.

Managers must identify three sets of factors at the start of the intelligence collection effort, and must ensure that they are clearly understood by their researchers and analysts. These are:

i. The Key Success Factors (KSFs) driving the business, the markets, or market segments, and the industry. KSFs, according to Leidecker and Bruno, are 'those characteristics, conditions, or variables that when properly sustained, maintained, or managed can have a significant impact on the success of a firm competing in a particular industry.'[8] These will include some of the more important aspects of market attractiveness, such as customer complexity, innovation, and market growth.

ii. Key competitor issues, such as core competencies, customer perceptions, differentiation, relative share, and relative quality.

Essentially, this is concerned with how firms compete in the industry, particularly at the served market level. For example, does the competitor compete on the strength of its competencies or, instead, on its product offerings?

iii. The strategic intent of the competitor, and its programmes and strategies for fulfilling its ambitions.

An effective collection activity begins with a review of the front-end analysis needs. While intelligence professionals are expected to possess excellent peripheral vision, they must not permit their focus to blur.

Primary research of external sources

Competitor intelligence which is not largely the product of, or validated by, primary sources is not intelligence, it is guessing. And it is therefore dangerous – dangerous because important decisions are made based on assumptions and information which are, at best, reasonably close to the truth, or worse, completely wrong. Facts, particularly those based on secondary sources, never speak for themselves. A firm that purports to build its strategic architecture and develop its strategic thinking on intelligence not reinforced by exhaustive primary research, and later analysis, may as well be building sandcastles in the sky.

Presidents and prime ministers do not make decisions on issues of national security on the strength of intelligence produced from desk research only; nor do generals prepare battle plans without first-hand intelligence on the capabilities, the strength, the disposition and the intentions of the enemy.

Interviewing primary sources outside the organisation is the cornerstone of an effective CI collection process. The volume of information gathered from external primary sources may represent a small proportion of the total quantity of data and information collected, but primary sources will always contribute the greatest added value to the competitive intelligence effort. This, in turn, helps prepare the groundwork for better analysis and more accurate projections.

Three questions to consider regarding the collection of intelligence from external primary sources are:

- Who should the firm (or its external consultants) talk to?
- What questions should the firm ask, and how?
- When is opinion or rumour classified as fact?

There is a wide array of potential sources available to the firm. These include:

- competitors (and their affiliates, partners, and subsidiaries)
- chambers of commerce
- credit agencies
- customers (both of the firm and of competitors)
- distributors
- government departments (local, national, and European)
- industry experts (investment analysts, trade journalists, etc.)
- information brokers
- market research organisations
- patent lawyers
- R&D centres
- regulatory agencies
- suppliers
- trade associations.

The most useful source of competitor information is the competitor itself. Although under normal circumstances a firm is not entitled to possess its competitor's strategic plan, the essence of nearly everything in the plan is available from legitimate sources. Mostly it is a matter of asking the right questions, in the right way, of the right people. It is also a function of time and money (are the costs of not having the information greater than the costs of obtaining it?). This is how one author on the subject of business intelligence put it:

> No business operates in a vacuum. Every transaction in which a company takes part discloses information about the firm's operations – information that may prove vital in competitive analysis. A supplier may know something about a new product design, a customer about production problems, a market research firm about marketing plans, a union representative about labour organisations.[9]

Gathering information from the competitor, and from firms associated with the competitor (advertising agencies, forwarding agents, suppliers, trade customers, etc.) involves a special set of skills. It also requires creativity, curiosity, a good tactical plan, persistence and sensitivity. The researcher (or manager) who interviews a competitor must be well prepared, must understand exactly what it is he or she is looking for, and should be trained in interviewing techniques.

The competitive intelligence researcher must always be alert to the danger of becoming 'so involved in stockpiling data that [he or she] misses clear warning signals that competitors are engaged in significant moves.'[10] He or she must also be prepared for rejections (not everyone is willing to be interviewed). The competitive intelligence researcher must understand that focus, persistence, and patience are necessary for success, and he or she must be willing to speak to anyone from the CEO to a plant foreman.

Business ethics in Europe require that executives and researchers should identify themselves and their firm at the outset of any official conversation with an employee of a competitor organisation. This is also a practice which top management and the legal department will (and should) normally insist upon.

The very nature of an intelligence project will usually determine who in the target organisation should be contacted first. If the focal point of the intelligence requirement is R&D, it is obvious that managers and staff in the competitor R&D unit should be contacted. If the questions centre around the terms of a strategic alliance between competitor firms, the researcher may possibly wish to speak to executives in the competitors' finance, legal and marketing departments.

The best sources are not necessarily the obvious ones. Once, while trying to learn more about the structure and goals of a pan-European marketing alliance in the healthcare industry (which comprised four family-owned firms), we were disappointed to learn that senior managers at one of the companies in the alliance were not prepared to talk to us at all. The other three companies each offered us something of what we wanted to know, but altogether not quite enough. We then spoke to the non-executive chairman of the alliance (who was responsible for overseeing the day to day operations of the organisation's secretariat). He spent 45 minutes on the telephone explaining, in considerable detail, the history, makeup, philosophy, objectives and medium-term plans of the alliance. When the information we found in published sources was combined with what we learned from our interviews with the three alliance partners and the chairman of the alliance, we were able to produce an intelligence report which answered every one of the client's questions. At least 80 per cent of the intelligence value came from the primary sources.

Researchers should contact known sources first. And the following sources in competitor organisations should not be overlooked:

- investor- and public-relations executives (they are paid to inform the outside world about their companies)
- customer service personnel (they know who the customers are, the company's strategy for customer support, and how successfully the strategy is being implemented)
- engineers (they like to talk about their work)
- sales representatives (there is very little they do not know about how sales really are going, how products are being positioned, discount practices, degree of customer satisfaction, and much more)
- scientists (they also like to discuss their work)
- secretaries (they know what the boss knows, if not more, they know where he or she is, and they know the boss's plans)
- senior managers (they can certainly tell you about what the firm should be doing, and plans to be doing, as well as why and how)
- telephonists (they know who everybody is, and they know every department).

There is no one individual in the competitor organisation who should be excluded as an information source. If one particular source cannot, or will not co-operate, the researcher must persist until he or she finds someone who will. Companies who do not wish to contact competitors directly should retain consulting and research firms who will undertake this work on their behalf.

Needless to say, in Europe the approach researchers take to human intelligence sources will vary from country to country. Senior managers in big French companies are generally less accessible than, say, their counterparts in Switzerland, and so on. Research on any scale in Italy, and to some extent France, is virtually impossible without the language skills.

Needless to say, the questions which researchers put to managers and staff at competitor firms must mirror the intelligence needs defined by the project brief, or plan. However, researchers can do two things in order to reveal as little as possible about what their real intelligence objectives are. The researcher should:

- avoid asking any one source everything he or she wishes to know, even if the source might be expected to have all the answers
- camouflage the 'real' questions with a series of other, entirely unrelated questions.

The issue of how questions should be asked is more complex. Managers and researchers who carry out interviews with competitors should be trained in interviewing techniques, they must be given the opportunity to practise these techniques and their interviewing styles in simulation exercises. If the interview of a source is not managed professionally, there is a high probability that the source will cease to remain a source – it will be 'blown'. Primary research for competitive intelligence purposes is mainly about dealing with people, and must therefore be executed with skill and great sensitivity. A competitor employee who believes he or she has been deceived, used, or, worse, has disclosed company information to 'the enemy', cannot be used again. If researchers are to be successful they must be trained in the craft. The competitive intelligence activity cannot otherwise be effective.

CI researchers should not, if possible, phrase questions as questions; they should use 'neutral', or 'non-threatening', phrases. Below are four techniques – including brief examples – used by researchers when talking to sources at 'target' organisations:

'Bracketing' technique

This technique is useful for narrowing down the boundaries of a number. Many people who will refuse to answer a direct question concerning, for example, development times, financial performance, manufacturing output, or sales data, are quite happy to comment on a given data range.

> *Example* – interview with an executive at a software publisher:
> Researcher: 'Would you expect to complete the beta testing programme for your new software application [within the next 12 months?] [. . . six months?] [. . . three months?].'

Respondent: 'Oh . . . sometime within the next year.'
Researcher: 'So you could be finished within six months?'
Respondent: 'Let's say between six and 12 . . .'

Challenging technique

The natural response to an incorrect statement by most people is to correct it. By 'challenging' the respondent with a statement that is wrong, the researcher can expect to be corrected.

Example – interview with a consumer products company executive:
Researcher: 'I understand you've just taken over PineFresh Products in Norway . . .'
Respondent: 'No . . . we've formed a marketing alliance with them.'
Researcher: 'So you'll be marketing their products in Europe.'
Respondent: 'No . . . PineFresh Products will be marketing our new range of household cleaning products in Scandinavia.'

Restatement technique

This technique involves repeating back to the respondent information he or she has already provided in the interview. The aim is to subtly suggest to the respondent that the researcher is interested in additional information.

Example – interview with a clinical research director at a pharmaceutical company:
Respondent: 'Up to now, the side effects of the drug are negligible.'
Researcher: 'Negligible?'
Respondent: 'With this compound patients aren't suffering the problems of drowsiness and nausea typical of this class of drugs. So far the results are good.'
Researcher: 'Good?'
Respondent: 'Much better than competitor compounds . . . especially with children and older patients.'

Suggestive statements

Suggestive statements are designed to elicit answers without asking direct questions. This technique is particularly useful when the researcher is still somewhat uncertain of his ground.

Example – interview with an executive at a manufacturer of cordless telecommunications systems:

Researcher: 'I know the telecommunications industry is growing fast. You must have a wide range of new products under development.'

Respondent: 'Not much at the moment . . . apart from a new radio-based system for personal paging.'

Researcher: 'I see . . . I suppose you must be looking closely at new developments in the cordless telephones sector.'

Respondent: 'Well . . . we are working on important security enhancements for our range of compact handsets, but these won't be announced until Telecom '95 in Geneva. Maybe you should speak to the Product manager . . . she can tell you more . . .'

These techniques get results. They enable the intelligence researcher to navigate efficiently through the information maze which characterises every intelligence project. In each of the examples above the researcher learned something new (or had certain assumptions validated), and discovered a new doorway to more information.

Careful planning is required before sources at the competitor firm, or at firms linked with the competitor (customers, distributors, suppliers, etc.) are contacted. As part of the advance preparation it can be helpful to rehearse the interview. Researchers must know exactly what they are going to discuss, the approach they intend to take, and who they wish to speak to. Researchers should not rely on a single source, they should not misrepresent themselves, and during the interview they must be alert to new opportunities (e.g. reference to a new development not directly related to the project at hand, but possibly important for the company to know). And all interviews should be conduced with a smile in the voice.

Where consultants are employed to carry out the intelligence study they must be given comprehensive briefings that clearly articulate the project objectives. A typical briefing to consultants will include:

- background information, including the rationale behind the project, and relevant technical or industry-specific data
- details about what the firm already knows, including assumptions and rumours
- deadlines
- the objectives of the study, including the specific questions to be answered.

Gathering competitive intelligence is time-consuming, painstaking work, and 'frustration levels' are often high. Unfortunately business managers have no time. They want answers, they want solutions to problems, and they 'want it yesterday'. When a management board convenes to receive a presentation from the firm's CI co-ordinator or manager it expects answers. The management board also expects to be told where the information came from, how timely it is, and how reliable the sources are. Top management does not wish to know how difficult intelligence is to collect or analyse, and they certainly do not wish to be told it is not available. Therefore, in order to meet the demands and expectations of management, the collection and processing of intelligence – the vital second and third steps in the intelligence cycle – must focus not only upon obtaining the most valuable information, from the best sources, quickly, relentlessly, and efficiently, but it must be accomplished by seasoned researchers skilled in the art of intelligence gathering.

Lastly, researchers, analysts, and managers must continuously ask themselves during the collection process: Is the information relevant? Is it urgent? Is it accurate? As Porter observes, 'Gathering data is a waste of time unless . . . used in formulating strategy . . .'[11]

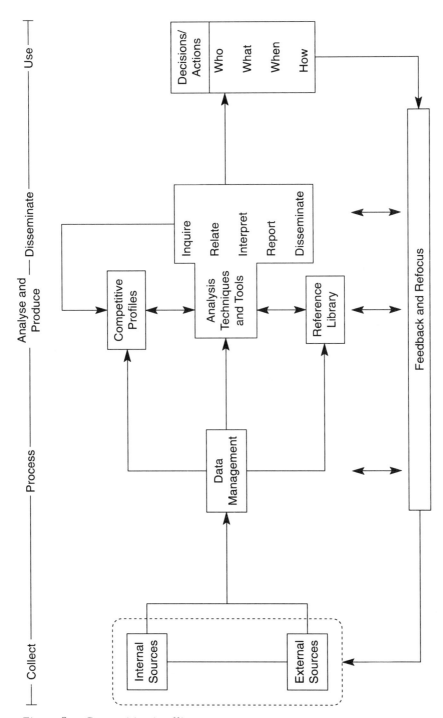

Figure 8.1 Competitive intelligence system

NOTES

[1]Samuel B. Griffith, ed., *Factbook on Intelligence.* (Washington, DC: CIA, 1991), p. 13.

[2]Ibid.

[3]Leonard M. Fuld, *Monitoring the Competition* (New York, NY: John Wiley & Sons, 1988), p.64.

[4]Everett H. Brenner, *Competitive Information Programmes – a Research Report* (Luxembourg: European Association of Information Services, 1991), p. 20.

[5]John Hagel, III. 'Keeping CPR on Track', *The McKinsey Quarterly,* Number 1, 1993, p.59.

[6]Fuld, op. cit., p. 4.

[7]See, for example: Kirk W. Tyson, *Competitor Intelligence Manual & Guide* (NJ: Prentice Hall, 1990) and Fuld, op. cit.

[8]Joel K. Leidecker and Albert V. Bruno. 'Identifying and Using Critical Success Factors', *Long Range Planning,* Vol. 17, No 1, February 1984, p.24.

[9]John M. Kelly, *How to Check Out Your Competition* (New York, NY: John Wiley & Sons, 1987), p.128.

[10]Ibid., p. 151.

[11]Michael E. Porter, *Competitive Strategy: Techniques for Analysing Industries and Competitors* (New York, NY: The Free Press, 1980), p. 74.

9 COMPUTERS AND COMPUTER SOFTWARE FOR COMPETITIVE INTELLIGENCE

This chapter is contributed by Michael A. Sandman, Senior Vice President of Fuld & Company Inc., Cambridge, Massachusetts. Fuld & Company is a business intelligence consulting and research firm.

INTRODUCTION

The major advantage of using computer technology in competitor intelligence is that the computer can make it easy for people to file or contribute relevant information, easy for them to search for information, and easy for them to organise the information for purposes of analysis. In this chapter, we will focus on just those three tasks, and on the structure and some of the products needed to accomplish them in a cost-effective manner.

The cost of acquiring computers and software has dropped sharply in the last few years. At first glance it often seems as though the computer should be used extensively from the outset of a competitor intelligence programme. After all, there is so much data floating around in a business organisation. Isn't it cost-effective to somehow 'put everything on the computer', especially since the computer can be acquired so inexpensively?

The answer is 'No'.

In fact, beyond using some simple stand-alone software applications, a computer system should be the last element to be put in place in a competitor intelligence programme – the capstone, not the foundation of the programme. Therefore, the first part of this chapter will be an effort to restrain the reader's enthusiasm for computerising competitor intelligence too early in the game.

WORDS OF CAUTION

First of all, no one should be under the illusion that computer technology can analyse information about the competition. There is no artificial intelligence available at this point to take the place of the human mind in this field of endeavour. Even though your physician's diagnostic expertise can be duplicated by software, no mere computer programme can discern all the relevant patterns in so complex an area as the competitive marketplace. The computer's primary use is as an intelligent file cabinet. Even then, it will need quite a lot of initial instruction. At the beginning of a competitor intelligence programme, it would be better to invest time in building the involvement of a large number of people across a company rather than on building and fine-tuning a computer-based filing system.

Even a matter as simple as sorting out and editing newswire service reports by area of interest cannot be fully accomplished by software. For example, there is an excellent service called 'First' available from an American company (Individual Inc., Cambridge, Massachusetts) which filters newswire service reports according to the subscriber's interests. The user submits a profile of his or her interest, and the company develops a thesaurus of words and phrases to look for in the wire service reports.

The service uses a software 'filter' to sort out news articles that contain the terms in that particular user's profile. The company that provides the service edits the stories into a newsletter-like format, and sends them to the user by fax or electronic mail.

Thus, a manager in the telecommunications industry might direct that articles containing both the word 'network' and some reference to his or her firm's competitors should be included in the newsletter. The client and the publishers of 'First' work to build a thesaurus or set of synonyms for 'network' – 'communications infrastructure', 'ISDN', 'fibre optic cable', etc. The thesaurus serves as a 'filter' that is supposed to let only the relevant articles through to the client. The publisher of 'First' suggests that the firm has a software programme that develops sophisticated sets of synonyms so that the user's profile can be constantly refined.

The process appears to be ideally suited to the computer, which has the ability to sort through information so quickly. The company that prepares this information gets high marks from its clients, but in fact it uses computer software only for the first level of sorting. It relies heavily on skilled editors who work from the early evening until around midnight each business day to read through the articles selected by the computer software. It is the editor, not the 'artificial intelligence' of the computer, that ultimately decides which articles have real value to the client, and it is the editor who puts them into a digestible format.

This expensive human intervention is necessary for two reasons. First, from time to time a totally irrelevant article will get through even the best software filter. Perhaps a competitor's socially prominent managing director will be cited as someone who is 'wired in' to the arts scene in her home town. Or the competitor will be cited in an article about 'networking' for executives who have been made redundant. It takes a human reader to see that the article is irrelevant. Second and ultimately more important, the editor looks at the stream of articles for new names and terms that should be added to the client's thesaurus. For example, the thesaurus would miss a newswire story about that newly founded firm in Dresden who has just announced 20 year credit terms for its range of telecommunications switches.

Firms like 'First' have every economic incentive to substitute computer software for human editors, who regularly take vacations, move to Bora Bora, or find positions with more traditional publishing houses. Yet these firms still choose to rely on people; as good as today's software is, the publisher of 'First' knows it will not sort *out* all of the irrelevant articles, and it will not 'sort in' all of the relevant ones that do not fit the client's original criteria.

One lesson: computers are literal-minded – they do precisely what they are programmed to do, no more and no less. And humans are not quite organised enough to give them an absolutely complete set of instructions.

A second lesson: a competitor intelligence system that relies totally on software to sort and analyse information will quickly get stuffed up with a great deal of irrelevant information, and it will miss new classes of data, the very sort of information that is often of the greatest value.

There is one more cautionary tale that needs telling. In the early 1980s, an American based electronics giant, one of the few truly global companies of that era, decided to use its considerable data processing resources to build a database of information about its competitors, who were located all over the world. The competitor intelligence group was inundated with data – news articles, financial reports, internal memoranda. In its effort to manage the flood of data, the group tried to get everything into the database, and it spent virtually all of its efforts over a two-year period – and well over $1 million – keying in data. As a result, there were no resources left for analysing the flood of information, and so there was no usable output from the effort. After a couple of years of financing this, the directors of the corporation killed the programme, because it did not give appreciable return on their investment.

Two more lessons emerge. First, it is virtually impossible to acquire and store 'everything' about the competition, even in the era of cheap computer technology. Priorities must be set. Are you concerned about technology? Distribution? Market strategy? Manufacturing cost? It's not possible to track all of the variables, especially in a dynamic marketplace. Track closely the competitors and competitive issues that are most important; gather information less intensively for the others.

Second, a competitor intelligence programme has to produce something of demonstrable value if it is to attract continued funding. Spending too much time and money on computerisation early in the life of the competitor intelligence programme will drain away resources that should be applied to producing a useful stream of output. At each point when you consider adding computer resources to the CI programme, make sure that the computer will add enough value in the short run to justify the costs. Your calculation should include total costs of acquiring, installing and maintaining both the hardware and the database or other software you are considering. It should also include the cost of training, especially if you are considering the sort of multi-user system we will describe later in this chapter.

DEFINITIONS

Although this chapter is written for the slightly computer literate rather than the expert, there are a few terms which the reader will want to understand.

Boolean logic

You may remember this from your early training in algebra. Boolean logic allows one to define a desired set by identifying where several broader sets intersect. Boolean logic is used by software applications that search computer files for specific data.

If you had a file drawer full of sales call reports, and you wanted all of the reports that mentioned BOTH low-pressure widgets AND your arch-competitor, Technische Widgeten AG, but you were not interested in reports that were written by salespeople in France, you would want a group (or set) of call reports defined as follows:

Low pressure widgets AND Technische Widgeten; NOT France.

The diagram overleaf illustrates the way Boolean logic operates to find the desired set of call reports.

File (or record file)

For purposes of this chapter, a file is defined as a collection of electronic records, rather like the electronic equivalent of a box of index cards or an encyclopaedia. A computer record file has the capability of being searched, so that the individual records can be put in without regard to the order in which they are entered. Software applications make it possible for the computer to sort through the file and search for the particular records or groups of records for which one is looking.

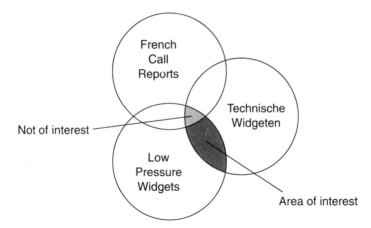

Figure 9.1 Boolean logic search results: search of call reports database

Note that 'file' is also used in a somewhat different context to identify a spreadsheet or word processor document. In that context, we may speak of a spreadsheet file or a graphics file.

Record

A record is a single entry in a file. It might be something as simple and structured as the name, address and telephone number of a person, or it might be as unstructured as a long document created with word processing software. In most computer files, the records have a 'key' at the beginning that identifies them to the searching software.

Field

A field is one of the entries in a record. Taking index cards with names and addresses as the example, the box of cards is the file, each individual card is a record, and each entry on a card is a field. The first name of the person might be one field, the last name a second, and the street address another.

Database

Strictly speaking, 'database' could be a single file. However, in the context we will use it, a database is a collection of files. In their most flexible incarnations, databases include files of varying types, such as files of addresses, files of word processing documents, and files of spreadsheets.

On-line databases and on-line newswires

An on-line database is typically a large file of information that is maintained by an outside party, often a publisher. For example, the text of the *The Economist* or *Financial Times* (FT) is available from an on-line database. One gets access to this information by connecting the computer to the database via a telephone line. The database publisher will have a set of rules that the user must follow to search the database. For example, if you want to search for all the articles published in the FT during 1992 that include the terms 'ICI' and 'fibre', you could do so.

Most on-line databases are actually accessed through a third party such as Dialog Information Services or FT Profile which allows the user to search numerous on-line databases. Third parties such as Dialog and FT Profile are called 'gateways' or 'hosts'.

Newswire services such as Reuters can also feed information to a computer via a direct telephone link. (The company that publishes 'First' obtains newswire articles through that type of link.) Any company or individual can subscribe to a newswire service via computer in much the same way as one can subscribe to a newspaper. There are software systems that a subscriber can use to build an interest profile, or filter, so that only the articles of interest are passed through to the individual subscriber. (These are described later in this chapter.)

Software program or application

Software programs are sets of instructions that tell the computer what to do. At the lowest level, when you turn a computer on, a program permanently resident in the computer tells it to display some basic information on the computer screen, and tells it how to interpret the keystrokes from the keyboard. Higher level programs tell the computer how to build a document or a spreadsheet. In most cases, we will use the term 'application' rather than 'program', since the latter term is used frequently in its non-computer context.

File formats

Software applications usually use a proprietary scheme for recording information on disk, in the same way as different individuals might arrange file folders differently. Software companies that make several types of applications, such as Microsoft, try to use common file formats so that their word processing application can 'read' a file created by their spreadsheet application. Applications that run under Windows™, OS/2™ or other umbrella software packages use common file formats so that pieces of, say, a spreadsheet can be pasted into a word-processed document.

Often, however, a document or record created by one software application will not be readable by another application. In these cases, the file can usually be translated into a common format called ASCII. The problem with ASCII is that it strips away most of the special formatting and spreadsheet formulas. For example a Lotus 1-2-3 file that is translated (or 'exported') into ASCII will retain all the numbers and spacing, but the formulas and cell addresses are lost. ASCII is useless when it comes to translating graphics images, since it relies completely on text.

Some e-mail systems and virtually all on-line databases and news-wire services transmit information in ASCII format. Those sources are usually significant in competitor intelligence work.

User interface

The user interface is the menu structure that allows the user to tell the software what to do. If the interface requires you to enter a string of letters or characters to make the menu work, it is called a text inter-face. If it allows the use of a mouse and the manipulation of little pictures on the screen called icons, it is a graphical user interface, or GUI.

GUIs are regarded as being easy to learn, but they put a greater drain on the computer's resources. Because of this, a computer with an Intel® 386 processor or its equivalent is the minimum needed to make use of an application that uses a graphical user interface. Text-based interfaces are more difficult to learn, but experienced users often find them faster than GUIs. Most proprietary competitor intelligence software applications use a GUI, and as fast computers become less expensive, most off-the-shelf applications will also be written with a graphical user interface.

LAN (local area network)

A LAN is a group of two or more computers are connected to each other within the same facility. Connecting the computers through a LAN allows them to share files with each other, which eliminates the need to move diskettes around when someone wants to take files from computer to another. LANs are created by cabling computers together, using special wiring and connectors at each computer. The network is controlled by LAN software.

When 20 or more computers are connected in a LAN, one computer is usually set aside to act as the repository for the record files and the application software, and it is called a file server. LANs without a dedicated file server are called peer-to-peer LANs, and they are adequate for groups of two to 20 or so computers. A peer-to-peer LAN that links a half-dozen analysts is a very reasonable first step in computerising a competitor intelligence programme. An enterprising and computer-literate person might well try to set up a peer-to-peer LAN, but it would be best to obtain some professional help from the LAN vendor.

Printers and other devices are usually connected to a LAN, and one printer may serve several computers in such an arrangement. LANs are usually capable of connecting different types of computers together. A large mainframe computer might be the file server for a LAN made up of Sun™ work stations, PCs, and Macintosh™ computers.

Artisoft Corporation's 'Lantastic'™ is highly regarded for networks of under 25 to 50 computers. Novell's 'NetWare'™ is the dominant product for larger networks, and it requires professional installation and ongoing internal support.

WAN (wide area network)

A WAN connects two or more LANs that are physically separated. A WAN might connect the LAN in the R&D facility in Watford with the LAN at company headquarters in Slough. The task of managing communications between LANs over a WAN is complex, and a whole category of products have been developed to control the flow of traffic. Similarly, a whole category of information technology practitioners has arisen to manage WANS and large LANs. When the competitor intelligence programme requires access to networks of this nature, it is necessary to have access to the firm's MIS or I/T specialists for both installation and ongoing support.

E-Mail (electronic mail)

E-mail is a software application for sending messages from one person to another using a network of computers. In most e-mail systems, each party has a 'address', and the message is sent to a 'mailbox' with that address. The recipient can pick up his or her mail from any computer in the system by entering the correct mailbox address on the computer's keyboard.

APPLICATION SOFTWARE SOLUTIONS FOR COMPETITOR INTELLIGENCE PRACTITIONERS

There are several categories of software that are potentially valuable to the competitor intelligence programme. What follows is not intended to be an exhaustive listing of products, but rather a representative listing. The software applications that are mentioned are generally well regarded, but they are not the only appropriate solutions. Omission from this list does not mean that a product should be excluded from consideration – quite the contrary. New software products, and indeed new categories of products, appear regularly, and existing products are frequently improved.

Most of the computer solutions that are accessible to competitor intelligence managers are designed for desktop computers – the IBM PC family, work stations, the Apple Macintosh™, and networks of these devices.

While larger computers certainly have the capability of supporting a competitor intelligence programme, the most cost-effective way to get started is on a desktop. As a practical matter, desktop computers also offer the quickest path, since it is possible to start up a useful suite of software applications without having to rely heavily on support from the MIS or I/T professionals in a firm.

Single-user and small group systems

As a general rule, the competitor intelligence manager should start with a single desktop computer or a small number of computers linked via a LAN to all the analysts in the group. The manager should start with off-the-shelf software and learn what the real information needs and resources are. A start-up period of six months or more is quite reasonable before any consideration is given to more elaborate systems. Many people already know how to use the applications they need for this first phase of computerisation.

Spreadsheets

Most people who are familiar with desktop computers know how to use a spreadsheet (or a word processor). We normally think of spreadsheets in the context of their ability to calculate and re-calculate sums and produce graphs. However, spreadsheets such as Lotus 1-2-3™ Excel™, and Quattro™ have useful data sorting capabilities that can be quite effective in helping to store and manipulate the kinds of competitor data that often are readily available within the firm.

Below is a simple spreadsheet for Essex & Newark Widget plc (E&N). E&N's sales director uses the spreadsheet to view win/loss results for products for which the main competitors are Euro-Widgets

Customer	Location	Win/Lose	Winner	Our Price	Winner's Price
Billets Ltd	UK	Win	Essex & Newark	19,67	19,67
Metal Formers	UK	Lose	Technische Widgets	19,67	22,16
Finchley Works	UK	Lose	Widgets SA	19,67	18,34
Taugus Metals	Portugal	Lose	Pusan Widget	19,89	16,54
Ferro Iberia	Spain	Lose	Pusan Widget	19,89	16,78
Bilbao Ferric	Spain	Lose	Pusan Widget	19,89	17,56
Vlamm BV	Neth.	Win	Essex & Newark	19,97	19,97
SNCA	France	Lose	Widgets SA	19,97	20,10
Mugg & Cie.	Belgium	Lose	Technische Widgets	21,09	21,45
Neth. Grinding	Neth.	Lose	Technische Widgets	21,09	21,08
Saxe Metal	Germany	Lose	Leadmine Ridge	21,25	22,10
EDM Werke	Germany	Win	Essex & Newark	21,65	21,65
Dynamo Systems	US	Lose	Leadmine Ridge	23,10	18,65
Eretz Blaster	Greece	Lose	Leadmine Ridge	24,43	23,14

Figure 9.2 Spreadsheet sorted by 'Our Price' column

Customer	Location	Win/Lose	Winner	Our Price	Winner's Price
Mugg et Cie.	Belgium	Lose	Technische Widgets	21,09	21,45
SNCA	France	Lose	Widgets	19,97	20.10
Saxe Metal	Germany	Lose	Leadmine Ridge	21,25	22,10
Eretz Blaster	Greece	Lose	Leadmine Ridge	24,43	23,14
EDM Werke	Germany	Win	Essex & Newark	21,65	21,65
Vlamm BV	Neth.	Win	Essex & Newark	19,97	19,97
Neth. Grinding	Neth.	Lose	Technische Widgets	21,09	21,08
Taugus Metals	Port.	Lose	Pusan Widget	19,89	16,54
Bilbao Ferric	Spain	Lose	Pusan Widget	19,89	17,56
Ferro Iberia	Spain	Lose	Pusan Widget	19,89	16,78
Billets Ltd.	UK	Win	Leadmine Ridge	19,67	19,67
Metal Formers	UK	Lose	Technische Widgets	19,67	22,16
Finchley Works	UK	Lose	Widgets SA	19,67	18,34
Dynamo Systems	US	Lose	Leadmine Ridge	23,10	18,65

Figure 9.3 Spreadsheet sorted by 'Location' column

SA, Technische Widgeten GmbH, Leadmine Ridge Widget Works, and Pusan Widget & Electronics Corp.

The first view shows the spreadsheet sorted by competitor. That view doesn't seem to reveal any useful patterns. The second view shows the table sorted by region, and it is more revealing. It turns out that Euro-Widgets is quite successful in the Danish and Spanish markets. However, the company has not made a dent in the Benelux countries. Pusan Widget's prices are low, but for some reason they are not making much headway except in the Netherlands.

The second view can be obtained by using the 'DATA/SORT' function of applications like 1-2-3. For simple databases where you want to sort entire lines of information, a spreadsheet application is perfectly adequate. You probably have it and know how to use it already, and so do your colleagues. If you can collect their spreadsheets of useful data and combine them, you can extract some useful information without a great deal of trouble or expense.

Because very large spreadsheets take up a substantial amount of a computer's memory, and because sorting large spreadsheets can be slow, spreadsheets are not adequate for records that include more than a few words of text or for databases with more than several hundred records.

Flat-file database software

You could also use a spreadsheet to build a list of internal experts on competitor issues within your firm, or a comparison of competitor's product features and prices. However, in situations like these, where you may want to search for a limited group of records, or where you may want to look for individual data elements, or where there are more than a few words of text, 'flat file' database software is probably more functional than a spreadsheet application. Off-the-shelf applications such as Q&A™ or Alpha 4™ (both for the IBM PC-compatible standard) and Double Helix™ (for the Apple Macintosh™) will let someone who is already comfortable with spreadsheets build a very flexible database such as the one illustrated by the records below.

Here, the records do not have to be kept in straight lines, and it is easier to provide for multiple lines of text. An example of a record from a file of competitor's products is reproduced below.

WIDGET PRODUCT SUMMARY

MANUFACTURER: Technische Widgeten GmbH

MODEL NUMBER: 65B-66532   TYPE: Circular

DATE INTRODUCED: 1/6/93

COUNTRY OF MANUFACTURE: Germany

EX-WORKS PRICE: £24.60   F.O.B. POINT: Rostock

WEIGHT: 9.75 (Kg)   ESTIMATED Mat'ls. COST: £10.90

MAX. SPEED: 3200 (RPM)   ESTIMATED ASSEMBLY COST: £8.95

ADVANTAGES Very light weight; low maintenance

DISADVANTAGES Restricted availability due to problems getting 0.036 mm ball bearings

---

The primary advantage is that the database can be sorted in many ways:

- look for a single piece of data, such as a product name or model number
- look for a word phrase, such as 'low maintenance'
- print a report sorted by the date the product was announced, including only those products with prices over £20 that were introduced after 15/11/92.

This type of off-the-shelf application software with a cost of less than £300 per copy can also be used for indexes of printed documents, or even for storing short documents themselves, provided that they are in computer-readable format and that someone builds an index by assigning keywords to each article. It will take the average spreadsheet user surprisingly little time to begin using these products, partly because the documentation that comes with the software is superior to the manuals supplied with most spreadsheet applications.

Some flat-file databases slow down when they have to sort through more than a few thousand records, or when they search for strings of words in the midst of large text fields.

Relational databases

The next level up in cost, capability and learning time is the relational database. Products like dBase™, Paradox™, and Access™ can be purchased off the shelf, and the MIS or I/T departments of most larger organisations may well already be using one of these products. Their major advantage is that they can draw reports and data out of two or more files, provided that the files have some common field, such as a product model number. The major disadvantage is that they slow down appreciably if you are trying to handle more than several thousand records.

Off-the-shelf relational databases are priced in the £500 range, but they have a substantial hidden cost. It will take three or four times as long to 'get up the learning curve' of a relational database than it will to learn how to use a word processing, spreadsheet or flat-file database application. Even then, you may not be able to do much more than you could with the flat-file application, unless you are working with several thousand records.

As a general rule, the boundary between flat-file databases and relational databases coincides with the boundary between inexpensive, informal uses of the computer and more expensive, more formally funded computerisation efforts that require real software expertise. If there is assistance outside the competitor intelligence group to help set up a relational database application, this type of application is worth considering. However, even that outside assistance has a cost. At the very least, the competitor intelligence manager will have to spend several days working with a database programmer, even if the programmer's time is not charged back to the group.

Beyond the off-the-shelf relational databases, there are several database products that can quickly store and retrieve tens of thousands of records, including large records such as full-text reports and articles. A partial list of products includes Oracle™, Sybase, and Ingress™, all of which can run on both desktops and mainframes, and Basis Plus™, which is designed primarily for mainframes. To justify using this level of software, the competitor intelligence group must be planning to build the in-house equivalent of an online database of the sort available through Dialog™. A typical budget for a project of this nature would be in the £100,000 range.

PIMs (personal information managers)

This is a class of software that is still in the process of forming. These products function as electronic Filofaxes, and they work well for a single competitor intelligence manager or analyst. The more sophisticated versions enable one to search for files and documents using a form of Boolean logic. The less sophisticated versions are little more than appointment books with electronic reminder pads. As of this writing, the most functional product is 'Ask Sam', which is available off the shelf. PIMs are fairly easy to use, but their appeal is limited to situations where only one person will have to access computerised records.

Scanners and OCR (optical character recognition)

Scanners are devices that 'take a picture' of a document. The picture, or image, is stored electronically, and it can be displayed on a computer screen, using an appropriate software application. For example, many word processors will 'import' a graphic image, as long as it is stored in a file format that the application software can read. Scanners are especially useful for storing images of competitors' advertisements and product literature. One can also write a few words or lines of text to tag the image and store the text and image together. That makes it possible to retrieve all the images tagged with a particular company's name or a particular product designation, or all the images dated February 1993, for example. Using software that

can sort with Boolean logic, one could find images of all the competi
tors' product literature from the June 1993 Cologne trade show that
showed new products. The one caveat is that scanned images take a
great deal of disk storage space. If one is planning on using a great
deal of scanned information, it is probably necessary to store the
images on CD-ROM or on magneto-optical disks.

Scanners can also be tied to computer software that will read the
image and determine what the text in the image says. This type of
application is called 'OCR' or optical character recognition software.
In theory, one could scan articles cut directly from a trade magazine,
file them in a database, and then go at a later time back and search for
all of the articles in the database that contain some term or terms of
interest. Using the right application software, one could take text
from several of those scanned articles and combine it with images of
pictures that were published, thereby producing a composite summary
on some topic of interest.

OCR software has improved to the point where its accuracy is
better than 99.9 per cent, provided the document is reasonably clear.
It is still difficult to accurately scan and recognise a faxed document,
or a document with unusual type faces. The scanner and OCR software have a definite place in the competitor intelligence programme's
toolbox. They provide the ability to enter documents into files that
can be searched in the future in some way not imagined when the
documents were entered.

Dedicated competitor intelligence software products

There are at least a half-dozen firms who supply software that is
specifically designed to reach into large databases and collect related
records. These applications allow one or more users to accumulate
many classes of records – newswire articles, internal memoranda
written with word processing software, spreadsheets, e-mail messages, and even scanned images of brochures. When you or a coll-
eague want to gather together all of the information on a particular
competitor, a particular regional market, or a particular product line,
this class of application software will allow you to look for just those
items that are of interest. Perhaps even more important, these systems

allow people elsewhere in the company to contribute information painlessly – a critical success factor in any competitor intelligence programme.

Usually, the vendors of these applications will work with the competitor intelligence group to design a appropriate user interface – a screen or set of screens with menus that help lead people through the process of locating what they want. The user interfaces are typically based on Microsoft® Windows™, and they are user-friendly and relatively easy to learn. Nonetheless, when you embark on installing one of these over-arching applications, you must allocate budget to the printing of training materials, and to training time for everyone who will use the system. Managers of competitor intelligence systems report that casual users quickly forget how to use the systems' more sophisticated features, and that constant re-training or help lines are required. Two robust applications in this class are Quest Development Corporation's 'Incite'™ and Henco's 'Synchrony'™. Both products are designed specifically for managing competitor intelligence files. They can be installed on a single computer, or on a LAN. When they are installed on a LAN, they promote the collection and distribution of competitor intelligence, because they allow all the users to contribute records to the CI files. Using Boolean logic, users can also search for records, documents, spreadsheets, etc., that have common terms. Dedicated competitor intelligence applications of this type make it easy for users to search by providing a list of keywords and an easy way to construct a Boolean logic rule for the search.

You should plan on a mid-five-figure budget to acquire the software, set it up properly, and teach ten or 20 people how to use it. While these applications are not inexpensive, the larger cost will be the investment of time needed to set up the lists of keywords and the time needed to train and retrain people to use the application. The vendors can provide a number of success stories, and they have done an excellent job of improving their products over the last couple of years. Most of them work with a graphical user interface, and they can retrieve files written in many common formats. They are superb tools. However, installing them absorbs time and budget. It is very important to work with lower-level software (such as flat-file databases) and to build broad involvement before bringing dedicated software into the competitor intelligence picture.

If you get to the point of considering dedicated software of this nature, make sure that the vendor you choose can support the product in all of the locations where you intend to install it.

Lotus Development Corporation's 'Lotus Notes'™ goes a step beyond dedicated CI application. It allows users who are linked together in a LAN or WAN to share both source documents and working documents. For example, someone in the London office might write a memo analysing the latest competitor product line. Another person in Birmingham could retrieve that document and also retrieve earlier documents related to that competitor or that product line. She could then draft a plan for a change in sales strategy, share the plan via the WAN draft with colleagues in Manchester and Brussels, read their comments on her screen, look at documents in their local databases that relate to the same issues, and produce a completed plan for submission to the director of sales in Frankfurt.

This type of application is called 'workgroup software', and it has many uses beyond competitor intelligence. It is a harbinger of the software systems will use to work effectively together from separate sites in the next decade. Lotus Development Corporation provides some initial consulting services to companies who install 'Notes', but the sensible way to proceed is to purchase a package of software and consulting from a 'Notes' re-seller. The initial cost will be higher, but without some experienced assistance and training, 'Notes' users will not get as much out of this very sophisticated tool as they should. The initial cost of installing 'Notes' is comparable to the cost of installing dedicated competitor intelligence application software. 'Notes' will co-exist nicely with the dedicated application, and it adds an extra dimension of communications and sharing capabilities to products like Quest's 'Incite'.

As with any customised, complex application software, workgroup products like 'Lotus Notes' and Microsoft's 'Windows for Workgroups™' are very functional once they are installed and operating, and once people are trained in their use. The costs of getting to that point are high, and the initial cost is only the tip of the iceberg. One must build an understanding of the competitor intelligence programme's real needs before committing to one of these all-singing, all-dancing software solutions.

TYING THE PIECES TOGETHER

At the simplest level, computer software can help an individual competitor intelligence analyst organise his or her own records. There are at least four levels of complexity beyond that, each of which involves some of the software applications described in the previous section.

The first level is to bring on-line newswire feeds into the competitor intelligence picture. In this instance, software is needed to sort out the articles of interest from the great mass of information than can be provided by Reuters or Dow Jones. Typically, the information is filtered through specialised software, and the software uses a profile or filter determined by the user. The stream of filtered information may be provided to one or more individuals. Software applications that provide filtering may also provide extensive database search capabilities, but at the most basic level, they simply pass a narrow set of (hopefully) desired information through to the user. The user may read the articles on his or her computer screen, print them on paper, or send them to an electronic file for later reference. The software may operate in the background while the user does something else with the computer. Some software will notify the user when an article of interest has been passed through. Note that internal sources of information could also be used in this scheme or in the more elaborate versions that follow. For example, a filter could be used to look at the flow of call reports from sales people or R&D reports, etc. (see Level 1 diagram).

The next level up is typically series of profiles or filters for two or more users. The person or people in marketing will get the articles that meet their criteria, while the people in R&D will get the ones meeting their criteria. In a competitor intelligence setting, the articles of interest to one analyst will be passed through his filter, and the articles of interest to another analyst will be passed through hers. Other articles will be excluded (see Level 2 diagram).

At Level 3, the information that passes through the interest filters goes into a database. When an item of interest is received, the software will notify the user by sending a message to his or her computer. In addition, the user will be able to inquire of the database and sort through it for other items of interest, using Boolean logic. Most of the time, users will be linked through a LAN or through an e-mail system, so they can send each other information they generate themselves (see Level 3 diagram).

Level 4 is a comprehensive system linking competitor analysts (the 'Business Information Unit'), external sources of information such as on-line databases and newswire services, internal sources of information, and people elsewhere in the organisation ('the Field') (see Level 4 diagram).

All parties have the ability to contribute information electronically, to search for and retrieve what they want, to assemble new documents by cutting and pasting together pieces of the items they find through their search, and to communicate with each other through an e-mail link. A LAN, and possibly a WAN linking several LANs together, is a prerequisite. A database serving a configuration of this sort would almost certainly need database software such as Oracle, Ingress or a similar application that allows the storage and sorting of large masses of data and simultaneous access by large numbers of users.

Level 4 is the complete, closed-loop linkage of sources, analysts, and consumers of intelligence. It is a feasible goal for organisations with a strong information technology infrastructure. It is only sensible for organisations in which there are large numbers of computer-literate managers. Ideally, the directors should be comfortable using computers to access competitor intelligence. If they are not, it will be more difficult to get funding for the care and feeding of so elaborate a system. If they are, they will be able to readily obtain the competitor intelligence products they need in the course of running their business.

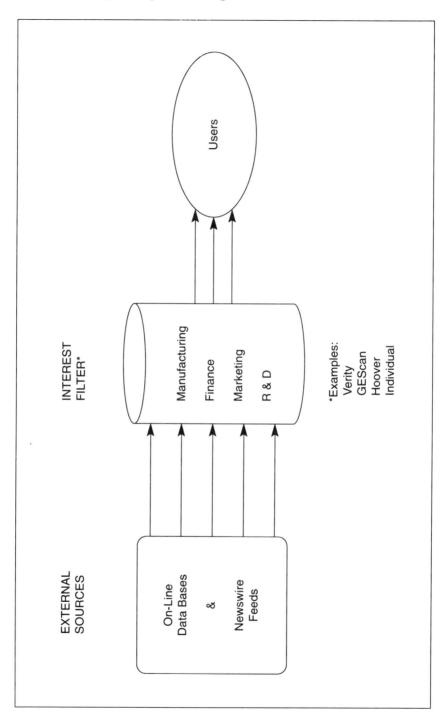

Figure 9.4 Level 1

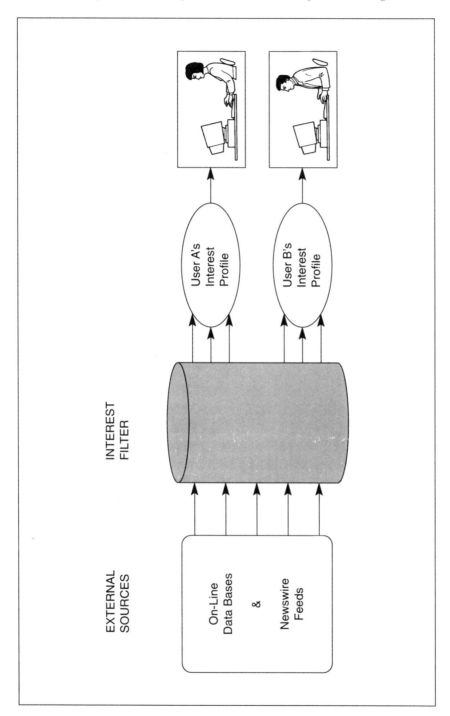

Figure 9.5 Level 2

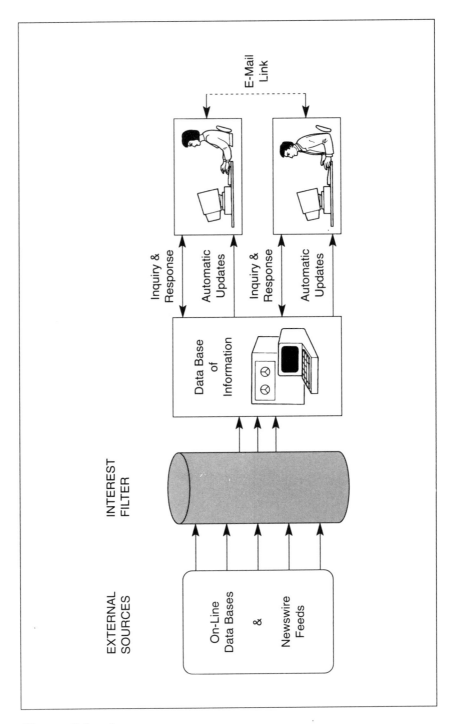

Figure 9.6 Level 3

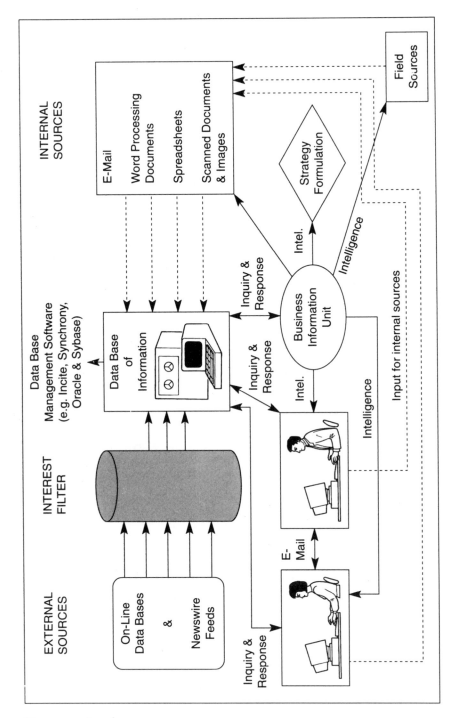

Figure 9.7 Level 4

ENTERPRISE-WIDE COMPUTER SOLUTIONS FOR COMPETITOR INTELLIGENCE

An enterprise-wide solution is one that ties the software and databases used for business intelligence into the broader information systems used throughout the enterprise. Level 4 is such a system. Unfortunately, although an enterprise-wide solution is the ideal, it can be difficult and expensive to attain. The greatest problems come when various parts of an organisation have adopted incompatible or nearly-incompatible hardware, operating systems or data file structures. This often happens quite casually, over a period of years. It is particularly apparent in companies that have been using mainframe computers, since many mainframe systems use operating systems and software that are proprietary to the mainframe manufacturer's products.

Incompatibility problems sometimes crop up in surprising places. For example, one of the regional US telephone companies decided to invest in customised software for the 150 or so people involved in competitor intelligence. The manager of the competitor intelligence programme decided that people in this group should communicate with each other through e-mail, which on the face of it is a very sensible approach, since all of them were already linked to one or another e-mail system.

The manager expected that she simply had to arrange for an appropriate database to be designed as a repository for the information her 150 correspondents would use. Unfortunately, she found that the company – a telephone and communications giant – had 17 different e-mail systems, many of which were incompatible with each other. Ultimately, she had to commission the design of an expensive, very simple, very dull, ASCII text-based interface to overcome the incompatibilities.

There are at least three lessons here. First, the computer-based system used for business intelligence ought to make use of the I/T or MIS resources already in place, where possible. Second, it may be necessary to accept some significant compromises in order to do that. And third, systems designed from the ground up must be assembled in a way that will make them compatible with the organisation's current and future approach to information systems.

This is a time of rapid change in information technology, and many companies are moving towards systems with open architecture. In theory, this will make it easier to link specialised business intelligence application software to the rest of the enterprise's information system. However, managers would be wise to make sure their business intelligence computer system is built around the specific databases and hardware that will be in broad use across their companies. If the company uses Ingress as its primary database, use Ingress, not Oracle, no matter what advantages Oracle may appear to have. 'Open architecture' is a relative term. Communicating from one computer platform or software file format to another is invariably an imperfect solution.

SUMMARY

Anyone contemplating the design of a computer-based system to help gather, store, sort through and interpret business intelligence needs to start with a low level of time and budgetary commitment to computerisation. Computers are excellent tools, but they will not 'automate' the task of gathering information or producing competitor intelligence from that information.

The key lesson is to start modestly and build slowly. Develop a network of people before trying to develop a network of computers. Have substantial resources available when the time comes to embark on broad computerisation program, and don't commit to that type of programme until the competitor intelligence effort has a constituency that is pleased with the output.

10 COUNTERINTELLIGENCE: DEFENDING YOUR COMPANY'S SECRETS

This chapter is contributed by Lawrence B. Sulc. Mr. Sulc served for more than 23 years as an operations officer with the Central Intelligence Agency (CIA), mostly outside the United States, and later for six years on the staff of the House Committee on Foreign Affairs. He is a member of SCIP.

INTRODUCTION

It is clear that as never before business and industry present increasingly rich targets for both government and corporate intelligence, not to mention a host of other forces. Threats come from the usual suspects, of course, but also from new and unexpected quarters – probes for information business would rather keep to itself, attempts at manipulation, theft, attacks on its personnel (physical and otherwise), counterfeiting, sabotage, denigration, computer intrusion, communications intercept, extortion, and on and on. It's a kind of war.

In this war as in others, intelligence is the first line of defence – either of a nation-state or a corporate entity. Counterintelligence (CI) is the first line of defence of the first line. Defending on the one hand its people and its management capability (including the intelligence function), and, on the other, its property, production, service to the community, its very reason for being, CI's mission is to protect the entire entity – whether government or corporate – from outside (or inside) harm.

Unfortunately, the initial letters CI are widely used in business circles to mean competitive intelligence. For many years, however, among government intelligence professionals CI has meant counterintelligence. To avoid confusion, CI will be used here in the latter sense, and BI will mean business, or competitor intelligence.

At least a general awareness of intelligence is important for managers – whether government or corporate. He or she must know what is going on out there. The realisation that intelligence activities, possibly quite hostile, sponsored by others – governments, corporations, whoever – are directed against one's own firm – or even oneself – should also prompt an appreciation of the place of CI in corporate operations.

A 'CI mentality' is a must to understand and to be able to counter the intelligence and the intelligence-like measures of opponents, such as computer intrusion, surveillance, stakeouts and counterfeiting, to name but a disparate few. A CI mentality is essential for one's health. Security, for its part, is integral to any organised activity, especially to BI and CI, keeping out no matter what and no matter whom – the spy, the saboteur, the mole, the manipulator, or merely the unduly curious. The three are closely linked (see Fig. 10.1) and like business itself, BI, CI and security are – certainly should be, anyhow – dynamic processes.

More and more businesses are becoming the objects of attention of others. Industrial and commercial targets are increasingly more important to certain foreign intelligence services than are military or political targets. 'Although the risk of a single cataclysmic threat to the United States is substantially lower than it was . . . the number and complexity of very serious threats . . . has grown, not shrunk . . . ' the new American Director of Central Intelligence (DCI), R. James Woolsey, says.

This view of the US intelligence community, widely shared by others outside United States government circles, should be heeded by business executives everywhere, whether American, European or otherwise. Industrial espionage by foreign intelligence agencies in the US is 'rampant' and often is carried out at the request of their domestic corporations, Alexander Michael, computer CI analyst, warns American industry.

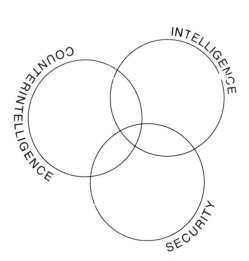

Figure 10.1 Reaching out – Looking inwards

'During the periods of Cold War detente, Soviet intelligence activities against the United States increased,' observes Edward O'Malley, a former high CI official of the Federal Bureau of Investigation (FBI) the American internal security service. 'Now they are increasing again.' 'It is a great challenge for the FBI to convey the seriousness of the foreign intelligence threat to the American public, including business, at a time when many Americans no longer perceive that there is a threat,' W. Douglas Gow, then assistant director of the FBI's intelligence division, told the Association of Former [United States] Intelligence Officers (AFIO) as far back as in early 1991.

The intelligence threat from the former Soviet Union, the FBI warns, is even more difficult to counter than before. The Soviet KGB's successor organisations continue to recruit scientists and businessmen for economic information. These targets remain, despite political liberalisation, top priorities, including within the [former] Soviet Union, itself. The role of Soviet [now Russian] military intelligence, the GRU, has increased also, with the GRU choosing particularly persons with access to sensitive technology.

According to Wayne Gilbert, head of the Intelligence Division of the FBI, in the 1980s more than US$1.5 trillion was invested in research and development in the United States.

The United States, accordingly, 'hosts more foreign official representatives interested in S&T [science and technology] than any other
industrial nation,' he points out. Troubled by the perceived threat of
technology protectionism and/or the creation of a technological bloc
among the G-7 countries, other nations, Mr. Gilbert says, 'find it
imperative to use whatever means available to keep pace with new
technological developments in United States business and government.'

Foreign intelligence operations against American economic interests, however, go well beyond collection on S&T, explains Mr
Gilbert, including gaining 'access to U.S. government policy deliber-
ations concerning foreign trade, investments, loans and positions on
bilateral economic negotiations. Several governments also seek information,' he says, 'such as company bids for contracts, information
that affects prices of commodities, financial data and banking information affecting stock market trends and interest rates.' Mr Gilbert's
list will be useful to the reader having CI interests.

Many foreign governments and/or corporations, Mr Gilbert continues, 'collect economic information on corporate negotiating positions, costs, economic feasibility studies, and marketing plans. Theft
of these confidential corporate trade secrets or reports can in some
situations more directly affect the competitive position of United
States firms than the theft of the firm's technology' or hardware, he
says.

Mr Gilbert, citing serious losses of American economic strength,
says that in 1982 piracy of intellectual property rights in five selected
American industries cost them an estimated six to eight billion dollars
in annual sales and 131,000 jobs. In 1987, he adds, worldwide losses
to American industry were estimated at $23.8 billion. In 1991–1992,
a 'US computer company estimated the loss of just two technical
manuals relating to a new computer chip could cost billions of
dollars in lost business,' he points out. Economic espionage is big
business. It means big losses for the victim and big gains for the thief.
As a consequence of rethinking its counterintelligence strategy, the
FBI has developed a list of CI perils for the United States. The new
National Security Threat List (NSTL), signalling the bureau's departure from its 40-year Cold War mission of focusing on the Soviet

Union and its allies, designates issue threats, 'no matter where the threat comes from or what country is involved'. The NSTL enumerates seven CI threats, the first two being 'foreign intelligence activities directed at US critical technologies . . .' and 'foreign intelligence activities directed at the collection of United States industrial proprietary economic information and technology, the loss of which would undermine the US strategic industrial position.' The prominence of 'critical technologies' and 'economic information' at the head of the NSTL demonstrates their importance to the US government.

'The FBI,' moreover, 'has broadened the scope of its counterintelligence effort to include some friendly nations,' *Political Warfare* magazine of Washington quotes Harry Brandon, a high FBI CI official, as saying. 'A number of these non-traditional intelligence adversaries,' Mr Brandon claims, 'currently conduct intelligence operations against the United States, directly against US firms, which go far beyond their defence needs.'

The new government of Russia having jumped into the international economic intelligence arena with both feet is determined to use economic intelligence gained from its reorganised foreign collection efforts for the benefit of its national business interests. Any doubt about this was dispelled when TASS, the Russian news service, announced agreement between the intelligence chiefs of Russia and Belarus to co-ordinate their activities to collect 'mostly economic information abroad'.

The CIA, for its part, is helping American business to sort out the former Soviet security services, 'now beginning to stabilise under Russian jurisdiction', as the agency puts it, from the state of flux which existed after the coup attempt of August 1991. *Security Intelligence* (SIR), the respected Washington-area newsletter, says that as the intelligence structure in the former Soviet Union more or less stabilises, of the new organisations to emerge in Moscow the two to watch are the Russian Foreign Intelligence Service (SVRR) and the Federal Agency for Government Communications and Information (FAPSI). The job of the SVRR, essentially the First Chief Directorate, or foreign intelligence collection unit, of the former KGB, SIR says, is to monitor 'terrorism, international economics and nuclear proliferation.' Its chief, Yevgeny Primakov, as it happens, 'is an expert in international economic relations'. SIR reports.

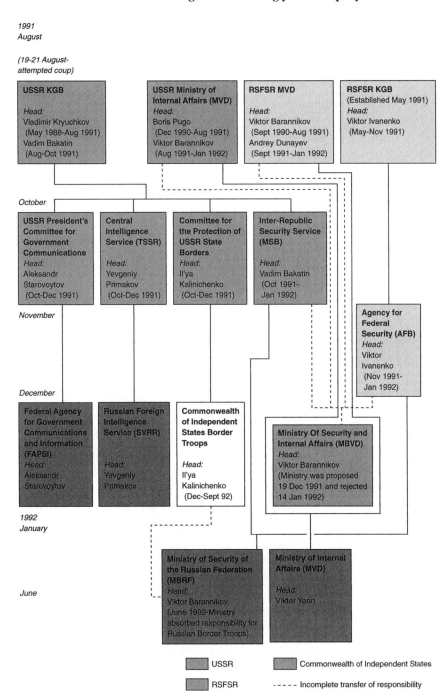

Figure 10.2 Evolution of the Russian Security Services (August 1991 – September 1992)

Source U.S. Central Intelligence Agency

'FAPSI, headed by Alexandr Starovoytov,' SIR points out, 'is the Russian equivalent to the US National Security Agency, and . . . has openly offered its services to Russian industrialists, traders and bankers to help them improve the Russian economy.' (See Fig. 10.2.) 'It takes little imagination,' SIR says of FAPSI, 'to see the threat represented by an agency whose job is to monitor communications for economic benefit, and a competitive global economy where critical information and money move electronically.'

In sum, the intelligence services of the former Soviet Union are increasing, rather than decreasing, their collection efforts. Their emphasis is on S&T and economic intelligence and on the recruitment of foreign scientists and businessmen to get it. They are determined, moreover, to share the 'take' with their national business interests, including that acquired by electronic means, for which the GRU and the former KGB have great worldwide aptitude.

Russia and the other former Soviet republics, not to mention the former Soviet satellites, are not alone, of course, in the quest for economic intelligence. Other countries, including 'non-traditional intelligence adversaries,' as the FBI calls them, are on the prowl. Japan, a major economic power, has major economic intelligence interests. Japan was a pioneer in the collection and analysis of information and controls a formidable modern intelligence system. In fact, the Japanese have added 'information' to 'land, labour and capital', as the important factors of production, says Dr John Prescott, formerly president of the Society of Competitive Intelligence Professionals (SCIP) in the United States. JETRO, the Japan External Trade Organisation, established in 1957 to promote trade under Japan's Ministry of International Trade and Industry (MITI), has long been considered one of the world's best intelligence services. JETRO, however, is merely prolonging an intelligence tradition beginning in the late 1860s.

Ron Morris, a specialist on Japan for the United States Library of Congress, thinks that country's main foreign affairs concern is '. . . making sure nothing happens to [its] relationship . . .' with the United States. Whatever its motivation, 'Japan is quietly and deliberately moving to expand and strengthen its capabilities in intelligence,' writes AFIO's *Periscope,* in response to '. . . the perceived need to lessen Japan's dependence on American analysis of threats to Japan's security.'

The world's most sophisticated economic intelligence network is not run exclusively by its government, however; Japanese business is very much involved, although it 'does not necessarily share the government's priorities and interests at all times,' *Periscope* says. 'Reportedly the Foreign Ministry intends to create a regionally-oriented information bureau, while the Self-Defence Agency plans to train hundreds of new analysts and to allocate large sums to improvement of information collection in both human and electronic areas.'

The additional Japanese intelligence capabilities to be provided by Foreign Affairs and Defense would, of course, complement (or compete with) those of JETRO on the economic side, providing Japan with a most formidable array of intelligence assets.

Of special interest, though, apart from JETRO's intelligence collection are its other undercover activities. A former intelligence official (presumably American) told *The Washington Times* of JETRO's 'working behind the scenes' in the American Congress in the aftermath of the Toshiba scandal to forestall congressional hearings and legislative sanctions against Japan. Toshiba's illegal diversion of milling machinery to the Soviet Union during the Cold War had seriously strained US–Japanese relations.

If the allegation of 'behind the scenes' lobbying by JETRO in the US Congress is accurate, it would have been a good deal more sensitive than collection by Japan of economic intelligence in the United States. 'Influence' activities of the kind described would have amounted to a Japanese 'covert action' operation against its American ally. Following on the Toshiba scandal, such 'lobbying', had it been officially noted by the US government at the time, would have further strained Japanese–American relations.

Countries once 'friendly', or at least 'neutral', towards the United States, are increasingly more active in the economic and S&T intelligence scramble. Others are quickly joining in. The intelligence services of nearly a hundred countries ' . . . are now running industrial espionage operations . . . ' in the 'Silicon Valley' hi-tech centre in California, the FBI told Norm Alster, writing for *Forbes* magazine. They want ' . . . everything from laser research to rocket engine test data to marketing plans, contract bids, . . . cost analyses and proprietary software,' the FBI said.

Prominent in the intelligence 'scramble', although not necessarily in the Silicon Valley whirl – although there is no reason to doubt it, either – is France. 'In the fall of 1991, former French external intelligence chief Pierre Marion announced that he personally ordered the creation of a special unit of 20 agents soon after the Socialists came to power in 1981, to obtain information on American multinational corporations for the benefit of French state-owned enterprises.'

Mr Marion's admission is described by Hans-Ulrich Helfer, former Swiss police and military intelligence (SSA) officer, in Intelligence Briefing of Hamburg. Among other things, says Mr Helfer, French operatives tapped telephones and searched the baggage of American businessmen in hotels. US specialists later claimed the French bid to sell Mirage jet fighters to India was successful only because the French knew the intentions of their American and Soviet competitors.

In this connection, a former senior US intelligence official told a Washington Post reporter that the 'French were passing . . . information on to the French private sector.' The Bush administration, according to the former official, made 'a great effort to make them stop. They would stop for a period of time, but they would come back.' Mr Marion, for his part, made his country's position on these matters quite clear. 'In technological competition we are competitors; we are not allies,' the French intelligence chief told a television audience in 1991.

Israel is another nation gathering intelligence from the United States for a number of purposes. That small, beleaguered country is torn. Needing its alliance with the United States to survive and economic intelligence from the United States to prosper, it appears to be clever enough to manage both. The People's Republic of China (PRC), for its part, with its immense and burgeoning population is determined by means of intelligence to 'leapfrog' the industrial development process. Israel and the PRC, although hardly 'non-traditional intelligence adversaries' like some of the others, are nonetheless formidable opponents in the intelligence 'game.'

Added to the CI irritants mentioned here is the aroused curiosity of the 'NICs', as the Canadian Security and Intelligence Service (CSIS) calls the Newly Industrialising Countries. '[T]here will be rising demands,' from the NICs, 'for access to restricted technologies for competitive commercial and military use,' the CSIS says. Many of these demands will be for dual-use civilian technologies, such as minicomputers or pharmaceutical manufacturing equipment, the CSIS says, anticipating '. . . an increasing requirement for international commercial intelligence, including proprietary corporate technical information, international financial data and foreign trade reporting.' More items for the executive's CI list.

To underscore the seriousness with which the United States views foreign intelligence efforts against American firms – abroad or within the United States – an advisory panel to the Overseas Security Advisory Council (OSAC) of the US State Department in late 1992 reported details about the 'strenuous efforts' of foreign intelligence services against American companies for the benefit of their own national industries. 'These efforts included eavesdropping, hotel room burglaries, and introduction of "moles", as well as other sophisticated intelligence techniques.' OSAC thus echoes the observations of Mr Helfer, the Swiss former intelligence official, quoted above. 'Our foreign competitors' interest in our information,' OSAC says, 'has never been more intense.'

'Economic espionage, serious today, will certainly continue to increase as international relations become more and more a matter of economic rather than military competition,' OSAC declares. For their part, American businesses want to know the kinds of technology and techniques used against them and which companies are targeted, says Robert R. Burke, businessman and chairman of OSAC's Committee on Information Protection, an advisory group of American firms and government agencies.

While American firms by and large do not seek US government intelligence on foreign firms for their benefit, they do want its assistance in counterintelligence. 'We want help when we are targeted,' says Mr Burke, speaking for American businesses operating abroad. OSAC, founded in 1985 to counter terrorism abroad, is now focusing on counterintelligence as American firms realise the importance of CI to their survival.

It is interesting to note that FBI officials now refer to the 'foreign intelligence threat', rather than to 'hostile spying', the term they used for so many years. It seems that while foreign opponents in intelligence, whether government or business, may pose a 'threat', they need not necessarily be 'hostile' about it. The lack of 'hostile' intent on the part of an opponent in the global intelligence/CI contest means the latter need not necessarily seek to damage or destroy, or even dominate the object of its interest. It may merely want some 'simple' advantage, such as a larger market share or prior information on next week's price changes or something in that vein.

In view of all these developments, the European business executive will see that his own country, his own firm, and he himself are subject to unwanted attention from many quarters. However, not all of this vigilance need necessarily be 'hostile'. The Japanese, after all, were seeking to improve relations with the United States by their alleged post-Toshiba lobbying activities in Congress, not to harm them. 'They're really concerned about maintaining access to the American market, and assuring that the United States will uphold its defence of Japan,' explains Mr Morris, the expert in the US Library of Congress, mentioned earlier.

'Corporate intelligence and thereby corporate counterintelligence is the new battleground of the 1990s,' says Neil C. Livingstone, widely-respected counter terrorist consultant in Washington, D.C. 'There are a lot of unemployed "spooks" who find the only marketplace for their skills are in corporate intelligence. This is the business today,' he says. 'In the 1950s a guy in business counter-intelligence wore thick-soled shoes and carried a clip board, checking the safes at night.'

'In a 40-year span, simple corporate security has changed into a sophisticated profession with some corporations today having security approaching the level of that in the CIA,' Mr Livingstone says. 'Some corporate executives are even protected in a manner befitting the President.' According to Mr Livingstone, 'the computer industry worldwide is on "fast forward" with hundreds of millions of dollars being spent on research and development. Obviously in such an environment, competitors seek to learn what others are doing. A company today without an aggressive collection capability and an effective CI capability will not be particularly competitive in a few years.'

'There is a revolution taking place in business intelligence today,' Mr Livingstone claims. 'Corporate security was not even mentioned at Harvard Business School 20 years ago – or even ten. Corporate security is not just a factor of the cost of doing business; today it is a matter of future profitability or even corporation survival. Interestingly, the United States is ahead of the world in the matter of security,' he says. 'Eighty per cent of large American corporations have some dedicated security element; fewer than 20 per cent of Japanese companies do.'

Here is Mr Livingstone's list of CI security essentials:

i. *Security access control*. A field in a state of revolution, today. Advanced systems 'remember' hand geography or the pattern of veins in the eyes.

ii. *Secure conversation*. Technology as usual is driving the needs in this area. Electronic eavesdropping, not very expensive, creates new counterintelligence requirements which, unfortunately, are very expensive.

- Secure communications, such as telephone conversation and fax scramblers. In many cases, only short-term, and thus relatively inexpensive security, is needed in this area.
- Secure document destruction. Shredders, for example.
- Secure computers. Reasonable codes and secure access.
- Secure filing systems.
- Secure corporate employees. Especially secure executives, perhaps most important of all. The adequate screening of employees cannot be overemphasised.

One can add to the above list, of course. Good security is of utmost importance. Sensitive material, in the form of notes, rubbish, telephone books, logs, files, blackboards and training materials must be protected. Cleaning crews can pose considerable risk and are particularly vulnerable to outside recruitment. Of supreme importance is that a security consciousness on the part of all be created and maintained.

There is no end to a firm's vulnerabilities, it seems. Computers and telecommunications systems increasingly fall prey to an expanding variety of threats, as Lisa Corbin, writing on corporate CI, points out. Computer intrusion, for example, whether for espionage, extortion or sabotage is a serious threat. So is the interception of communications. Facsimile machines, copiers and computer software are all vulnerable to damage and theft, as Ms Corbin says.

Natural disasters, electrical outages, dust, heat – even spilled coffee – are catastrophic for computer and communications systems. Ignorance and error also take their toll. 'A misdialed digit caused sensitive documents to be faxed to *The Wall Street Journal* instead of one of the companies involved . . .' in important merger negotiations, Ms Corbin reveals. An inexpensive fax-number verification device would have prevented the disaster, she says.

Changing passwords, using computer virus-detection programs, installing power-protection devices, employing removable drives and encrypting communications are but a few of the measures available to protect computers, while access control, proper training and careful hiring practices are only some of the many means to make a firm more secure. Education and contingency planning can prevent much loss, yet security is often viewed as an expensive – and expendable – nuisance by American corporations, Ms Corbin says, tending to confirm similar observations mentioned elsewhere, here.

Examples of CI and security problems abound but there are remedies to improve the survival prospects of those firms with the wit and will to employ them. Uncaring or careless corporations, on the other hand, will continue to suffer loss, some of them never knowing why. A survey conducted for the American Society for Industrial Security (ASIS) by Daniel T. Swartwood and Richard J. Heffernan, security analysts, in mid-1992, shows that the theft of proprietary information in the United States 'has increased dramatically in recent years', with many firms although aware of losses ignorant of the details.

Of the 500 American firms queried in the ASIS survey, mostly aerospace-space, electronic, computer, telecommunication and utility firms, 246 replied. They reported 619 cases of 'misappropriation of proprietary information'. Firms earning the most money reported relatively lower losses, probably reflecting, Messrs Swartwood and Heffernan believe, a greater commitment to security by larger corporations. The reported thefts were carried out by employees and former employees (58 per cent), other US firms (8.4), foreign governments (8), consultants (6.3), vendors (3.8) and foreign businesses (3). 'Unknown entities' were responsible for 12.5 per cent of losses. Of special note is the finding that more than a tenth of the thefts were carried out by foreign interests.

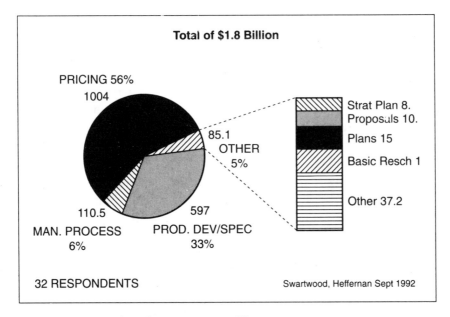

Total of $1.8 Billion

PRICING 56%
1004

85.1
OTHER
5%

110.5
MAN. PROCESS
6%

597
PROD. DEV/SPEC
33%

Strat Plan 8.
Proposals 10.
Plans 15
Basic Resch 1
Other 37.2

32 RESPONDENTS   Swartwood, Heffernan Sept 1992

Figure 10.3 Loss by info category in millions

The thieves' methods varied from unauthorised use of data and electronic surveillance to break-ins and bribery. The information sought included customer lists (19 per cent) and data on pricing (11), product development (8), basic research (8), sales (7), manufacturing processes (6), proposals (5), compensation (5), costs (5), and strategic plans (4). The results of the ASIS survey may be added by the reader, if not already there, to the CI list of areas business should protect.

The impact on the victims from the 'misappropriation of information' described ranged from 'embarrassment' to a loss of market share. Some companies increased security in response and some 'stepped up administration'. A quarter of the respondents, however, had no programme whatever to safeguard their secrets. Ten per cent said that the programmes they had were ineffective. A third felt management support for their programmes was 'less than adequate'. It would appear that the CI culture is not uniformly appreciated.

Of special interest is the survey's finding that many companies are unaware of the extent of their losses or even their cause, suggesting a bleak future for American business. On the other hand, perhaps CI itself faces a brighter future. In any case, the theft of proprietary information is a growing problem affecting competitiveness. Thirty-two firms in the ASIS survey lost as much as $1.8 billion among them, a lot of money even in Washington (see Fig. 10.3).

The systematic collection and analysis of information to protect the firm – its CI effort – is an integral part of the overall BI function. A very important – perhaps vital – aspect of CI is, of course, security. Overall corporate security should be a part of, and supervised by, a viable CI unit. Relevant information of a security nature should routinely and immediately be shared with the CI unit, whose analysts are trained among other things to predict terrorist activity, in so far as possible. Ideally, security personnel will be integrated into the CI unit but, in any case, should be equipped to deal quickly with security matters. One of the most serious of these, of course, is terrorism, about which more below.

The United States Central Intelligence Agency defines CI as 'intelligence activity intended to detect, counteract, and/or prevent espionage and other foreign clandestine activity, sabotage, international terrorist activity, or assassination conducted for or on behalf of foreign powers.' 'Sabotage', 'terrorism', 'assassination', not to mention espionage and all the other things described above, demonstrate that CI is serious business.

Until recently, it was widely held in the United States that while US intelligence would continue to focus on world economic trends, new far-reaching technological developments and attempts to restrict trade or create trading blocs, government economic intelligence would not be passed to private American firms. Robert Gates, Mr Woolsey's predecessor as DCI, opposed such sharing, believing 'it was not the government's responsibility and would pose questions of fairness,' as R Jeffrey Smith of *The Washington Post* describes his position. Mr Gates also believed that 'disclosing information to private firms could compromise secret intelligence sources and methods,' says Mr Smith.

With a new administration in Washington, however, Mr Woolsey may have another view. The issue of sharing is 'the hottest topic in intelligence policy', the new DCI told the Senate intelligence committee during his confirmation hearing in February. The Clinton administration would have to examine the 'complexities, legal difficulties [and] foreign policy difficulties', involved in sharing, he told the senators.

In view of increasing foreign intelligence efforts against American corporations, the United States government has been pressed to reverse itself. Whatever the administration's decision on sharing economic intelligence, however, the US intelligence community is certain to continue to work closely with business on CI matters to help it protect itself from the intelligence efforts of others in the international arena.

Business – or competitive – intelligence is, as the reader will know, the practice of gathering, analysing and disseminating useful information in a timely manner to help in making informed decisions. With good intelligence, crises can sometimes be avoided or perhaps even prevented. But as business executives know, crisis situations and threats arise no matter what. A good BI/CI system in place permits the inevitable to be managed wisely.

The threat to a given company may range from the theft of its secret glue-making formula or its new marketing plan to an attempt to kidnap its chief executive or a plot to poison its product. The firm may be the target of either a government or private seeker of information or an entity with more dangerous motives – a terrorist group, for example – or indeed all of the above. A 'CI mentality', mentioned earlier, is critical to its defence and perhaps to its survival. Security, to reiterate, is crucial to both the BI and CI functions.

Security, it should be pointed out, has many uses and benefits beside keeping the lid on the pot of gold. Some firms, for example, use their security staffs to investigate name-brand counterfeiting and oversee the prosecution of offenders. Such tasking is really closer to CI than to security, but the two disciplines, as we have seen, not only complement each other but overlap. Other firms – and here the tasking is actually closer to the security function than to CI – assign to security the monitoring of safety programmes, all intended to reduce profit loss.

In any case, it is the job of managers to manage. Among the things they must manage from time to time are crises. Crisis management (CM), a subject of considerable depth and breadth of itself, is worthy of not only a chapter but a book and a good deal more. Crisis management is more than just a project or programme. It stems from the awareness of the need to be prepared for trouble. Both BI and CI help immeasurably and can play a key role as managers ponder problems and prepare to deal with them.

Multiple crisis management plans are desirable to address the numerous and diverse contingencies that will arise. Flexibility and resourcefulness are essential, throughout. If there are CM rules they are these: plan, prepare, rehearse. It is important also to keep adequate records, readily recoverable (not totally on a computer system that might fail). For example, files on trusted employees keyed to their knowledge of languages, diverse cultures, special subjects, and so on, can be invaluable in emergencies and are often helpful in non-crisis situations, as well. Finally, good internal communications and a good public information system must be established early and maintained.

The first step in setting up a CM capability – and key to its success – is to win the participation and understanding of senior officials of the firm. The next step, writes Donald Sanford, management consultant, is 'to identify the critical departments of the company through a risk analysis and determine what it would take to keep them in business or re-establish their business function after a disaster.' As Mr Sanford reminds us, 'contingency planning is a process, not a project . . .'

As part of this process, a firm should know itself as well as its adversaries. It should determine its vulnerabilities and what should be protected, and from whom (or what) and for how long. It should decide, if possible, the objectives, motivation and capabilities of its adversaries and calculate the costs and benefits of protection. 'It is possible that a firm's intentions can be protected rather than its capabilities,' says Daniel Swartwood, the security analyst mentioned above. These tasks are precisely the job of CI.

Many businesses – the small and medium-sized ones being relatively new to the field – use outside management and security consulting firms to provide or help provide CM programmes. Many accounting and insurance companies, moreover, want their clients to have a CM capability, says Michael Guidry, head of The Guidry Group, management consultants in Houston, Texas. The Guidry Group, well-versed in all areas of corporate CI and security, is the premier American security firm in combating cellular telephone fraud, having to its credit a number of large criminal 'busts' in conjunction with law enforcement agencies.

A prototype CM team, says Mr Guidry, would have a representative of top management, but not the chairman of the board or the chief operating officer, themselves, who are needed to run the company. Human resources (personnel), finance, public relations (or advertising), and, obviously, BI/CI/Security would be represented in the CM unit. This skeletal team, no more than, say, five people, would expand if and when necessary.

The 'permanent CM team' might have as few as two or three members or as many as 15. The 'expanded team' – expanded only for the duration of a particular contingency – if too big, creates its own problems, says Mr Guidry. A big team is difficult to manage and 'you might end up finding one of the people on the team is a "competitor"', Mr Guidry warns. The CM team should be kept as small as possible, he advises.

Vendors (public relations firms, accounting companies, insurers and consultants) as well as company employees should be required 'to go to school' on CM, Mr Guidry believes, if there is a chance they might be called in. Vendors can be very helpful. As a matter of fact, insurance companies can take care of 99 per cent of the problems of a kidnapping case or hostage situation, he points out. 'Many important issues, such as paying ransom in kidnapping cases, are determined by the terms of insurance policies,' he says. Insurance firms often have considerable expertise in such matters.

Crisis Management manuals are often several hundred pages long; the Guidry Group's manual has 20 to 25 pages, depending on a client's needs. The basic CM team should meet regularly, daily or twice daily, on schedule, Guidry tells its clients, if only to assure itself that there is no crisis. Regular meetings do not signal crisis – special meetings do, he says. Team members – and their secretaries – should discuss nothing substantive on the telephone.

'The kidnapping of executives is rare, although, obviously, it happens,' Mr Guidry says. 'Responding to natural disasters is mostly commonsense and, of course, the need for a CM team in such situations is obvious,' he points out (here again insurance companies can help). 'Espionage because of leaks,' however, 'is incredible. More than anything else, companies need to be aware of CI – they never see anything until a problem arises.' They must protect their information and the newest area of concern, their communications, Mr Guidry insists.

To thwart espionage, these are a few of the things The Guidry Group advises executives to do:

- shred documents at desks, using 'dot' not 'strip' shredders (the use of companies providing shredding services is very risky)
- be cautious with copy clerks and cleaning crews
- be aware that scrambled faxes are insecure
- leave note pads in meeting rooms which should then be collected by trusted employees
- realise that executive lap-top computers are security 'disasters'
- never conduct substantive conversations over cellular telephones.

In this connection, Mr Guidry tells of certain enterprising people, who, from vantage points near computer companies or stock brokerage houses, monitor cellular telephone traffic for as little as a few hours a day. What is thus 'picked up' on product design, stock tips and so on is worth millions of dollars. Ironically, the target companies are oblivious, unable to 'manage' a crisis of which they are unaware. Not only is a 'CI mentality' absent in these firms but the most basic security instincts, as well. People simply talk too much on the telephone, says Mr Guidry. The losses are staggering.

In likely and unlikely places around the world, 'multinational corporations and their executives have become the leading target for terrorists, according to Kroll Associates and Business Risks International,' *The Los Angeles Times* reports. Threats may come from criminals, political extremists, ethnic separatists, narco-terrorists, political guerrillas and 'even from militant wings of anti-abortion, environmental or animal rights groups', directed against business and business executives. To this litany must be added the disgruntled former employee and opportunist who need a 'quick extra buck,' mark, peseta, lira, or franc . . .

To protect itself from terrorists and guerrillas in Colombia, Occidental Petroleum employs 'an army of counter surveillance experts', a source told *The Times*, emphasising again the importance of counter surveillance to security and CI concerns.

CI policy is integral to overall corporate policy, helping to determine what is to be protected – for not everything can – and for how long. If there are rules in all of this they are to be flexible and constantly to re-examine one's objectivity. With respect to security, everyone in the company should be trained to observe and report, especially 'front line personnel' – salespeople, warehousemen, delivery and service employees. Attention to security matters should be considered in employee performance evaluations. All should be enjoined to believe. After all, the welfare of everyone is at stake. A 'CI culture', or even a 'security culture', is not easy to establish, witness the apparent difficulty of doing so in the US Department of State, a major component in the nation's security structure.

The State Department, especially its Foreign Service, has suffered mightily from war and terrorism. Since the end of World War II more American ambassadors than generals have been killed in the line of duty. Yet, at '. . . the State Department many Foreign Service Officers believe the "diplomatic culture" leads diplomats to regard security as incompatible with traditional diplomacy . . . ' a White House official told *The Washington Times*, some time ago. 'But the fact is you can't conduct successful diplomacy without security,' the official said. Of course, he was right.

'It's a lot easier to break an egg than to put it back together,' commented George Carver, a former senior official of the CIA, in the same *Times* article. 'The dominant culture in the State Department says you basically achieve ends by accommodation,' Mr Carver explained. 'People outside the Foreign Service clan, like the FBI or the CIA, are regarded as interlopers who have to be repelled.' Mr Carter's appraisal of the State Department's culture applies to many other entities as well.

A firm will have a 'CI culture' or it will have some other kind. The organisation, wisely led, minimises its 'broken eggs'. It does not 'repel' its BI, CI and security personnel, but warmly embraces them. Such a company makes BI, CI and security integral parts of its culture and attempts to persuade everyone in the firm to participate in the missions of BI and CI. Security problems and intelligence are everybody's concern. To proceed as if they are not is to court disaster.

No dissertation on intelligence is complete without a quotation from Sun T'zu. 'If you know yourself and know the enemy, you can win the battle,' the Chinese strategist said. 'To defeat the enemy psychologically is the superior strategy. To defeat the enemy militarily is the inferior strategy.'

Sun Tzu's lesson is relevant to the hard-pressed manager operating in today's perilous world. Deprived of military means to deal with his competitor – or 'enemy' – he must outfox him. A corporate-wide commitment to counterintelligence will help immeasurably in achieving this task.

APPENDIX 1

STRATEGIC MARKET AND COMPETITOR ANALYSIS AT DEUTSCHE AEROSPACE

Deutsche Aerospace (DASA), a DM17.3 billion unit of Daimler-Benz, is today a major force in the European aerospace industry. It is also a key element in the integrated group of Daimler-Benz high technology companies.

DASA was created in May 1989 by joining plane maker Dornier and engine maker Motoren- und Turbinen-Union (MTU) with Telefunken Systemtechnik (TST), the aerospace and military electronics division of AEG.

Seven months later DASA acquired an 80 per cent stake in Deutsche Airbus, formerly a subsidiary of Messerschmitt-Bölkow-Blohm (MBB), and the German partner in Airbus Industrie. In January 1992 DASA acquired the remaining 20 per cent in Deutsche Airbus, which is now a full division of the group. At the end of 1992 the company claimed a total of 81,872 employees worldwide, over 90 per cent of which were based in Germany.

In March 1991 the company entered into a joint venture with Pratt & Whitney to develop new engines, and in May of the same year DASA joined Aerospatiale of France to form Eurocopter (of which DASA owns 40 per cent), to develop and manufacture civilian and military helicopters. The next big moves for Deutsche Aerospace took place in early 1993 when the company:

- linked up with Boeing to study a new super jumbo airliner
- rolled out the first widebody jet ever assembled in Germany (the Airbus A321)
- bought 51 per cent of the Dutch firm Fokker, making DASA Europe's biggest producer of aircraft for the 80–130 seat regional sector.

Deutsche Aerospace also has a one-third stake in the European Fighter Aircraft (EFA) project, through its Military Aircraft Division.

At the Spring 1993 Conference of SCIP (Europe), which took place in Cologne, Dr. Horst Schmidt-Bischoffshausen, head of Marketing and Innovation Management, Deutsche Aerospace, Munich, presented an overview of the Deutsche Aerospace approach to 'Strategic Market and Competitor Analysis'.

The slides used for the presentation are reproduced in this appendix with the kind permission of Dr. Schmidt-Bischoffshausen and Deutsche Aerospace. They offer a useful insight into how one major European organisation views and integrates the CI function in its strategic marketing process. As Jürgen E. Schrempp, Chairman of the company's Board of Management, observes, DASA will in the future 'have to get better than our competitors who are less hindered in competition than we are'.

Deutsche Aerospace

Competitiveness
by (R+D) intensive innovations

"Today we make 50 % of our current turnover
with products which did not exist 5 years ago.

Thus if we are not creative in time, we cannot
employ 50 % of our workforce within 5 years.

This is the continuous burden of innovation for
our company."

Dr. Kaske/Siemens
8/1990

1.

Deutsche Aerospace

What can we learn from internationally successful companies?

- They are **competent** in a certain product area

- They operate **close to customers** (sales and service)

- They are **innovative** i.e. they constantly try to improve the products and services („Kaizen")

- They **organize** themselves **flexibly** i.e. they continuously adapt their organization to market requirements

- They have **highly motivated** and engaged people/**employees**

- They can offer **cost and time benefits** to their customers

- They have a **clear company strategy** and **communicate** it **internally and externally**

2.

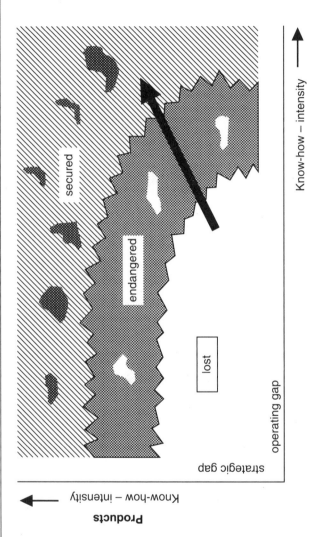

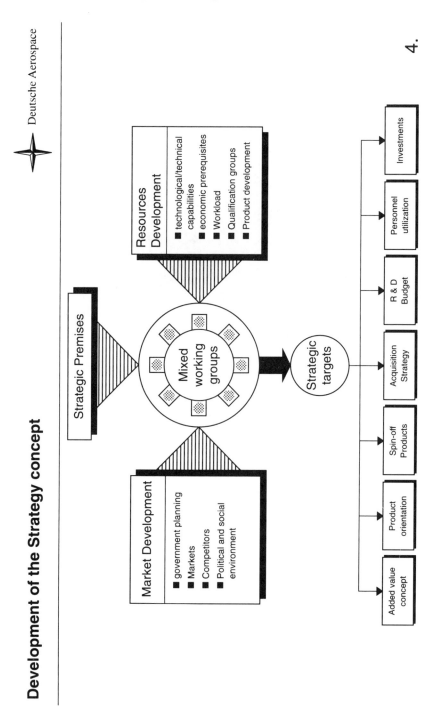

Development of the Strategy concept

Deutsche Aerospace

4.

 Deutsche Aerospace

Strategic Procedure

5.

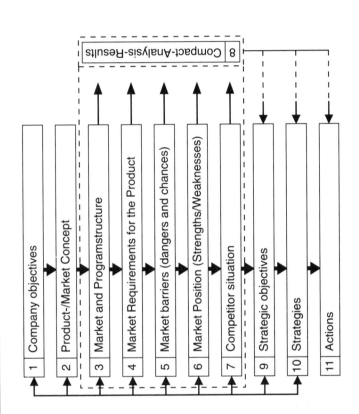

1	Company objectives
2	Product-/Market Concept
3	Market and Programstructure
4	Market Requirements for the Product
5	Market barriers (dangers and chances)
6	Market Position (Strengths/Weaknesses)
7	Competitor situation
8	Compact-Analysis-Results
9	Strategic objectives
10	Strategies
11	Actions

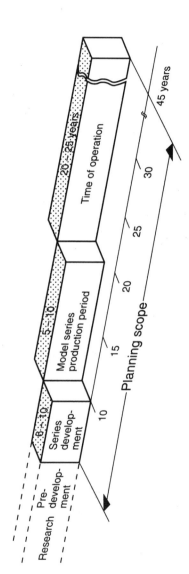

Longterm Planning Strategies

Example: Aircraft industry (commercial aircraft)

Research
Pre-
develop-
ment

Series
develop-
ment

8 - 10

Model series
production period

5 - 10

Time of operation

20 - 25 years

10   15   20   25   30   45 years

Planning scope

Deutsche Aerospace

Model series cycles require decisions with long-term impacts

6.

 Deutsche Aerospace

Specialities of aerospace business

- Product lifecycles are beyond industry average

- Product recoupment periods are in many cases beyond 10 years

- For some business areas with high risks there exists a strong dependance from **one** or **only few customers**

- The civil aviation markets are US-Dollar contracted markets (how can we reduce the US-currency risk?)

- New product developments require extreme capital resources (i.e. high risk decision with only longterm recoupment)

 **Essential aerospace projects can in general only be done in cooperation**

7.

Orientation Figures for our strategy development

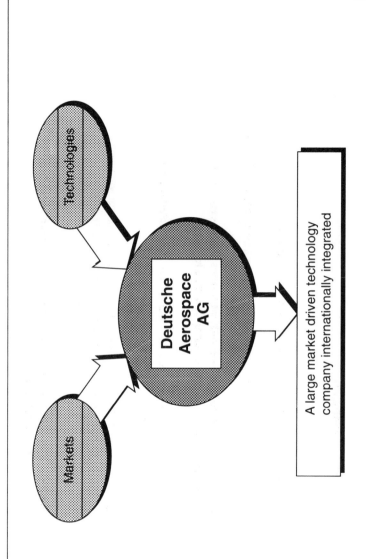

Deutsche Aerospace

Technologies

Markets

Deutsche Aerospace AG

A large market driven technology company internationally integrated

8.

Strategic triangle: Establish your own unique customer and competitor benefits

Deutsche Aerospace

9.

Market Analysis
- Market segmentation
- Market volume/development
- Customer requirements
- Key buying factors

Price/performance/value

Customers/Target groups

Competitors

We (own company)

Price/performance/value

Competitor benefits

Competitor Analysis
- Market position
- Product range
- Cost structure
- Added values
- Marketing mix
- Technologies
- Patents
- Services
- Relationships

Deutsche Aerospace

Establishing of competitor advantages by strategic alliances

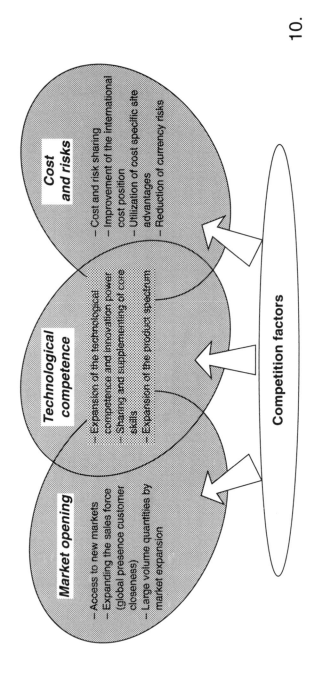

Market opening

– Access to new markets
– Expanding the sales force (global presence customer closeness)
– Large volume quantities by market expansion

Technological competence

– Expansion of the technological competence and innovation power
– Sharing and supplementing of core skills
– Expansion of the product spectrum

Cost and risks

– Cost and risk sharing
– Improvement of the international cost position
– Utilization of cost specific site advantages
– Reduction of currency risks

Competition factors

10.

Strategic Positioning of Businesses

→ Deutsche Aerospace

11.

Rolls	Characteristics	Consequences
Core Businesses:	■ Essential Contribution to the main purpose of the Company ■ Management of core skills ■ Dominant Player in relevant market ■ Permanent Cash generator ■ Expandable business development concept, if position not yet fulfilled	Claim for higher priority attention and supply of resources and management
Special Businesses: – Integrative Businesses	■ Important contribution to the sucess of core businesses ■ Not necessarily market dominant ■ No large cash consumer ■ Competitive economics	Only limited claim for resources; Resource allocation and business success are measured acc. to their importance for core business and their external market pos.
– Individual Businesses	■ No relations to other businesses ■ Attractive profit contribution	Minimal allocation of resources
– Provisional Businesses	■ Allowing access to potentially essential technologies and markets	Time limited and principally limited resource allocation

Strategic growth potential inside and outside of the core businesses
Example: DASA-Helicopters (EC)

Deutsche Aerospace

Forward Integration

Backward Integration

Horizontal Integration

Diversification
Expansion into Non-HC-related areas

Stepwise Expansion (Sales, Marketing and Product Support)

Takeover of supplier- and/or equipment manufacturers

Core business, Development and Manufacturing

BO 105

Build-up of a HC-Family

Takeover or cooperation with competitors (Compatibility of product line, of resources and capabilities)

12.

Deutsche Aerospace

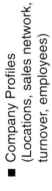

Which data are we collecting?
Suppliers/Competitors data

- Company Profiles
  (Locations, sales network,
  turnover, employees)
- Company relevant
  Production programs
- Production specific data
- Product developments
  Product policy
- Market/sales strategy
- Cooperations, Joint ventures,
  capital shares

- Licence manufacturing programs
- Main markets
- Major target groups
- Image
- Sales force/network by country
- Service network
- Scope of service
- Prices/Price policy
- Production rates
- Sales/deliveries
- Export shares
- Market shares

13.

Deutsche Aerospace

Which data are we collecting?
Customer/Demand data

- Company Profiles of major customers
- Structure of demand
- Typical applications ("mission profiles")
- Inventory of company relevant products
- Demand/demand development over the next 5 years
- Major procurement projects

- Potential customers
- Purchasing power
- Purchasing behavior
- Decision makers (buying center, etc.)
- Preferences for certain suppliers
- Image of suppliers
- Key account for...

14.

── Deutsche Aerospace

Sales market data by country/region

- General market conditions (economic, political, geographic, infrastructural, socio-/demoscopic)

- Market access conditions Import laws, legal constraints, economic protectionism, technology transfer constraints)

- Offset conditions

- Import/export constraints

- Product related market data
  - market structure
  - market segmentation
  - market volume
  - market demand
  - market development
  - competitor structure
  - competitor strengths/weaknesses
  - competitor strategy

15.

Examples of strategic market and competitive analyses

 Deutsche Aerospace

(1)

16.

Strategic Studies on... (1)	Produced for... (2)	Frequency per year (3)	Examples (4)
1	Market segmentation studies including competitor comparison	Marketing Dept (MD)	Unique	Helicopter Segments
2	Market and Sales Forecasts (longterm, shortterm)	Marketing Dept (MD) Sales Dept (SD)	Once (1/2 year revision)	Helicopter Forecast
3	New product developments (Market and competitor inputs)	Engineering Dept (ED)	Unique, Update (once per year)	BK 117-HC, HC-question-naire
4	Strategic competitor analysis	TOP-Management, SD, ED, MD	Once p.a.	Commercial A/C (AI-Boeing)

Deutsche Aerospace

Examples of strategic market and competitive analyses

(2)

17.

	Strategic Studies on... (1)	Produced for... (2)	Frequency per year (3)	Examples (4)
5	Sales/Marketing and Market strategy	SD, MD	Once p.a.	Advertising of HC
6	Studies on cooperation scenarios	TOP-Management	On demand once p.a.	Military A/C
7	Studies on international licencing programs (part of marketing)	TOP-Management MD, Manufacturing Dept	On demand, revision once p.a.	
8	Studies on aerospace services (scope, inventory, suppliers...)	Product Support Dept (PSD) MD	Once p.a.	
9	Cost analyses (Products, equipment, services, ...)	Top-Management ED, MD	On demand, Once p.a.	Cost structure analysis method

Examples of strategic market and competitive analyses

(3)

→ Deutsche Aerospace

18.

Strategic Studies on... (1)	Produced for... (2)	Frequency per year (3)	Examples (4)
10	Pricing analyses (Products, equipment, services)	MD, SD, PSD	1/2 a year	HC pricing
11	Comparative studies on competitor organizations	MD, SD, PSD	On demand	
12	Country analyses (Relevant key data...)	MD, SD, PSD	Once p.a.	Country strategy chart; HC-inventory
13	Aerospace supplier profiles/studies	Top management MD, ED, Manufacturing Dept	On demand	
14	Patent analyses	ED, MD	On demand, quarterly	

19.

Deutsche Aerospace

Corporate (centralized) marketing functions

1. Market Analysis
   (Analysis of branches, countries, competitors, suppliers, exogenic factors, ...)

2. Marketing Planning, Coordination and Control
   (Integration of decision plans in an overall business and marketing plan, marketing audits)

3. Export Marketing

4. Overall Strategy Development
   (Cooperations, acquisitions, R+D, ...)

5. New Business Development
   (military into civil products conversion...)

6. Company Communication

◆ Deutsche Aerospace

Commercial aircraft competition:
1. Company related competition factors

■ These company related factors are evaluated and compared to the largest competitor, Boeing

Legend:
+ competitive advantage
(+) limited competitive adv.
− competitive disadvantage
(−) limited competitive disadv.

	Deutsche Airbus/ Airbus Industries	Boeing	Remarks
1. Organizations	(−)	+	AI must be further optimized
2. Flexibility	(−)	+	Diversity of AI-Partners and national interests are limiting factors
3. Rationality	+	+	
4. US-Dollar dependence	−	+	AI-Partner are highly $-dependent (up to 80 %)
5. Infrastructure	+	(−)	The European infrastructure exceeds the American one
6. Product Support	+	+	Equivalent
7. High speed marketing	+	+	Equivalent
8. Highly motivated and qualified employees	+	(−)	The qualification of European employees is better

Conclusion: The present comparative evaluation of the company factors demonstrates some competitor advantages of Boeing

20.

Deutsche Aerospace

Commercial aircraft competition:
2. Product related competition factors

■ These product related factors are evaluated and compared to the largest competitor, Boeing

Legend:
+ competitive advantages
(+) limited competitive adv.
– competitive disadvantage
(–) limited competitive disadv.

		Airbus Industries	Boeing	Remarks
1.	Aircraft prices	+	+	No difference
2.	Direct operating cost	+	(–)	Airbus A/C have lower DOC
3.	Product quality	+	(–)	European product quality is better
4.	Technology lead	+	(–)	Airbus A/C are technically better
5.	Product variety (family)	(–)	+	Boeing has advantage with the B737 and B747
6.	Product commonality	+	+	
7.	Environmental suitability	+	(–)	Airbus A/C are with respect to fuel consumption and noise better

Conclusion: The present comparative evaluation of the product related factors demonstrates some competitor advantages of Airbus Industries

21.

Meeting the requirements of a new product: Helicopter

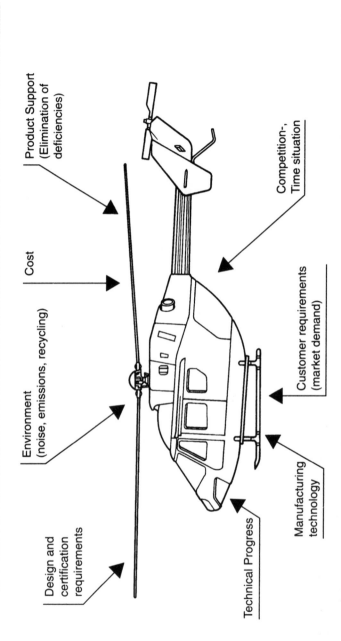

Deutsche Aerospace

Product Support (Elimination of deficiencies)

Cost

Environment (noise, emissions, recycling)

Design and certification requirements

Technical Progress

Manufacturing technology

Customer requirements (market demand)

Competition-, Time situation

22.

Importance of Characteristics in Next Generation Helicopters

MBB
Deutsche Aerospace

23.

Characteristic	Very important	Number of Responses Less important	Not important
Range/payload envelope	21	3	—
Cruise speed	13	10	1
Power margin-clearway reqt.	16	7	1
Hot day performance	17	4	3
Weight and size	7	11	4
Reliability safety	23	2	—
Maintenance downtime	23	2	—
All-weather capability	13	8	3
External noise	7	16	1
Internal noise	16	8	—
Vibration	19	6	—
Cabin volume	14	9	—
Baggage volume	13	10	1
Fuel capacity	15	9	—
Pilot workload	6	18	—
Passenger comfort	18	7	—
Passenger/cargo versatility	10	9	5

* Based on 26 total questionnaire responses.

HC-Marketing Concept/Structure

Deutsche Aerospace

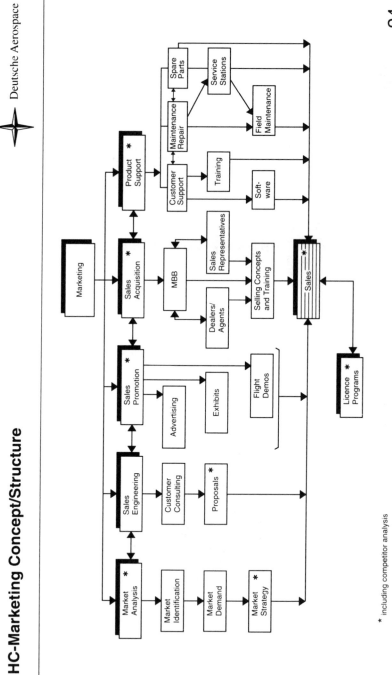

* including competitor analysis

24.

25.

Market Analysis: its tasks within the HC and A/C-Division

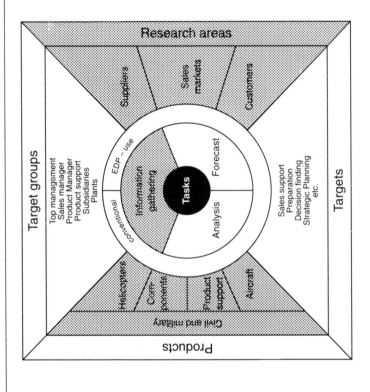

Deutsche Aerospace

Key Factors in commercial aircraft competition

■ In the 90s the following unique selling propositions (USP) will be relevant for the commercial A/C-market worldwide

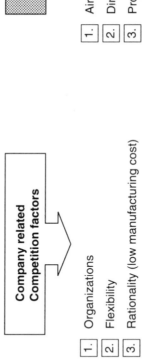

Company related Competition factors

1. Organizations
2. Flexibility
3. Rationality (low manufacturing cost)
4. US-Dollar dependence (US-$ leading currency)
5. Infrastructure/logistics
6. Product Support (Spare Parts service, documentation, training, technical service)
7. High speed marketing/sales
8. Highly motivated and qualified employees

Product related Competition factors

1. Aircraft prices
2. Direct operating cost
3. Product quality
4. Technology lead
5. Product variety (family)
6. Product commonality
7. Environmental suitability of the product/product family

26.

Method of comparative cost analysis

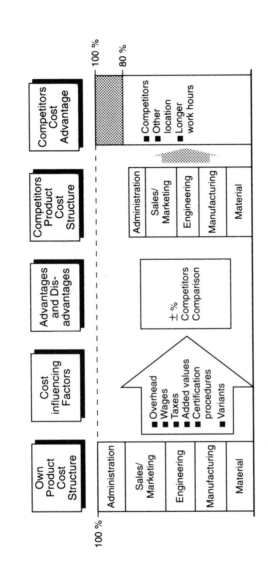

Deutsche Aerospace

27.

Deutsche Aerospace

28.

Corporate

Divisions (Product)

Overall Strategy

Strategy

New Business Development

Market Analysis Planning and Control

Sales Offices Coordination

Marketing

Market/ Competitor Analysis

Sales Sales Support

Marketing/ Commercial Planning and Control

Product Communication

Product Support/ Logistics

Company Communication

* Competitor intelligence necessary

Deutsche Aerospace

29.

Decentralized (Product divisions) marketing functions

1 Market Analysis
(Markets, Competitors, Products, ...)

2 Marketing Planning and Control
(Objectives, Marketing mix, actions, controlling)

3 Strategy (cooperations, licencing, product development, ...)

4 Sales and sales support

5 Product support/logistics

6 Product communication
(PR, advertising, trade shows, flight demonstrations/presentations)

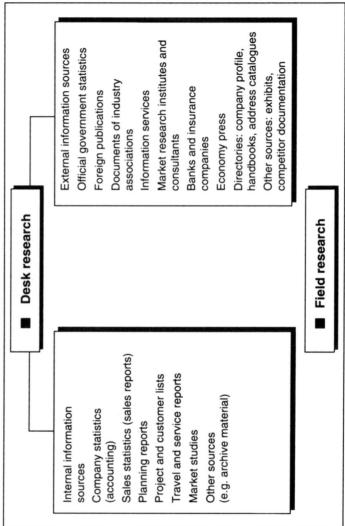

Data collection/Information sources

━━━◆ Deutsche Aerospace

30.

■ **Desk research**

External information sources
Official government statistics
Foreign publications
Documents of industry
associations
Information services
Market research institutes and
consultants
Banks and insurance
companies
Economy press
Directories: company profile,
handbooks, address catalogues
Other sources: exhibits,
competitor documentation

Internal information
sources
Company statistics
(accounting)
Sales statistics (sales reports)
Planning reports
Project and customer lists
Travel and service reports
Market studies
Other sources
(e.g. archive material)

■ **Field research**

 Deutsche Aerospace

Customer – Supplier-Relationship changing for the future

1. The customer **has to take** what he **gets**

2. The customer needs to do nothing, the supplier must deliver correctly (without defects and in time)

3. The supplier satisfies the requirements of the customer

4. The supplier **exceeds** the customer requirements and its demand

5. The **winning** supplier however **exceeds** the **customer requirements and** the offered performance of all competitors

Supplier   Customer

Market   Market

31.

APPENDIX 2

INTRODUCTION

No two firms produce intelligence briefs in quite the same way. Similarly, no two briefs in a single company will necessarily share exactly the same format. Each intelligence brief reflects the specific needs of the consumer for whom the intelligence is required, and of course no two intelligence projects are the same.

To the extent that intelligence needs differ, the scope and format of intelligence briefs will also differ. But this does not mean we cannot learn from examples.

The following is based on a consultant's brief prepared by a manufacturer in one sector of the telecommunications industry. It could also be used as an internal briefing document.

This consultant's brief is offered for purposes of illustration only. The names of firms are fictitious.

CONSULTANT'S BRIEF

COMPETITIVE MANUFACTURING CAPABILITY ASSESSMENT

Overview of the project

EuroFunFones (EFF) has decided to retain a firm of consultants to undertake a study of the manufacturing capabilities of four major players in the fun fone manufacturing sector. The purpose of this study is to ensure that future manufacturing investment is targeted towards areas of strategic importance, in order to maintain EFF's competitive advantage.

The company anticipates that the consultants will work closely with executives and staff of EFF, particularly on the topic of product cost analysis.

Time scale
The assessment and preparation of results must be completed within a period of 60 days beginning 1 June 1994. The project will conclude with a final presentation and report in the first week of August 1994. Regular progress review meetings will be held throughout the period.

Scope of analysis
The fun fone design and manufacturing operations of:

- Big Electronics (Taiwan)
- Rapid Communications (Australia)
- Inter Link (United States)
- Swift Overseas (Portugal)

Demographics
- Sales
  - US Dollars by region
    - Actuals last two financial years
    - Projected next two financial years
  - Units by region
    - Actuals last two financial years
    - Projected next two financial years
  - Units by segment
    - Actuals last two financial years
    - Projected next two financial years
- Number of employees
  - Salaried by region/facility
  - Hourly by region/facility
- Number / size (m3) / type of facilities by region
  - Warehousing
  - Offices
  - R&D
  - Manufacturing
- Output volume by product type by facility
  - This year (estimated)
  - Last year
  - Five-year average
- Total capacity by facility
  - This year

- Last year
- Five-year average
- Total flexibility by facility
  - Can production facilities be used to produce other products?
  - How easy would it be for the competitor to add capacity?
- Total throughput by facility
- Capital investment by facility
- Productivity
  - Utilisation (as a percentage of production divided by capacity).
  - Revenues per employee.

Strategy/policy
- Declared manufacturing strategy
  - Traditional (based on low wages, scale, or focus)?
  - Flexible (time based)?

Organisation
- Manufacturing organisation
- Engineering organisation
- Command & Control structure
- Relationship to parent
- Relationship to other internal groups

Human resources practices
- Personnel philosophy
  - Paternalistic?
  - Participative?
  - Contractual?
  - Hire/fire?
- Compensation and benefits costs/rates
- Reward system
- Recruitment strategy
- Turnover/absenteeism

Sourcing
- Organisation/structure
  - centralised?
  - decentralised?

- Total spend
- Sourcing practices/strategy
- Sourcing trends
- Number of vendors by commodity by region
- Delivery/scheduling methodology

Cycle time
- Time to market – that is, average time from concept to product launch for the last four product families.
- Manufacturing cycle time by facility – that is, average vendor lead time + average raw material/work in process + average production cycle + distribution to customer cycle.

Product cost
Estimated manufacturing costs for each product (material cost estimates based on reverse engineering will be provided by EFF).

Process technology
- Degree of vertical integration
- Technologies employed
- Process equipment manufacturers
- Technology trends
- Test methodology
- Approach to customisation

Management information systems (MIS)
- Materials management
- Finance
- CAD/CAM/CIM
- Physical distribution
- Level of system integration

Physical distribution
- Distribution methodology by region – channels
- Order processing system (centralised? decentralised?)
- Distinct competencies
- Design/technology
- Sourcing

Process
- Organisation
- Technical expertise in zoom widgets and stargazer technology

Physical distribution
- Distribution methodology by region
- Order processing system
- Centralised?
- Decentralised?

Core competencies
- Design/technology
- Sourcing
- Process
- Organisation

Technical expertise in megachip technology
background data to be provided by EFF Technical Department

INDEX